The Ideology of Failure:

How Europe Bought Into Ideas That Will Weaken and Divide It

STEPHEN PAX LEONARD

THE
IDEOLOGY
OF
FAILURE

HOW EUROPE BOUGHT INTO IDEAS
THAT WILL **WEAKEN** AND **DIVIDE** IT

ARKTOS
LONDON 2018

Copyright © 2018 by Arktos Media Ltd.

All rights reserved. No part of this book may be reproduced or utilized in any form or by any means (whether electronic or mechanical), including photocopying, recording or by any information storage and retrieval system, without permission in writing from the publisher.

Printed in the United Kingdom.

ISBN	978-1-912079-28-5 (Softcover)
	978-1-912079-27-8 (Ebook)
EDITING	John Bruce Leonard
COVER	Tor Westman
LAYOUT	John Bruce Leonard

Arktos.com   fb.com/Arktos   @arktosmedia   arktosmedia

CONTENTS

ACKNOWLEDGEMENTS — viii
PREFACE — x

INTRODUCTION — 1

I. THE GROUPTHINK TRAP — 8
II. THE POLITICAL CORRECTNESS FOLLY — 27
III. FREEDOM OF SPEECH — 64
IV. LOSING THOSE ESSENTIAL CONNECTIONS — 87
V. WHAT IS GOING ON IN SWEDEN? — 98
VI. SWEDISH AIR WAVES — 141
VII. SOCIETIES AT RISK — 160
VIII. DON'T JUST POINT THE FINGER AT RUSSIA — 172
IX. THE GLOBALISTS IN BRUSSELS — 202
X. IN DENIAL — 215
XI. OVER THE BROW OF THE HILL — 229

Bibliography — 243
Index — 249

Norman and Saxon (A.D. 1100)
Rudyard Kipling

'My son,' said the Norman Baron, 'I am dying and you will be heir
To all the broad acres in England that William gave me for share
When he conquered the Saxon at Hastings, and a nice little handful it is.
But before you go over to rule it I want you to understand this:-

'The Saxon is not like us Normans. His manners are not so polite.
But he never means anything serious till he talks about justice and right.
When he stands like an ox in the furrow — with his sullen set eyes on your own,
And grumbles, 'This isn't fair dealing', my son, leave the Saxon alone.

'You can horsewhip your Gascony archers, or torture your Picardy spears;
But don't try that game on the Saxon; you'll have the whole brood round your ears.
From the richest old Thane in the county to the poorest chained serf in the field,
They'll be at you and on you like hornets, and, if you are wise, you will yield.

'But first you must master their language, their dialect, proverbs and songs.
Don't trust any clerk to interpret when they come with the tale of their wrongs.
Let them know that you know what they're saying; let them feel that you know what to say.
Yes, even when you want to go hunting, hear 'em out if it takes you all day.

They'll drink every hour of the daylight and poach every hour of the dark.
It's the sport not the rabbits they're after (we've plenty of game in the park).
Don't hang them or cut off their fingers. That's wasteful as well as unkind,
For a hard-bitten, South-country poacher makes the best man-at arms you can find.

'Appear with your wife and the children at their weddings and funerals and feasts.
Be polite but not friendly to Bishops; be good to all poor parish priests.
Say 'we', 'us' and 'ours' when you're talking, instead of 'you fellows' and 'I'.
Don't ride over seeds; keep your temper; and *never you tell 'em a lie!'*

Acknowledgements

This book is a revised and updated edition of a previous book published with the title *Travels in Cultural Nihilism: Some Essays*. The changes and revisions to the text were made whilst serving as a Senior Research Fellow at St Chad's College, one of the Colleges that make up the University of Durham. I am very grateful to the Principal and Fellows for offering me a Fellowship, and for allowing me to work in an atmosphere so convivial to scholarship for one year. I am also pleased to have had the opportunity to discuss the contents of the book with so many students and like-minded people at the College, in particular Bill Apedaile, James Page, Mark Roberts, Callum Bennett and Julius Berrien. In such viciously polarising times as these, fellow-travellers soon become close friends and I am pleased to say that this was very much my experience at Chad's. There are few rebels who are prepared to challenge the prevailing discourse and orthodoxy of their own tribe. Those that do soon find themselves on a lonely path of sunken dissidents. If you meet a fellow-traveller on that pot-holed track, then you soon form a cast-iron bond with that person. Happily, that has been my experience in writing this book.

The original text was written during my time as a Fellow at Exeter College, Oxford. As always, I am grateful to the College, its Rector and Fellows for providing such a wonderful place to work. It was a great privilege. The idea to write such a book (which is admittedly quite far removed from my normal ethnographic pursuits, although I have a long-term interest in ideology) came to me after a summer spent in Sweden, but the real intellectual stimulation emerged after subsequent lively discussions with friends in Oxford. I should like to thank in particular Therese Feiler, Cosima Gillihammer, Peter Harris, Jason Carter, Hugh Wybrew and Charlotte Bannister-Parker — all at Oxford — for their unrelenting support, opinions and critical analysis.

During my time at Oxford, I was fortunate enough to host Sir Roger Scruton who gave an excellent paper at Blackfriars on a topic tangential to the thorny issues I tackle in this book. I am grateful for his advice and support these last years. I should also thank Professor Jonathan Haidt for his comments and for his inspiration for the subtitle of the book.

Finally, I should like to thank John Bruce Leonard at Arktos for proof-reading the book and for his efficiency in helping bring this book to its fruition. Some may wish to infer that by publishing with Arktos, I should be considered as a member of the alt-right, identitarian movement. That is not the case, but I do support the anti-globalist cause. I do not belong to any groups or political parties and do not approve of identity politics of any kind. To be frank, discussions without labels seem to be often richer too. I wish to do away with the fixation on group identities, and by doing so bridge the yawning ideological chasm that has become so destructive in Western societies. In the current climate, that seems to me to be the duty of any responsible intellectual. Sadly, I doubt that I have achieved that aim in this particular book.

SPL
Durham, May 2018

Preface

> For if you do not understand a man you cannot crush him. And if you do understand him, very probably you will not.
> — G. K. Chesterton

These last years I have become puzzled by some of the developments that I have witnessed in academia, and now increasingly in society at large. In particular, I am disturbed by the blanket groupthink and the culture of fear and silence that has somehow become a feature of life in the West. I think any intellectual should be a passionate supporter of freedom of speech, but many seem all too happy to accept Stasi like infringements to the freedom of expression. At the same time, beyond academia I could see how the democracies we live in were becoming more and more polarised by the day, and how all these problems were being amplified by social media. With the *#MeTooMovement*, we seem to have slipped into an absurd and irrational cultural panic. In my opinion, the toxic, binary zero-sum identity politics that currently plagues western universities has gone too far. It has to end now, before the culture wars or whatever you want to call the current epistemic paralysis morphs into something more sinister.

These are strange times. To discuss political ideologies these days is to dive into a polarised, neurotic and bawdy scrum. It is nigh impossible to be heard and the voices are unforgiving. This is a book about the suppression of alternative voices in the context of a clash between politics and culture. As I will go on to demonstrate, these voices have been suppressed through both groupthink and what as a linguistic anthropologist I perceive to be linguistic corruption.

This book is arguably a polemic, but it should not be. I might be prorogued somehow, but somebody has to speak the truth about developments in the West, and Sweden in particular for so seldom do we actually get to hear what is going on in that country. The very future of Sweden, and the West generally is at stake here. I am taking the long-term view of things and asking readers to reassess their teleological priorities although the people that actually read this book will probably have their priorities absolutely right. We tend to read things which we think might appeal to us, anything that might be tinder to those inflammatory thoughts locked away in the empty cabinets and dusty drawers of our mind.

It is surely the duty of a scholar to attend to the big questions, and not just the micro-niches of his own field. It is a matter of extreme responsibility. As an ethnographer, I wish to question not just the ideological values outside of the Western domain, but also very much those within it. When I do so, I do not speak with a vatic energy; but there is a falsehood that must be unmasked and brought to light. I wish to posit the absolute, not relativism, and expose the hidden cultural and linguistic codes which I believe are the sources of oppression. That is all I have done here, but because the truth is often glossed as 'racist, xenophobic bigotry' by the dullards who have succumbed to this arsenal of commoditised language, — the rhetoric of anti-communication —, it might feel like a revelation for some. I believe we are living in an atmosphere of stifled public dissent, the kind of atmosphere that lingered before the establishment of the notorious totalitarian regimes of the twentieth century.

Politicians cannot bring themselves to state the obvious: that multiculturalism, as the ideology dictates we call it, has been a disaster everywhere. The metro-liberal Left's despisal of any sense of tradition and shared social bonds is an attempt to render us rootless, leaving our societies looking like little more than a Hamletian 'sterile promontory'. It is extraordinary to think that Marx himself rejected the 'values' (by which I perhaps mean the psycho-social facts that a group fall back on in times of conflict; the very word 'values' implies a culture of moral whim) of the French Revolution (especially equality and liberty) as too abstract. The contemporary Left takes the idea of emancipation to such extremes that it absolutises Janusian terms such as 'diversity' and 'inclusivity'. It is a betrayal of the non-State socialism that was at the heart of the Left until the late nineteenth century, and is the core of the problem that the essays in this book attempt to address. The constant mischaracterisation of those that stand for tradition and cultural continuity will come undone, and perhaps in a rather spectacular fashion. I believe we are rapidly reaching this point.

Words can suddenly become weapons in times of crisis, in the blizzard of fundamental uncertainty; the communicative ground shifts under one's feet and conversations on this topic, if they took place at all, became during the migration crisis, the most recent US Presidential election and the Brexit debate dichotomised and polarised. Following geo-political events of such magnitude, our world has become deeply politicised. Friendships (and relationships) are now formed and their fate might be determined on the basis of where one stands on these issues. The struggle and 'information war' we are implicated in goes beyond our own lives, and speaks to the future of our entire society and social norms. Communities are now created along lines of political discourse. There is an onus on linguistic and moral consistency. Terms such as 'diversity', 'inclusion', 'minority', 'race', 'gender' are the new shibboleths for probing and identifying the opposition. These terms are indicators of political compliance, be it for individuals, groups, institutions and even communities. As we will see, more or less every public institution in the West goes out of its way to incorporate these terms in all forms of communication, public or private. Communities and institutions around the world scramble unthinkingly to incorporate these words into their discourse. There is a curious belief that they can only be credible if they use this kind of language. The response is robotic and near-universal. People are forming political communities on the basis of the use of these words, dividing up the moral territory. They then moralise these communities along binary terms. Communities are thus no longer fixed entities, but are open-ended amorphous groupings based on a finite set of politicised buzz words that refer somehow to certain 'rights'. These intellectual communities are playing an important role in the epistemic shaping of our world leading to a kind of social polarisation not known since the 1930s. As a society, we have now subsided into an awkward culture of anxiety, one that I believe is not so radically different from that which prevailed in the East German Stasi era.

It is not surprising therefore that the issues I deal with in this book can be extremely divisive, and the discussions agonising. Some of the topics are almost by definition dissensual. The 'refugee crisis' in particular raises many ontological conundrums, but I hope to have shown here that the 'refugee crisis' has meant that Europeans must now ponder their moral universalism and reconsider their Christian values even if they live in ostensibly secular States. The West—Germany and Sweden especially—have brought home the problems of war-torn countries that were best left alone. The migration crisis of 2015/16, and its subsequent ongoing permutations, could (and I suspect will) entirely threaten the establishment of order in Western Europe, and that may even be the intention of some of the globalists who might be plotting a conspiratorial, destabilising agenda. Either the globalists' liberalism will have to redefine itself when for the first time in twenty-five years it is confronted with a non-liberal ideology, or a new ideology will develop. Whatever it might be, I just wish that we were not living in these times. How I wish my mind could rest on some more pleasurable, less sinister *ideé fixe*!

These issues are admittedly subjective; there is perhaps little point trying to grasp for some kind of objective truth, at least when it comes to dissecting such crises. These polarising topics (the migration crisis, Brexit and the election of Trump in particular) have exposed deep divisions between members of society which have previously lain fallow. Some of these divisions which have now come to light in America are so deep, there is even talk of civil war.

These last years, I have spent much time in Sweden. I have watched political events unfold with a sedulous eye. I have witnessed at first hand how successive Governments have forced so-called 'multiculturalism' on a kind people that are liberal-managed with the aid of a mendacious, Government-subsidised media. As an outsider, but as a good *flâneur* of the North, I have seen, objectively, how the multiculturalist project has failed in the most spectacular fashion and how its failures have been covered up time and again. If Leftist politicians are able to continue on this clandestine, deceitful path, I believe a model society described previously by the UN as 'the best place to live in the world' and presumably therefore redolent of all things that are superlative, could be transformed into a troubled State within a generation or two. That is why this book has to be written now, by somebody who has observed, but not been tainted by the statist air and the totalitarian mindset induced by the Swedish media and politicians for whom conformity of thought is the first imperative. But, also Sweden is a microcosm for the world, always one step ahead in terms of 'progressive' thinking. It is the future; it marks the direction the West is going in.

I want to do whatever it takes to remove the ideological blindfold from the Swedes, and make them see sense, because unlike some of them, I think this country is worth saving from the kind of laissez-faire multiculturalism that some countries publicly ditched years ago. Liberalism (when I speak of liberalism in this book, I am primarily talking about socio-cultural liberalism that 'promotes individual rights and equality of opportunity' [Milbank and Pabst, 2016: 13] and not economic-political liberalism) subscribes to the idea that the past is *always* worse than the present, but I love the Sweden that was, the Sweden that can still be found amongst the battalions of birch and the moon-lit antique farmhouses. I feel a Faustian restlessness, a desire to speak up for the Swedes, to show them that theirs is a country worth fighting for. Sweden has no Solzhenitsyn, nobody who is prepared to say, as he did about the Soviet Union 'in our country the lie has become not just a moral category, but a pillar of the State'.[1] And yet, once again, we are living in Solzhenitsynesque times.

Forgive me if this sounds like a *cri de coeur*, but I am talking here about cultural pathology and the regression of humanity, for we in the West at least are living 'in an age of unsettled beliefs and enfeebled tradition' (Eliot, 1933: 62). It is the crisis of secular modernity, an anti-traditional globalist liberalism steeped in moral disorder and its imminent

---

1   See *The Observer*, 29th December 1974.

clash with absolutist Islam. This is a book that tries to tackle the Socratic question in the light of a fundamental binary between globalism and localism, between tradition and continuity on the one hand and State-sponsored rootlessness on the other. But I hope it is something more than just a farrago of -*isms* that an uncouth Slovenian philosopher might cough up in a tubercular spasm.

The essay 'The Globalists in Brussels' considers the question of whether we are going to empower local communities by giving them the freedom to choose their own composition, or whether we are going to give this power to far away technocrat elites who like to think that only they can address global issues. Future political battles may well be fought along these lines. Brexit and Trump have at least shown us that there are alternatives to the prevailing discourse and ideology, and that we must not inevitably succumb to the oligarchs in Brussels.

The Swedish Government did its best to meddle in the response to the Brexit result, telling us that it disapproved of the apparently xenophobic tone of the Brexit campaign and broadcasting absurdly partisan radio documentaries on how Boris Johnson apparently had managed to dupe a national electorate. Irrespective of one's political views, the fact of the matter is that the key political figures in the Swedish Government who voiced these complaints are amateurs whose opinions are not worthy of the headlines they receive in the newspapers that they sponsor. The current Prime Minister, Stefan Löfven, is a former welder who became a trade unionist and then a politician. Basically, Arthur Scargill with a heart of gold. He had not held a single Government post before becoming Prime Minister. And so when hundreds of thousands of migrants headed towards Sweden in the summer of 2015, his Government just simply did not know what to do. Many of them had wanted this for many years, but never dreamt that the change could happen so quickly. Their ideologised liberal conscience told them that they should unquestioningly let them all in on an indiscriminate basis, but they were overwhelmed.

The migration crisis was such a mess that when the Swedish Prime Minister announced the reversal of his idiotic open-door policy, he and his deputies cried like babies in front of the cameras. Apparently, the 'multicultural dream' was not such a dream after all. Two years later, a failed asylum seeker drove a lorry down one of the main thoroughfares in central Stockholm, killing five people and seriously injuring many more. In times like this, our leaders showed themselves to be totally feeble and helpless. They have lost their way, unable to draw the obvious conclusions even when they stare them in the face. The consequences of these disastrous actions show what we should make of these stooges who have attempted to force people to accept the perverse moral diagnosis that their traditional way of life is flawed, and that their society is inherently based on evil prejudice.

Very similar events took place in Germany: thick crowds of tearful Germans embracing 'refugees' on railway platforms were months later dealing with mass rapes, suicide bombers, machete-wielding immigrants, lorries being driven into Christmas markets and an Afghan asylum seeker with axe in hand whose actions were inspired by the brutal atrocities in southern France (Nice) a week earlier. In the month of July 2016, Bavaria, the part of Germany that took in most of the Syrian asylum seekers, looked like it might slip into some kind of *intifada*. With each attack, the German media tried to persuade the public that the attackers were mentally ill, and that they could have just as easily have been Germans. It is a familiar pattern in Germany (and Sweden): there is a 'refugee' induced terrorist event, the German media blames its own people and the politicians respond by slowly chipping away at the freedom of the ethnic population with odious hate-speech legislation or censorship of social media, which is put in place to criminalise the discourse of the *Alternative für Deutschland* (AfD) opposition. Unwelcome political opponents will be rendered illegitimate, but this will be dressed up as a measure to protect helpless minorities. Merkel who wears a solemn personality made for a Requiem Mass, and her globalist peers seem with these initiatives to wish to aspire to a European-wide oppressive mass guardian-state which they can therapeutically control through managerial government. The cultural Left seems to wish to use immigrants to change fundamentally society in the West. There appears to be a desire amidst certain groups on the Left to use immigrants as an instrument to turn upside down the social order in Europe.

In this book, I deal with the issue of obfuscation. One example of this is when a terrorist ran his lorry into a heaving crowd of party-goers celebrating Bastille Day in Nice, killing eighty-six people and critically injuring many more, and the police responded by destroying the CCTV footage of the event. Perhaps we should just pretend the atrocity never happened. This book does not attempt to detail or describe the long list of horrendous attacks by Islamists who were invited to our countries, but instead attempts to understand the reasons why our political leaders have turned against us in this fashion, feeding us lies and misinformation and using the 'racist' slogan as a means of closing down all discussion. It tries to show that our democracies and the principles that define them are in danger. The book is a collection of short essays, a factory of ideas and thoughts, written at a time when political events are changing faster than anybody could ever imagine. There is a sense of urgency here; a feeling that in the West we are losing control, that we are sliding into an age of techno-authoritarianism. I am writing at a time of crisis and that is perhaps reflected in the book's style. The essay style has been chosen as short self-contained chapters are nimbler than discursive argumentation, and permit me to move from topic to topic with pluralistic thought. Some of the essays are enlivened by the occasional *aperçu*, interlaced with short ethnographic vignettes. I deal with a multiplicity of subjects in an anti-systemic way (one might say with a distinctive *timbre*) without forcing these into a single object of enquiry. I prefer not to organise my thoughts into tight, logically ordered systems, but instead to tip-toe between illusion and disillusion.

In July 2016, the Pope declared the world to be in a state of war, and had said previously that he believed this might be Christianity's last Christmas. This is not a war of religion, he pointed out. Indeed, that is so. This is a civil war; a war between people who want to preserve their traditions, cultural heritage and freedom and those who preach liberalist multiculturalism and who will defend a whole schema of freedom infringements in order to achieve it. *Home* has become the locus of a silent, uncanny war. European nations are divided between those who want to preserve historical modalities of belonging, and those who wish to extirpate them; those who want continuity and identity, and those who aspire to a Rousseauesque social *tabula rasa*.

There will no doubt arise in some readers the temptation to accuse me of hyperbole, but President Putin has said himself repeatedly that we are on the brink of nuclear war; and yet this is curiously never reported in the Western media. One might think if the President of Russia gathered journalists to tell them about what he believed was the nuclear threat, then that might be worthy of an article, especially given Putin's reputation for speaking frankly. Journalists are quick to gloss over anything that might disturb the image of the safe, world order that President Obama insisted we enjoy even if mass shootings in America now seem to happen on an almost weekly basis. 'Unorthodox' views are not welcome which in itself tells us something about the relationship between Western Governments and the media.

Islamist atrocities have been committed in places where just a few years ago they would have been unthinkable. The arrogance shown by some immigrants towards their host society is a new phenomenon, and not a feature of previous refugee crises. Our politicians are in denial about the threats that face us. The former Swedish Prime Minister told Swedes to 'open their hearts' to the 'refugees', and now some of the migrants are committing rape and murder on a daily basis in the parts of Germany, Sweden and France which accepted the highest number. Those who spoke out about what they perceived to be a gross error were called 'racist bigots', and were subject to verbal abuse. Legislation was introduced to silence them, so that the project could continue unheeded.

But, the real theme that connects the click-clacking pieces of this book is the increasingly wooly notion of globalist liberalism and *in extremis* its orthodoxy of cultural nihilism, a concept which is explained fully in the 'Introduction'. In terms of the latter, the critique is simply that one cannot begin to integrate people from very alien cultures into Western society if one educates them by telling them that their European hosts (be it Swedes, Britons or Germans) are collaborators, racists, colonialists and fascists. That is no way to establish fraternity. And yet Europe has bought into the notion of cultural nihilism, and such an ideology of failure is weakening and dividing the Continent.

Having prowled through the geo-political shrubbery, some of my thoughts have emerged as a Nietzschean plea (without the anti-Christian features) to think for oneself, to rise above the herd. Nietzsche would have believed that the ideals of contemporary Western society (equality, tolerance and diversity) favour the unexceptional and the mediocre. Equality has no place for genius. It is fine to raise valleys, but why try and lower peaks? We have created the society of the autonomous herd where greatness is regarded with suspicion, where feeling pleased and proud as a champion is not an altogether-good-thing. But, it is herd-like in another way: people dare not question these ideals even if, as I hope to show, they are far more contentious than they appear. They dare not speak out about the changes happening in our societies. We risk creating a society that is doubly weak: it is based on flawed social truths, unquestioned and supposedly irrefutable ideological truisms; and the herd enmeshed in these ideals will not challenge the truths.

The liberal herd morality has become too strong in our societies, dismissing independent thinking and undermining our freedom. The essays in this book explore in a roundabout way some of the mechanisms by which this has been achieved. It concludes by saying the West needs to resurrect the 'noble' instinct, the feeling of power without having to rely on the moral ideal of universal equality. It needs to remember that basic social structures such as the nation-state, the family and a faith do actually matter.

I hate being a pessimist. One cannot change the world by telling people that they are all going to die, that their herd morality will end up in cultural loss. One has to trudge through the *Weltschmerz*, and make sure there is a hook at the end. A hook to hang some kind of positive thought on.

I ask the reader not to perceive this as a Schopenhauerian thesis, but as an appeal to speak out, to rise above the herd, to trust one's instincts and for Swedes to take immediate action to save their fine country from collapse. In that sense at least, I have a smidgen of something positive to say, and attempt to look 'over the horizon' in the final essay to days where the world takes on a blush hue in the context of recent anti-globalist successes.

I support a multi-polar world, an anti-universalist, anti-globalist political philosophy that does away with the herd consciousness as a form of self-preservation and promotes individual actions. I am promoting creative autonomy *hic et nunc*. Western politicians like President Obama talked about 'universal values', but I doubt they exist. I wish to promote localism, and not globalism which feeds off this herd consciousness. We should be empowering local communities, and not giving power away to bureaucratic strangers with Bond-villain-like dreams. The localism/globalism distinction underpinned much of the Brexit debate, even if the Bremainers insisted on framing it in a different way. There were those who wanted political accountability to be local, and those who were comfortable giving power to an unelected elite in order to have a stronger collective 'say' in the world. For many the rationale of voting for Brexit was at least to maintain the familiar structures of political accountability that have served us well enough over time in the context of a sovereign state.

Brexit showed that the Establishment could be beaten despite all the doomsday threats from the globalists and even President Obama. The opponents to this, those who were too keen to cede sovereignty to the likes of Merkel, Schulz and Juncker proved to be very bad losers indeed. Many signed a petition in the following days insisting that the result be overturned. They had become enemies of democracy, and now it is clear that many of the anti-democrats sit in the House of Lords (the upper house of the Parliament of the United Kingdom) and are hell-bent on stopping Brexit instead of doing their job and implementing it.

A person's view on Brexit now represents not just an index for an entire repertoire of political opinions. In accordance with the Left's attempt to correlate personality with world vision, it is also a gauge for what kind of person he is: good, educated and rational or irrational, irresponsible and ill-educated. We have discovered a tapestry of conflict, but it is a tapestry that goes beyond political thinking. A strange, and rather haunting chasm in our society has been suddenly exposed. Psychological walls built around the doubts and suspicions that linger in an environment of groupthink (a concept discussed in the essay 'The Groupthink Trap') leave people wondering whether they have been alienated and unsure whether it is acceptable to raise such and such topic. Many who describe themselves as 'tolerant' become immediately intolerant of opposing views.

The politicising ideology that is discussed in all of these essays affects every aspect of social life. It is oppressive and bordering on totalitarian. An extreme liberal narrative is being merged with institutional fascism to create some curious thought-bubble. But is the thought-bubble bursting? Mainstream media (MSM) ignored it, predictably enough, but the 2018 Italian general election result suggests people can see through the mendacious 'liberal' speech codes that make up the slogans of this ideology. The migration crisis has led to the emergence of slave markets in Libya and child marriage in Sweden. And yet it is clear that those that caused the migration crisis three years ago have not experienced any kind of *metanoia* about what they did. The consequences are far too traumatic to admit. In September of this year, Sweden will go to the polls again. This might be the very last chance to save Sweden from the scars of multiculturalism, censorship and the authoritarian Left — topics which are discussed fully in this book.

Introduction

> And we should consider every day lost on which we have not danced at least once. And we should call every truth false which was not accompanied by at least one laugh.
>
> — Nietzsche

This book is an ideological journey through the murky waters of cultural nihilism. The journey is a fragmented, non-continuous one with no itinerary, but it is real and not vicarious. It is an experiential, phenomenological wandering that drifts in and out of the Swedish woods, only to reappear in urban Russia, Oxford, Kiev, north-west Greenland, Paris and southern France. One might call it unconventional in that sense. It is a journey of solitude, a slightly Bergmanesque chronicle, undertaken by a man alone with his thoughts, rather preoccupied by the fact that something is not quite right.

By nihilism, Nietzsche had in mind 'a transvaluation of values' at the extreme of modernity. In the consumerist, globalist society that we live in, one might take this in a Nietzschean context to mean one desires what one desires and what one desires is the product of stimuli, not 'will'. However, my concern in this book is to embed Nietzsche's thinking into the contemporary politico-cultural framework where a nihilistic tendency vis-à-vis cultural categories has become something of an orthodoxy; and it is the nature of the orthodoxy which is of particular interest. What I am writing about here is the rejection of the authority of long-established social and cultural categories which have become somehow the symptoms of a defective Western mythos. These categories are being undermined by a collection of heavy politicised whims whose only appeal is often the destruction of the previous social fabric. Spengler (1991) showed how these features of nihilism were a feature of collapsing societies, and as an ethnographer I am keen to find out if he was correct.

By the orthodoxy of cultural nihilism in contemporary Western society, is meant a veiled imperative to devalue certain aspects of our cultural life if these features are not able to appeal to some victimology or other. The term nihilism in this book is used in the Nietzschean sense (and not the Heideggerian or Sartrean sense) to refer to a critique of modernity in an age where the highest (the sheer notion of higher values is anathema to liberalism) values have been problematised, and where mediocrity and conformity are privileged over individualism. Nihilism is where everything is permitted, and nothing is worth anything. To take one contemporary corollary to this, one might infer that we are approaching the ultra-liberal end game when pan-sexual promiscuity is so totally saturating that there is no thrill or *frisson* left. Nothing can any longer be illicit, for everything is available on the metaphorical supermarket shelf.

Cultural nihilism is an explicit anti-Western cultural typology, a product of cultural Marxist thinking peddled most aggressively by French intellectuals. It is selective in terms of the cultural categories it wishes to break down, and is full of contradictions. It is secularist and anti-Christian but supportive of an Islam which speaks in totalising narratives. Its enemy is well-functioning, developed, relatively homogeneous communities in the West: societies that have produced wealth for more or less everybody. It is difficult to find any philosophies as perverse and peculiar as this, but cultural nihilism might share something with Jewish anti-semitism in terms of structures of self-hatred. As part of cultural nihilism, secularisation undermines the highest values posited in Western culture, but also its foundations. It negates transcendental beliefs and replaces them with modernist slogans that collectively underscore liberalist thinking.

No attempt is made in this book to theorise nihilism beyond what has been written already from a rather monological perspective (Rosen, 1969; Löwith, 1995; Vattimo, 2004). But, instead the book intends to show how nihilism plays out in the twenty-first century, and particularly within a Swedish context which can only be described as *noir*. I hope it exemplifies how this kind of cultural nihilism can in fact be a danger to the human condition.

This is a meta-crisis because the values that imbue life with meaning are being undermined in the name of politically correct secularism at a time when the incoming culture (to Sweden at least), Islam, absolutises the same values. We are withdrawing from the rooted, autochthonous world of significance, the *Lebenswelt*, to the point that it is no longer clear what our basic cultural commitments are. At the same time, we are embracing a culturally nihilistic creed built on the narrative of emancipation, and labelling it 'progress': an oratorically persuasive way of saying 'change' (cf. Gehlen's 'Sekulärisierung des Fortschritts', 1967). It is an orthodoxy because the manner in which it is presented makes it extremely difficult to refute, as to do so one would simply be 'unprogressive' and thus in accordance with politically correct determined social norms 'illegitimate'. These essays look at how structures of meaning which have stood the test of time are being broken down, and being replaced with faux-connections. Reference will be made to academia where in some corners intellectual traditions are being perverted, and the prevailing discourse used to do it is both homogenising and silencing.

This book unpacks a little what ultra-liberal modernity in Sweden actually looks like. In this respect, Baudrillard's (1993: 133) likening of liberal modernity as hypertelic extension of spheres of culture to a vast orgy seems apt:

> The orgy in question was the moment when modernity exploded on us, the moment of liberation in every sphere. Political liberation, sexual liberation, liberation of the forces of production, liberation of the forces of destruction, women's liberation, children's liberation, liberation of unconscious drives, the liberation of art.

Woodward (2009: 145) notes that the 'effect of this orgy of liberation is that the distinctions between cultural spheres break down, and each sphere becomes totalising in itself: sexual liberation has made everything sexual, political liberation has made everything political etc.' It seems to me that we are living in such a totalising system today, and that the 'orgy of liberation' is happening at a time when there is an attempt to collapse some of the basic categories and social structures by which we organise our society: gender, family, the nation-state etc. This is part of the emancipatory teleology which dictates that such actions amount to deconstructivist 'progress'. It is my premise that such a teleology ends ultimately in cultural nihilism.

The implosion of the categories of modernity which undermines entirely notions of tradition, structure, convention and familiarity and the collapsing of the meta-narratives of history leaves us vulnerable and acephalous without existentially fulfilling forms of meaning. These uncanny developments go against Enlightenment rationalism and foundationalism. We have plunged into a meta-crisis, an ontological *mise-en-abyme*. Islam in Sweden does not engage with these concepts of modernity, and is instead more likely to be steeped in theocratic significance. This encounter could then be perceived as some kind of inexorable symbolic cultural exchange; an *amor fati*. And it is being done without a hint of nostalgia. One must simply accept it as an event that is taking place, as 'progress' towards a more equitable 'multicultural' society.

I hope to show that there are many contradictions inherent in this ultra-liberal, nihilistic path. But, the most obvious one is perhaps that secularisation is seen as part of the development of a socially 'progressive' society, but in Swedish society (or indeed any) Islam will never be able to accept the secularist dogma. The syncretic ideals of secularism and multiculturalism, emancipatory feminism and Islam are entirely contradictory and confuse cultural impulses, but are all equally promoted at the same time (in Sweden at least). There is no rational reason why the radical feminists of a country like Sweden are so supportive of Islam. They sit of course at the opposite ends of the egalitarian scale. This appears to be a case of the 'enemy of the enemy is my friend'. In this case, the enemy is the West based on a Christian tradition.

Cultural nihilism is not a state of being that can last beyond the short-term because self-evidently it leaves people with *nihilo*, 'nothing'. Nihilism means that the shared cultural state is one of denial. Ways of living that had previously been marginalised now take cultural priority, and the previously sacred life may now be rendered defunct. It is an extraordinary cultural and philosophical *volte face*, but it is my belief that cultural nihilism will be replaced by something more positive and identity-affirming. Like every typology, this is a simplification, but cultural nihilism seems to be more or less the best term to describe the current direction of Swedish society, but also society generally speaking in the West.

But before we abscond into the Swedish woods for some indulgent introspection, let us turn to the layout of this book, which is divided into a dozen mini-essays. Our attention is first focused on the important psychological dimension implicit in the conceptual orthodoxies that I will describe, and like good inclusive citizens we are all meant to embrace. The essay 'The Groupthink Trap' is concerned with the invisible and sometimes inaudible bundle of ideological expectations which make up what I call 'liberal' groupthink. The essay looks very briefly at how liberal groupthink manifests itself in an academic context in particular, and the mechanisms used to create a sometimes false consensus on ideological priorities. The following essay, 'The Political Correctness Folly', goes to the heart of the instruments used to enforce this apparent consensus. The objective of this essay is to show how political correctness has veered far from its original, well-meaning trajectory. Working in conjunction with groupthink, it creates instead an environment of rhetorical uncertainty, a verbal culture of over-manufactured slogans whose objective is to showcase victimologies and transfer cultural priorities to minorities through an ever more narrowly defined discourse. One of the arguments that runs through these essays is that this discourse is more than merely insidious. It is impacting negatively on our freedom — freedom to express ourselves, freedom to formulate contrarian opinions. The repercussions are *real*. There is now an unease about what can be legitimately discussed in public. The freedom of speech, and the ability to 'speak up' lie at the core of the following essay, 'Freedom of Speech'. In a context of Islamist terrorism, censorship, hate-speech legislation and so-called hate-crimes, the freedom to articulate any views which run contrary to the liberal groupthink has retreated to the private realm. The anti-discourse now belongs to the living room.

The next essay opens with an ethnographic vignette from the High Arctic, a place where social, familial and environmental connections have an absolute ontological priority, and a place where I have done long-term fieldwork as an ethnographer. Sitting at the top of the world, the Inuit hunters observe our cosmos from the point of isolated privilege. In contrast to theirs, they believe our world of liberalist fancies and disconnectedness can only be self-imploding in the long-term. They hold that to live in a place without *real* connections is to embrace nihilism. The next two essays are concerned solely with Sweden, and provide the reader with a few insights into culturally nihilistic developments in this country. The focus here is primarily political and looks at the potential re-emergence of European totalitarianism and the role of the media in its creation; this time it is a quasi-totalitarianism that appears benign, but nonetheless has taken shape in a context of mass surveillance and an anti-racist ideology that is advanced as if it were unassailable.

The promotion of multiculturalism is leaving our societies directionless, segregated and floundering in a convoluted teleology. The essay 'Societies at Risk' takes us back into the Swedish woods with the ever-circulating thoughts of what happens when we have nothing more *gemein* ('together, in common'), when as a society we have simply been blown off course. This malaise manifests itself at a meta-political level where some of our leaders have been for too long motivated by globalist ambitions, and not local concerns. It is argued throughout the book that one of the key contributing factors to this malaise is the EU and the way it has scandalously dismissed notions of democracy and accountability. The ambitions of the federalist EU have gone way beyond the mandate handed to them forty years ago when member-states joined in the interest of facilitating trade. The plan to create political union by stealth risks creating a dystopia because these actions are tyrannical, and tyranny normally results in dystopia for the many, and wealth and happiness for the few. This is thus the preoccupation of the essay 'The Globalists in Brussels'.

The next essay focuses on the rather morbid topic of terrorism and the West's inability to respond to it because of the moral relativism we have embraced. The essay 'Over the Brow of the Hill' is not by any means a conclusion (nor indeed an essay) in the conventional sense. But, it does bring together some of the key strands (there are admittedly many in this book) and finally considers on a more upbeat note how the West might begin to look forward given the deeply troubling paradigms that have been touched upon in previous essays.

I

THE GROUPTHINK TRAP

'Great is truth, but still greater, from a practical point of view, is silence about truth. By simply not mentioning certain subjects. [...] totalitarian propagandists have influenced opinion much more effectively than they could have by the most eloquent denunciations'

— ALDOUS HUXLEY

OPERATING AT AN ADVANCED LEVEL, groupthink and its bruising core assumptions can bring about silence because people are fearful of social isolation. In times of quasi-war and oppressive ideologies, potentially deviant opinions can linger in toxic silence. Toxic because this is a silence of coercive psychological barricades, hostile borders and prickly peripheries. The empathy for the political other has waned in certain liberal circles where deviant psycho-cultural thinking might be taboo and where the 'progressive' has to be internalised. This is the inclusiveness that we are all meant to celebrate.

Dissenters threaten the cohesion of the group, endanger the illusion of invulnerability and unanimity and thus risk the group's requisite social identity and the need to maintain it. Groupthink determines everything from our views on climate change to our response to terrorism. Opinions and reactions are pre-programmed to conform to a liberal, politically correct agenda. At its extreme, groupthink as part of a propaganda machine can become totalitarian. Then, dissent retreats entirely to the private realm. There might be examples of this played out on the State level. In 2011 at the funeral of Kim Jong-il of North Korea, thousands cried hysterically as the cortège drove through the snowy streets of Pyongyang lined with crowds of people. Women dressed in military uniforms swayed, on the verge of collapse. It looked like the scene from a badly made film, and perhaps it was. It is easy to assume that the outpouring of grief and the hysterical wailing was choreographed, but what if it wasn't? What if this is the power of groupthink and State propaganda in an isolated totalitarian state? A country so cut off from the rest of the world, it sits literally in darkness at night next to its ultra-electrified neighbour. Satellite pictures show North Korea to be invisible in the darkness. It looks as if there is a sea separating China and South Korea.

The cavalcade was led by a black limousine with a giant portrait of the leader balanced on the top. Behind the American-made 1975 Lincoln Continental Limousine drove another limousine decorated with North Korean flags and carrying the casket of Kim Jong-il on the roof. As the cortège wended its way past thick clouds of wailing mourners, the snowfall became heavier. Thousands flocked to the slowly moving car screaming: 'Don't go, General! Don't leave us'!'[1]

Ideologically speaking, the West is naturally very, very far from North Korea, but totalitarian mentalities begin with groupthink. Groupthink is the psychological phenomenon that occurs within a group of people, in which the desire for harmony or conformity in the group results in an irrational or dysfunctional decision-making outcome. Groupthink can be manipulated to act as a form of mind-control, and manifests itself in the new mega-churches with their irritating theatrical style of worship. Apparatchiks coerce individuals into adopting group beliefs by tricking an individual into thinking that the group's predetermined consensus was in fact the individual's own idea, and by making him think that he has input into the group's decision when in fact he has not.

It is irrefutable that groupthink as a pathology has been shown to lead to fatal flaws in group decision-making because the desire for group consensus overrides people's desire to present alternatives, and because the system of 'checks and balances' is effectively removed. Two well-known

---

1 Available at: https://www.youtube.com/watch?v=mSLJYbhXCkE

examples are the Challenger Space Shuttle disaster and the Bay of Pigs invasion. Engineers of the space shuttle knew about some faulty parts months before take-off, but they did not want negative press so they pushed ahead with the launch anyway. With the Bay of Pigs invasion, President Kennedy made a decision and the people around him supported it despite their own concerns. The same thing happened in the boardrooms of Volkswagen in the more recent debacle where the decision making process was psychologically corrupted. And that is the concern here: psychological corruption.

Groupthink (Janis, 1972) members see themselves as part of an in-group working against an out-group opposed to their goals. In the context of academia, groupthink is based on a presumed, but false consensus, the assumption that the person subscribes to a full programme of post-modern liberal views on everything from multiculturalism, the EU, gay marriage, and modern art, to climate change and Shostakovich. Totalitarian systems of thought might begin with such synchronised group thinking where psychological attempts are made to prevent dissent materialising. Liberalist groupthink appeals often to what one might call in-group culture snobs, the kind of Tartuffians who love to wax lyrical about social justice and diversity, but pepper their conversation with talk of rather undiverse pastimes such as contemporary opera and modern art. The conventional aim with this kind of liberal groupthink is for them to secure their place in the liberal intellectual elite with all its cultural manifestations.

Groupthink hinges on the power of the collective to perpetuate a worldview which could be entirely false. A biased selectivity in the interpretation of events is achieved through groupthink discourse which relies on a perversion of language, an unquestioned belief in the morality of the group and a complete lack of critical evaluation of alternative viewpoints. There is a loss of independent thinking, freedom of individual expression and creativity. If there is a competing groupthink, it is a shy, silent and suppressed one, unable to question things which seem to be beyond suspicion. The dominant 'liberal' groupthink is arguably as 'closed' as that of the jihadists who believe that the Qur'an states the absolute truth. They both work as forms of social endorsement.

Groupthink requires the appearance of a consensus of opinion; the *ummah* — the society of all believers — does the same thing for Muslims right across the world. It might seem excessive to think of a religion as groupthink, but radical Islam, as it is practiced in some parts of the world, is indeed that. It is fiercely oppositional: the in-group Muslims are working against the out-group (anybody who is not Muslim, or who does not accept their interpretation of Islam). If one is part of the in-group, one does not question this as it will leave one excluded, alienated and in the parts of the Middle East and North Africa where ISIS, Al-Qaeda and others have operated, marked for death. A check on the radical Islam groupthink could be a sign of heresy. But of course it is difficult to control the groupthink if your members run into the billions.

In the context of groupthink, the power of peer pressure is such that any dissent is socially unacceptable, and would lead to alienation. Any alternative thinking is persecuted, and thus groupthink always results in errors as those under its sway do not perceive any mechanism for 'speaking out'. There is, of course, but there are normally consequences if one does so. In an age of mass immigration from North Africa and the Middle East, a mindset that dictates that one must not deviate from the conditioned norms could come at an unquantifiable cost: irreversible changes to our societies, broad recognition of *shari'ah* law, an end to gender equality etc.

Those who are complicit in groupthink are effectively the 'enemies of freedom' because only one opinion is legitimate. A feature of groupthink is that outsiders are consistently negatively stereotyped. It is not surprising that this false sense of unanimous consensus can be particularly dangerous when introduced into a conformist society such as Sweden that is struggling with a sense of putative, collective guilt. Critical thinking might be eroded in such a context as we witnessed in Sweden's worst miscarriage of justice with the Bergwall case (2015), where a supposed serial killer ended up being cleared of all charges. Groupthink was considered to be one of the reasons for the errors in judgement.[2] Lawyers involved were accused of 'believing' the facts, rather than actually looking at them, which is a rather disconcerting development to say the least.

Ironically (as surely higher education is concerned with an open discussion of ideas), but not altogether surprisingly, groupthink can be acute in academia amongst at least the more ideologised left-wing intelligentsia. Here, groupthink can act as a coercive mechanism to suppress what they deem to be 'fascist' thought, a binomial in which everything that does not look or sound like democratic, globalist liberalism is fascist. In such a context, it is assumed that all 'good' people are politically liberal. It is considered normal for all Faculty members in a Humanities or Social Sciences department to be liberal, and normally far left of that. The opposite would be unthinkable, for one would be surrounded by heretics. The so-called liberals are not very liberal when it comes to their demands for liberality.

As we will come to see, it turns out that the quasi-religious advocates of 'diversity', the pillars of the diversity dictatorship, are often not very diverse at all. They are in fact monolithic, frequently blinded by their own ideology and engaged in a sensitising onslaught. They operate in an ideological echo-chamber, a monoculture ironically devoid of any view diversity whatsoever. The university bureaucrats that eagerly peddle this agenda spend their days filling out equality and diversity surveys, implementing gender equality charters produced by the Equality Challenge Unit, and asking themselves whether there are hidden or unacknowledged gender biases in their thinking. Various awards are given out to university departments for recruiting more women and minorities, and they get to call themselves 'champions'. Oxford University was recently given a bronze award. One wonders what one has to do to get gold. Social justice has been bureaucratised, and in the universities at least is the preoccupation of failed academics.

Nietzsche thought that the pursuit of truth was the highest moral value. Our universities should focus on truth and the achievement of academic

---

2   See *Dagens Nyheter* (*DN*) article (5th June, 2015).

excellence, not social justice and political conformity. University subjects such as sociology are based on the pursuit of social justice rather than truth to such an extent that the integrity of research and certainly teaching in such disciplines is jeopardised. However, people cannot always come to the truth unless they are able to express the untruth and have that criticised in public forums. One truth that many on the Left seem to have forgotten is that Marxists killed more than 100 million people around the world in the twentieth century. And yet so many academics in the Humanities and Social Sciences still cling onto the Marxist doctrine, never wishing to discuss such facts.

Social justice biases are hardly 'hidden': positive discrimination towards women and ethnic minorities is everywhere in the public sector, and is made absolutely explicit in some job advertisements. Women-only short-lists exist for appointments to certain academic posts. There are plenty of women in academia who have benefited from this positive discrimination. Unsurprisingly, this bias is particularly prevalent in disciplines which have historically been more popular with men, such as the sciences and engineering. It is a radical oversimplification of the historical story to say that women have been oppressed and that we now must make amends for it. Throughout history, males have been cannon-fodder in countless wars. They have been coal-miners and worse.

But now there is in fact a pseudo-war on men in academia, and probably much of the public sector, because the ideology dictates that one must perceive society to be *inherently* unfair to women. If one is a white, straight male, then the system might perhaps just work against one, because one has no chance of invoking minority status. It is really time for these men to fight back, but do not expect the feminist Swedish men with their handbags swinging from their arms to lead the charge.

If one disagrees with the feminist ideology — a key component of the liberal groupthink —, one risks being excluded and automatically subject to the accusatory atmosphere. Many students have embraced this hegemonic thinking and wish to increasingly censor people they disagree with, contemporaries or historical figures. This is no longer a righteous question of defending the weak and the marginalised. It is little more than a race to be the most politically correct, sometimes apparently for the sake of being just that: a group of activists who claim to wish to stop bigotry, but are amongst the most bigoted people you will ever meet. Anybody who disagrees with their views risks being labelled a Western imperialist, sexist, privileged or any number of things, even if such a description is often quite inaccurate. Armed with this 'bigoted tolerance', these uncritical thinkers tend to resort to a basket of amorphous ideologies and misplaced prejudices, rather than reasoned argument. They do not seem to understand the very basics of critical reasoning with their 'straw man' arguments and informal fallacies. They unthinkingly accuse people of racism in discussions on Islam, and thus fail to address the proposition by misrepresenting the opposing position. These so-called intellectuals seem to wish to live in an anti-intellectual world where stereotypes trump critical, independent thinking. They seem to be motivated by an anti-metaphysical imperative which implies they should discard notions such as abstract thought, causality and truth.

The result is that there is relatively little debate about anything at a time when cultural patterns are being bashed about. Groupthink creates a culture of silence and intimidation in universities and alongside developments such as no-platforming correspond to an anti-intellectual bullying. Nowadays, our universities are no longer bastions of free thinking and open debate, but are instead increasingly the wastelands of groupthink and anti-communication where the key issues of the day are seldom discussed.

Many academics, most of them educated at the elite higher education institutions, stand apparently for anti-elitism. They shudder even at the sound of the word 'elitist' because it encapsulates everything that doesn't have to do with moral victimhood, and would thus run contrary to the prevailing groupthink. And yet some represent the Leftist cultural elite and are thus the embodiment of another hypocrisy. Intellectually, they want to be an elite but must not be described as such, as their political views and philosophy are completely antithetical to the concept of elitism.

Many like to talk down all monarchic structures, but rush to Buckingham Palace to collect their OBEs. Some speak incessantly about equality and social justice, but are educated at the most expensive schools in the country. Schools that are nowadays beyond the reach of almost everybody except the ultra-rich.

These so-called 'Champagne socialists' are in fact the epitome of hypocrisy. They have a tendency to frame discussions in terms of diversity, inequality and human rights, the latter of which is often cited as the conduit for liberalism's alleged supremacy, even if it is based on abstract and very outdated principles. They are the face of the culture of repudiation that characterises contemporary Western society, and the groupthink that colours the teaching of Humanities (and some of the Social Sciences) in our universities. It is a culture that celebrates a post-Christian era, a penumbra of thought that dismisses the notion that the West was built on Christianity, that it is the pinnacle of human cultural and intellectual achievement, and is worth defending. It is a context which dismisses all kinds of rules and norms, wallowing in the anti-grammar of our time.

There is nothing wrong with elitism providing it is based on academic ability (and not wealth) and providing there is meritocratic mobility into it. At a political level, elitism must have national accountability, and not supra-national oversights. Throughout history, there have always been elites of some kind. Elitism provides society's next generation of leaders. The best and brightest should rule. So I am afraid that is Jeremy Corbyn out.

But to describe such opinions as unfashionable would be an understatement. To be a member of the liberalist groupthink, it is important that one is signed up to the multiculturalist agenda and to victim support. Academia and the Civil Service are no longer meritocracies; they are meritocracies gone too far. A system of positive discrimination is in place for those people who were perceived to be discriminated against in the past even if, relatively speaking, they are the new arrivals. Within this insular world, the value of what is said depends on who said it, and not on what was actually said. The orthodoxy of nihilism is at work, and the result is that we are moving towards a perverse minoritocracy, not a *bona fide* meritocracy.

It should be borne in mind that such ideology is grounded in psychological mechanisms which when left unchallenged can function to hide social reality. I believe this is the current state of affairs. We live in a world of warped paradoxes, but the social reality is concealed. As an example of this, in a society that claims to be built on free speech, it is more or less impossible to talk about the things that matter. A topic we will return to in the essay entitled 'Freedom of Speech'.

In such a blurred context, these terribly important thoughts about the 'big issues' become internalised because the omnipresent ideology has rendered them illegitimate. Internalised ways of thinking risk falling deeply at odds with the official mantra operationalised by the managerial liberal regime. This is ideology in the Marxian sense: false ideas representing the consciousness of the liberal elite used to legitimise its power. The ideas are false because they claim to represent everybody, but are in fact just the views of a group with control over the ideological mouthpiece. As with any effective ideological discourse, it has a subtle indirectness to it and belongs to the unconscious of a society. Ideology is apparent in the mass media, as we will see in Sweden, and in the language code used to generate these messages.

Monolithic liberalism with its claim of universality underpins so comprehensively the way all our public institutions function, it has almost become some kind of invisible film, a pernicious layer of imperialistic ideology that is so omnipresent in the West that some have forgotten what was there beforehand. And yet its effects are anything but marginal, innocuous or insubstantive. They are there to be seen in the education of our students. The totalitarian mindset is approaching some kind of sovereignty over language with regard to these issues. It might be assumed that liberalism stands above moral debate and argument by claiming to have a monopoly on legitimacy, and *eudaimonia* or 'human flourishing'.

Allow me to focus briefly on the question of diversity as a key feature of the liberal groupthink — 'diversity', the magical word that seems to be perpetually on the lips of the bureaucratic *primus pilus* whose battalions have taken over the management of our universities. Diversity is a particularly important part of this ideology that has been institutionalised with every institution having a 'diversity statement'. In the case of university diversity statements, an attempt is made to cover every thinkable variable which might be grounds for discrimination.

For its advocates, 'diversity' has become a sort of religion, some kind of intellectual creed based on a perverse self-hatred of the West, providing of course it is not diversity of thought. People are told 'diverse' workplaces are more 'productive' even if there is no good evidence for it, and frankly who cares if they are? Surely, the objective must be simply to employ the best people irrespective of their ethnicity and gender. Diversity has assumed the mantle of some kind of irrefutable truth, a celebration of tolerance, but its implementation is totally intolerant. We will see subsequently how the objective of this 'tolerance' manifests itself in the words of European Commissioners and former Heads of State such as Sarkozy. They wish to destroy the notion that a nation represents one culture. They have been absolutely explicit about this, and so it is wrong to equate liberalism with inaction and laissez-faire politics. In the words of our political leaders, diversity collocated with so-called 'tolerance' is cultural abandonment and ethnic dilution.

In practice, the sub-text regarding diversity states, 'It is fine that you don't look like us, but you must think like us'. You can be black, disabled or lesbian, but if you are a conservative thinker, then that is not 'diversity'. 'Diversity' is another Leftist catchphrase which provides a *quid pro quo* advantage to a particular person based on political considerations. It is part of the overall socio-political agenda that is the subject of the essays in this book.

As with so much of the language that makes up the liberalist speech code, diversity means in fact the opposite to what it should connote. When one hears people talk about 'diversity', one can be sure that they are promoting a hegemonic discourse which is completely intolerant of any 'diverse' opinions. They are the face of an ideologised public consciousness, a closed politicised mind that uses this kind of language to create and enforce a common sociality. According to the globalist, multiculturalism has nothing to do with ensuring the existence of a multiplicity of cultures. Get beyond the hermeneutical *legerdemain*, and one realises it is entirely antithetical to that, seeking to toss every ethnicity and identity into the cauldron of global consumerism. What is served up is homogeneity, and not heterogeneity. 'Multiculturalism' and 'diversity' are key terms in a dialectical process supported by multinationals and globalist politicians. It is a process which sets out to rule and dictate to a globalised, consumerised mass of people stripped of national identity, but endowed with secularism and a façade of fake, humanistic values. We no longer need heritage, culture or any sense of nationhood. Now, we have Hollywood, McDonald's and MTV. Now, we have one size that fits all, but in a typical nefarious manner we will call it the opposite.

In totalitarian regimes, language tends to be manipulated to the point that words signify the opposite of what they are meant to refer to. It becomes a kind of anti-syntax. With code-words such as 'diversity', 'progressive' and 'racist', the language of the liberalist regime sounds like a repetitive, totalitarian monologue with its ideological phraseology. It is becoming stagnant and denies any individual spirit. It connotes a teleological view of social development by coupling the positive connotations of the word 'progress' with any grouping of people who are 'ethnic' (i.e. not white). It operates therefore in a totalitarian fashion because it attempts to eliminate the scope for questioning or critical evaluation. If the scope for questioning something is suppressed, then it is reasonable to assume that a totalitarian mechanism is being employed.

Totalitarian language is built on implicit, axiomatic oppositions. Polarisation is mandatory for totalitarian discourse. 'Diversity' is part of this herding, polarising lexicon of ideological principles (every ideology has a group of labels which it uses for ideological purposes); institutions and the 'institutionalised' use it to herd up the unthinking sheep into the ideological pens. People accept these terms mechanically and unconsciously once the discourse becomes omnipresent and repetitive, especially when, as in the case of Sweden, the authority of an external editorial voice has been subverted. The alarm bells should be ringing, but they are not. Perhaps because talk of 'diversity' seems entirely innocuous, and of course as compared to the objectives of previous totalitarian regimes, it most certainly is. Collectively, such terms can reinforce an institutionalised authority by obeying the linguistic mantra. In the new totalitarian discourse, key words such as 'diversity' act as clever forms of virtue-signalling as they are seen to be a conspicuous expression of moral values. The *modus operandi* is hostile towards any other kind of reality which is by definition of being different, 'deviant' and thus politically incorrect.

One must sing the triumphalist paean of diversity. It seems that diversity advocates simply obey the rules in order to gain one another's grace; it is almost a crime to question diversity's apparent benefits, and nothing seems to spook the diversity advocates. In a secular society, it is surely a sense of community, togetherness and belonging that they seek. In a godless world, they long for the fraternity of shared abstract values, or at least are willing to appear to long for them. There is a need to be recognised as adhering to the new universal truth because that is the ideological blanket of the day. 'Be diverse, but not ideologically diverse' might be the slogan. But, of course, diversity is part of the social justice ideology, an ideology that is meant to act as an appendage to our consciousness.

Diversity is played out as a sort of competition to prove who is most opposed to racism, sexism etc. According to the new religion, 'diversity' is irrefutably correct and LGBTQPIA or whatever the latest all-inclusive group acronym is, is a fashionable obsession. Held as a transcendental truism, the anarchic implication is that the group that has no claim to marginalisation is in some sense culpable for ever having resisted the deprioritisation of their own cultural make-up, for ever having believed that being heterosexual was the default sexuality, for sanctioning gender distinctions and privileging heterosexual marriage. This aspect of our 'cultural grammar' is becoming increasingly ingrained, washing away our freedom of expression on such matters. With an expression of puzzled compliance, we have effectively lost the right to even comment on such dramatic changes and victimologies because the new cultural grammar forbids us from doing so.

Anybody who questions the gospel of diversity in the world of academia will be hung out to dry, but the truth of the matter is that diversity does not necessarily lead to more intellectually stimulating student communities. In many British universities, the Chinese student community who number in the thousands have on the whole very little to do with the Home students.[3] Diversity does not lead inexorably to seamless integration and cultural enrichment. Diversity is the dogma, and thus it is back to the problem of the pervasive groupthink and ideological dogmatism. One cannot debate the values of the robotically repeated speech code — diversity, tolerance, social justice etc. The speech code is the groupspeak, and must be employed unthinkingly. It is motivated reasoning. It is the utopian multicultural vision that matters, not the facts. At least with regards to student bodies, 'multicultural' is for once being used in its proper sense.

Diversity is the slogan, the unqualified truth, whose value must never be questioned. But, of course, it is not really about diversity as understood in its unconditioned sense. It is about bestowing a preferential value on minorities who are assumed to somehow be victims. Making people feel like victims is crucial if one wants to rack up votes as a 'progressive' politician. If it were about diversity, then we would respect the anti-gay legislation of Uganda. But, as it is about victims and not diversity, the gays of Uganda might instead be good candidates for asylum. And it is not multiculturalist either; it is the promotion of non-Western cultures and religions (typically Islam) and the undermining of our own. If it were multiculturalist, we would be encouraging Buddhist Monks, Masai warriors and the Maori to settle in the West. We would be celebrating polygamy, child marriage, honour killings etc.

The most enthusiastic advocates of diversity are those on the Far Left,

---

3   According to the UK Council for International Student Affairs, there are now approximately 100,000 Chinese students studying in the UK. There are more Chinese students in the UK than the rest of the EU put together.

such as members of the respective European Green Parties. In their public announcements, they tend to try and conceal their real objectives. They masquerade as tree-hugging environmentalists. If only they were that, then their efforts should be applauded. Instead, many of them have a much more sinister objective: to make our nations as 'multi-ethnic' (i.e. non-white) as quickly as possible and to replace a withering Christianity with a flourishing Islam. They are using mass immigration as a mechanism to capsise the current social order.

Sweden has been heavily influenced by this variety of post-modern nihilistic groupthink, which has become the common denominator for any politically correct discourse. In Sweden, and to a lesser extent in the UK, society operates increasingly on such scripted thinking. Codes and taboos are fabricated by an in-group, in the case of Sweden, a liberal elite of academics, journalists and public sector officials that continue to confuse nationhood with nationalism. Groupthink is powerful because the out-groups are, according to groupthink, unacceptable in some way as they have been coupled with stigmatised labels such as most obviously 'racist' or 'politically incorrect'. As a society that is thought to be more or less classless (even if that in no way applies in the major cities), there is a sense of co-dependency in Sweden and thus not to conform and be part of an 'outgroup' is disproportionately stigmatised. Huntford (1971) has shown how individual identity is weak in Sweden. He describes an ultra-conformist society where dissent is not tolerated, where very considerable power and control has been handed over to the State, but where on the whole (up until now) that control has been used benevolently.

Until recently, there was a conspiracy of silence surrounding immigration and multiculturalism in Sweden and some other west European countries. In Sweden, it is right to speak of a militant anti-racist cult for whom egalitarianism and multiculturalism are the axioms of the moment. There is their groupthink, which spawns socially patterned defects, and there is 'badthink'. This is the context in which people in Sweden, the UK and elsewhere in the West are engaging in self-censorship, because they do not want their careers destroyed. Even faintly unpleasant ideas can now cause great upset. This 'manufactured' hypersensitivity is another means of restricting an open debate by constantly guilt-tripping one's opponents. The hypocritical 'language police' who wish debate to be nothing more than a representation of a mono-perspective are the same people who expound the merits of living in an open society. As we will see, this is particularly the case in Sweden.

The 'language police' wish to persuade the public that the use of a word should disenfranchise some group or another. To preserve the freedom of speech, the language policers should either be just ignored, or better still ridiculed for their attempt to stifle free speech. If their fatuous thinking was accepted, the rich English language would be increasingly deprived of metaphor, and we would be left speaking in some kind of prescribed code. At an institutional level, that has already happened. The 'language police' will claim that the use of a word or phrase is either racist or sexist. If they are going for the first tactic, it will be alleged that the word discriminates against what they perceive to be a disadvantaged group. If the objective is to invalidate a statement on the grounds of sexism, they may criticise the use of 'objectifying' language which is perceived to be degrading to women, but women only.

The fear of 'enforcing stereotypes' and the fear of being caught using objectifying language has brought about what one might call a new 'way of speaking' where personal descriptions in their entirety are shunned. Describing a girl as 'gorgeous' is very likely to be seen to be a sexist, chauvinistic statement even if it is objectively correct and agreed upon by everybody. With such developments, we in the West have retreated behind a linguistic veil, tip-toed behind the curtain of reality to a backroom of stagnant bureaucratese.

Suddenly, every other comment made by a male is 'sexist', and any reference to somebody from another culture is 'racist'. The constant linguistic scrutiny and social engineering of these delusional social justice warriors threatens to rid well-intentioned people of their sense of humour. The atmosphere of conformism has become stifling, and threatens to leave us stranded in a heavy and inert world bereft of the slightest whiff of mischief that might manifest itself in a wry grin or a raised eyebrow. What ever happened to Platonic lightness, or even a soupçon of occasional silliness? Unchallenged self-censorship and a politically correct consensus will make England a country as boring as Germany.

Oversensitised nihilists risk turning society into a factioned group of mindless robots living in a culturally impoverished world where irony and banter have been reduced to the strictly private realm. That would be a tremendously sad day, but is a process underway on American university campuses where it would seem it is just a question of time before jokes are banned altogether, as jokes tend to play off the cultural differences that the linguistic cleansers are trying to expunge. Not so many years ago, one of my university professors used to take great pleasure in citing limericks to his students. But, presumably, regaling one's students with a limerick beginning with 'There was a nun in Peru…' might today get one sacked.

Objectification and stereotype enforcement is a notion central to feminists, and is another component of the liberal groupthink. A feminist would argue that it is humiliating that a woman might be lowered to the status of an object. It is oversimplistic and pandering once again to some kind of spurious victimhood to assume that men's speech *necessarily* 'objectifies' women, and that this supposed objectification has to be something negative and dehumanising. Women talk about the sexual organs of men in explicitly 'objectifying' terms, but surely no man would find that offensive. We use each other as objects of emotion, knowledge, conversation etc. all the time. In the most romantic and gratifying of monogamous relationships, a couple will use each other as sex objects even if they do no think of it in those terms. Providing of course that it is always consensual, this is not something negative. It should be obvious that speaking in a way that curtails any kind of language that might somehow be perceived to be objectifying is an unnatural way of being. Beyond the West, the sight of a beautiful woman would always be commented on. Men laugh and grin (but not before staring a great deal); women roll their eyes. That is the 'natural', non-ideologised way of being. In the West, we have been forced through artificial means to drift away from our senses.

Nor does 'objectifying' and using 'objectifying language' have to imply a loss of respect or autonomy. It is another case of feminists being hypersensitive to language to the point that people assume unthinkingly that any act of 'objectifying' is extremely negative. There is nothing intrinsically wrong with objectification. Any man that considers it demeaning for a woman to be the object of his polar attraction has been swept away by the androgynous, gender-free ideology and has lost his masculine core. He is adrift in a turbulent, feminist sea. The sight of a beautiful woman is absolutely electric, brings happiness, energy and makes the day complete. The problem is that we have become too embedded in the all-embracing anti-fascist worldview of alleged oppression, hanging on to any word or concept that may somehow be perceived as degrading to some group or another. It is important to realise that the new social norms that this lead to are detached from our 'natural' way of being.

We have become inculcated in a pseudo-world of fake values where people sign up to discrimination because everybody wants to be the victim, and ideally belong to a group of victims that have ideological currency in a context of cultural repudiation. This is not to say that there are not *bona fide* victims in society. Of course, there are. The wife that is being beaten up by her drunk husband, the short-sighted boy that is being bullied at school, the person rendered homeless after a domestic dispute. These are all individually victims, undeniably so. But, there is an important distinction to be drawn between genuine victims, who are individuals, and minority or 'marginalised' groups, who believe they are, by definition of their minority status, victims in a racist society of white supremacist capitalism. Scruton (2015: 61) has shown how the Left has a tendency to always transfer the concept of a right from an individual to a group to the extent that individuals are no longer considered as individuals when it comes to assessing their rights.

This constant language policing that we witness with so-called 'objectifying language' is a form of linguistic corruption and linguistic sterilisation; an attempt at homogenising our language into pre-packaged labels and slogans that conform with the supposed moral sensitivity and compassion of the liberal psyche. To escape from this, to travel to Eastern Europe, Russia, Africa or South America, is nowadays unbelievably refreshing, because one realises that the world has not yet drowned in universal sameness and victimless crimes that violate moral taboos. It is to discover again a refuge of sanity, a place where minds are open, where traditional values are respected, where language has not been hijacked, where thinking is free and not conditioned, where men are admired for their masculinity, where women are worshipped for their femininity, where feminism is laughed at or may even be a form of insult. But most significantly, it is to walk free from the liberalist groupthink and the psychological angst that increasingly characterises our apparently free and open societies.

The only way to beat repressive liberal groupthink is for the shy conservatives, the heterodox dissidents, the intellectual exiles to speak out against this orthodoxy which supposes always that its own values are superior, even if they wrap themselves up in the doublespeak of 'equality'. Liberalism does not have a monopoly over principles of liberality. Conservative academics who have been on the receiving end of intimidation, harassment, discrimination and denial of tenure (and indeed employment) should group together (as they are now finally doing with the Heterodox Academy) and expose the intolerance of liberalism, which is increasingly prevalent in our universities. This is now beginning to happen. Forgive me for being a gadfly, but principles really ought to come before careers. There is an obligation for intellectuals to challenge the tyrannical regimes enveloping us. Surely, nobody would want to work in an environment where only one opinion counts. That would after all be an affront to diversity. Groupthink opponents must break out of the mental prison, the Kafkaesque scenario that is unfolding. People in the West have been socialised to use a speech code that is perverse; perverse because the notions that it packages as 'progressive' are culturally nihilistic. They are teleologies that disband established social and cultural categories, and leave one with nothing except for a repudiating discourse and the canons of tragic memory.

In large parts of the West, we have become neurotically insecure to such a degree that people are being accused of 'sexist' behaviour for referring to a woman by her husband's surname. Others resign instantly for a slight slip of the tongue; victims of the ideological witch-hunt. These resignations intimidate people to the point that nobody feels as if they can speak their mind for fear of having their career destroyed. Such intimidation is happening in the context of the emergence of a 'mass society' without borders and with all its echoes of totalitarian bodies that disregard national sovereignties, with waning freedom of speech and with mass surveillance on a scale never known before. And now we have mega-tech companies that collect vast amounts of data on every aspect of our lives. Ultimately, such a society through legislation, totalising notions and an intrusive cultural grammar may become closed to the freedom of thought. We should be concerned.

II

THE POLITICAL CORRECTNESS FOLLY

> Political correctness never rears its ugly head independently. It always shows up as a series of actions designed, to this observer, to crush the souls of those blessed with common sense.
>
> — MILO YIANNOPOULOS

NAMED AFTER AN OFFENBACH OPERETTA, the multi-tiered Chinese pagoda-like building might look more at home in urban Vietnam. Its citrine and rouge coloured façades bring a splash colour to the wide boulevards of the 11th *arrondissement*. Here, late Haussmann apartments overlook busy streets where French cars wrestle *aux heures de pointe*. The nineteenth-century Bataclan theatre plays to crowds of young rock fans who throng the stalls at the weekends. That is until one winter evening when the theatre was turned into a coliseum of Domitian sadism, an arena for a kind of savagery that even Commodus might have baulked at.

With such events, it is clear that we are living at a time of crisis when there urgently needs to be open debate and discussion, but we are also living at a time when an open discussion has become impossible because of the pervasiveness of political correctness. Political correctness is not a trivial matter. It can be dangerous, as we saw when Islamist terrorism entered the *agora* of Western cities. Jesse Hughes of Eagle Death Metal was playing that night at the Bataclan theatre in Paris in November 2015 when Islamists massacred eighty-nine of his fans. He has repeatedly told the Press what he saw, the fact that there were insiders (the security staff were Muslims), the fact that it took an eternity for police to enter the building, the fact that he saw Muslims dancing in the Parisian streets afterwards, the fact that Muslims were booing during the minute's silence that were held, the fact that the Paris police closed down 450 mosques and found recruitment material in every single one of them. But, the Press insisted on contorting his message, sometimes relaying the exact opposite from what he told them.[1]

These inconvenient truths cannot be reported, not from a white Christian male at least, because they are deemed to be politically incorrect as they criticise Muslims. This is even the case when Muslims slaughter Westerners as happened here. What happened on that terrible night, and more importantly the response to it, is a metaphor for Western civilisation. As we will come on to see, we do not live in an open and free society, but instead we live in a falsified proxy of it. The society you live in is not the one you think it is. Appearance is not the same as reality: the sun 'rises', but in fact it is the Earth which turns.

Political correctness has moved far away from its original good intentions and has become an attempt at manipulating language and thought in order to prevent people talking about the things that matter. It is a mental and moral trap that attempts to stop people thinking for themselves. Say the wrong thing, and one drowns in the waters of moral fear. Seen in this light, political correctness is the scourge of our times. It operates as a form of emotional coercion where it is imperative to accept the manufactured appeal to ideologised group victimhood, and to pander to minorities. It serves up pre-packaged, oven-ready opinions that chime with all-encompassing and apparently friendly slogans to do with equality, diversity and openness. But the institutions that do most to promote these empty slogans have little interest in these values beyond mere discourse; for example the academy, which at least politically and ideologically speaking is totally un-diverse and promotes a closed system of thinking. As we have seen, diversity is one-dimensional. Public institutions are more focused on discriminating against anybody that refuses to follow their politically correct

---

1   Available at: http://takimag.com/article/surrending_to_death_gavin_mcinnes/print#axzz48gKLoVO9

regime. These speech codes are rhetorical devices to ensure that those who do not adhere to the 'liberal' ideology can be labelled as heretics because they fall foul of the tenets of their illiberal dogma.

It is difficult to formulate a response to political correctness because any response will be simply labelled 'politically incorrect' and thus illegitimate. Political correctness is a zero-sum game with the suppression of rational thought as its objective. Ironically, it is the number one enemy of tolerance, and represents little more than linguistic fundamentalism in ritual fashion — the intellectual fundamentalism in which language is caught. It is also difficult to respond to because it is packaged as a 'form of enforced niceness' (Žižek, *Big Think* presentation), and an opponent would therefore appear 'cruel' or 'wicked' in his questioning the moral high ground.[2] By definition, moral superiority can only be achieved by one party. As a discourse strategy, it is therefore rather effective.

Political correctness leads to a culture of over-labelling where suddenly every statement or opinion has to be qualified adjectivally. Everything is *-ist*; nothing can escape description. An example of this is the insistence of people on the Left to label Trump a 'misogynist'. Judging by his reported actions, one could in fact claim that he was the exact opposite. Once a point or comment can be described as 'racist' or 'sexist', then it has been deemed illegitimate and the discussion is 'dead'. If one can call somebody a 'racist' or a 'fascist', then one no longer needs to give them the time of day. This is an overused and anti-democratic conversation strategy. It is a means of closing down debate on false grounds, and playing into the anti-communication of manufactured liberal groupthink. Those who wish to prevent discussion do so by racialising disagreements which are not even 'racial' in nature.

We are faced with a dangerous combination of rampant extremism and a culture of fear, a fear of speaking out because the speaker does not want to be labelled negatively. Such an environment can only lead to escalating social tensions as the pressure in the 'verbal pressure cooker' becomes too much, and the gasket explodes. It is a 'verbal' pressure cooker because the disenfranchised groupthink sceptic has been biting his proverbial tongue

---

2 Available at: http://bigthink.com/videos/slavoj-zizek-political-correctness-is-fake

for so long, railing to himself at how flawed the ideology of the Left has become. Either that, or the power of liberal groupthink has rendered perfectly intelligent people into mindless sheep, just following the herd without being able to think for themselves. It is a refutation on a grand scale of the Cartesian principle *cogito ergo sum*. Speaking to university students, the sense of herd morality is clearly apparent. Many are wholly unwilling to challenge or deconstruct the panoply of contemporary social truths regarding diversity, free speech, feminism, equality, tolerance etc. Instead, they try to shoe-horn them into conversations. For students in the West, these have become the supreme moral principles, and by employing this coded language, they have unthinkingly become parties to these grinders of ideological axes.

It is as if their education coupled with significant exposure to social media amounts to an extended diversity training session. In short, they have been ideologised by authoritarian liberalism. Increasingly, they have been told what to believe, and the secularist, anti-particularist liberalism that they have been indoctrinated with extends to every aspect of social life. Instead, their minds should be open, totally open. They should be free to entertain the idea that rejecting the primacy of spiritual life is to abandon the entire basis of Western humanism. They need to be ideologically liberated of an intellectual pollution that has made so many of our words and ideas unfit for rational discourse, and then they will be able to reflect on the arguments being made and speak freely. Our students must have the freedom to question dogma, whatever it may be.

This issue of control will resurface many times throughout these essays. Authoritarian liberalism is unsurprisingly first and foremost about control and power. If this authoritarian liberalism is allowed to disseminate across Europe, then frankly the future of the West is bleak, as the metaphorical herdsman is an 'enemy of the open society' in the Popperian sense of the phrase. But the situation is a 'pressure cooker' for another reason: political correctness creates conflicting groups, the so-called 'persecuted' minorities, the victims and those who pledge support to this totalitarian ideology, and the remainder of the population who cower in silence, overwhelmed by the slogans. It is an ideology which is divisive and thoroughly alienating. We are living again in the age of ideological censorship: agree with our 'liberal' values or be quiet. We might be creating an atmosphere where everybody (unless one can claim minority status) is a potential 'thought criminal' in need of sensitivity training, where each can be inducted with the latest politically correct dogma. These tensions of psychological warfare in our society are part of the dialectics of the tragedy of modernity, and will surely become intolerable.

The multiculturalist rhetoric attempts to legitimise its ideology by defining any opposition as 'racist'. This word is part of the magical lexicon that delegitimises anything that does not conform to the liberal mindset. Those that insist on this language are not liberals; they are intolerant authoritarians who try to alienate those who disagree with their views. 'Liberal tolerance' is in fact quasi-dictatorial. The freedom to think for oneself is of inestimable value, and intolerant illiberals are trying to prevent people from doing so. Independence and the freedom to actualise one's potential are prerogatives of the strong. It is not possible to achieve transcendence at any personal level without them.

In a free society, holding unpopular opinions should not be reason for social exclusion. If one really wants a 'tolerant' society, one must become intolerant of the current 'negative tolerance' regime, because it in itself epitomises intolerance. One would have to show tolerance to opinions which have been outlawed or suppressed. It is essential that we reopen the mental space and extinguish the Marxian 'enlightened false consciousness' ('they know very well they are doing it, but still they do it') for it is the freedom of thought which really necessitates tolerance.

Racism is a red line; if one of the liberal parties can convince the electorate that the only anti-mass immigration party in Sweden is 'racist', then their group manipulation measures have succeeded and they can be excluded from debate. But, of course, 'racist' is a word whose meaning has been hijacked, and it is now applied to all manner of opinions that do not conform to the sensitivity standards of political correctness. If somebody is accused of saying something 'racist', one can almost assume the guilty comment has nothing to do with 'race' by virtue of the nature of the accusation. It is a kind of identity politics that is both illogical and destructive. Accusations of racism tend to be instantly believed, and the function of the 'r' word is more or less that of an Austinian speech act (Austin, 1962: 52). It is quite literally 'doing things with words' as the accused's role in the conversation has changed because it has been rendered illegitimate.

The ultimate objective with this accusation is perhaps 'thought control', a management of our perceptions of reality, to create a culturally Marxist mindset through value clarification where culture can only be discussed in terms of inequalities. Any thought or observation that fails to conform to the inexorable, but surely by now intellectually bankrupt cultural Marxism is typically painted as *racism, xenophobia, homophobia* etc.

Oversensitised safe-spacers use the social media cesspit, whose power as a means of bullying and puerile insult has become so strong and which evokes a false sense of community, to close down debate, to vilify, exclude and alienate anybody who is perceived as having crossed the line of political correctness.[3] Liberal thinkers are far more active on social media than conservatives, who are typically awkward in defence because they are made to feel unsure as to whether their views are outdated. Employing pseudonymous speech, some students use social media not just as a platform to raise self-esteem but to hastily fabricate a moral panic, and close down any debate which they consider to be 'offensive'. There are countless examples of social media being used to create a synthetic anger, but an obvious one is the resignation of the distinguished Noble laureate, Professor Tim Hunt, for making a few jocular comments at a lecture in South Korea. The flippant comment about the 'problem of falling in love with female colleagues' was perceived to be sexist, even if everybody laughed at the time. The discrepancy between the perceived wrong-doing and the vengeance wreaked is alarming to say the least. It seems as if barely a week goes by now without such an incident occurring.

The West has become curiously hyper-sensitive and this hyper-sensitivity is constantly nurtured. One of the obvious, but very malign consequences of this is that debate is drying up on a whole range of issues which might be considered sensitive in some way. We are moving away from freedom by incorporating the normative beliefs and thought processes of our society. It is obvious that we are losing our rhetorical freedom, as the spontaneity of

---

3   It is said that the outbreak of civil unrest in South Sudan in July of 2016 where at least 150 people were killed was caused by a post in social media.

expression has dried up. People rehearse a line in their heads first to make sure it will not cause upset; political stand-up comedy is threatened, perhaps endangered. At least, John Cleese thinks so. He has refused to do any more comedy gigs at universities. Debates are often no longer debates in the true sense of the word; questions are typically framed in the clichéd speech codes of a weak society whose members are suddenly so easily offended. Young people in particular are no longer sure how to operate linguistically in the world, and so they retreat into their own mini-groups where they feel more secure in expressing their opinions.

In academia, political correctness and the academic fad of post-modernism lies at the vortex of creating degrees in phony departments such as Women's Studies and Gender Studies, subjects which have a highly politicised agenda and which employ fake academics who work on issues of non-binary gender theory and social inequality and who invariably have both a personal and ideological axe to grind. The cultural whim of gender theory states that a person's 'gender' is whatever the person believes it to be. Such disciplines with their attempts at ideological colonisation of gender nihilism have had a highly negative impact on infinitely more thought-provoking fields such as anthropology, taking it away from its roots, its basic interest in 'other' cultures and moving it towards a highly politicised movement preoccupied with gender, migration, race and alleged social inequality. Women's and Gender Studies' lectures comprise often little more than a flagrant attack on conservative values. If it were not for the inequality they rage against, these elite institutions that the academics teach in would not exist. Women's Studies and Gender Studies' departments must be closed down, for they have zero intellectual credibility. They are built on an ideology, and the ideologues that teach this nonsense are completely disconnected from reality at the most fundamental level. They are programmes for activists. Nothing more. They are pathological to the core. We cannot use public funding to support vacuous subjects filled with nothing but politicised agendas.

The political bias in academia, the Humanities and Social Sciences in particular, is threatening the integrity of research. It has a radical atheistic, teleological, anti-capitalist agenda, constantly trying to eke out some source of oppression or other, but at the same time creating paradoxically an oppressive atmosphere of liberal groupthink. Its authors appear to be blind to the hypocrisy. Some students in the US in particular are being educated with the notion that the West has done something 'evil', and in order to talk about this they should reassign their values as prejudices; they are poisoned with the ubiquitous chimera that man can liberate himself from tradition and pre-existing meaning. It is not a noble objective to try and transcend these human realities, these bonds and powers that tie societies together. Students at elite universities have been inculcated with a fear of celebrating success because their achievements may have been due to some kind of inequality in society.

Some of the opponents to this discourse live in fear of being 'outed'. Academics are able to say 'we on the Left' without stopping to think that it would be totally unacceptable in a university context to say 'we on the Right'. This is the hegemony that the Left has over thinking in academia. One is expected to endorse the verbal confetti, the meta-drivel of certain French intellectuals who too often talk about culture exclusively in terms of oppression and power. But, their followers are unable to dispense with power. All they can do is create alternative social orders that revolve around power and domination.

Always on the look-out for the oppressed, Foucault (to take one of these French intellectuals) thought culture and knowledge are primarily discourses of power, 'structures of domination'. Foucault's goal is subversion. He wants to persuade people that truth is linked to a form of consciousness, the episteme, imposed by the class which profits from its propagation. It is these cultural Marxists and post-Marxists (who traded rather peculiarly the unemployed working class for gay rights as their focus point) that have a grip on universities, and whose cultural theory has convulsed the Western academy.

The post-modernists see society as a Hobbesian battleground of identity groups centred around the oppressor-victim paradigm. For them, group identity and conformity are privileged over individualism; mediocrity over exceptionalism. It has long been understood by the cultural Marxist Left that groups are a more powerful vehicle to claim ideological and victim status than individuals. These post-modernists have enormous power over bureaucratic structures. Within these structures, the motivation is empathy; empathy is the problem-solving mechanism. It creates negative communities of spurious victims. In a culturally nihilistic society, 'manufactured' victim status (for it is no way 'real') confers an array of advantages ranging from positive job discrimination to superior status as inscribed in the law, such as hate-speech legislation. This might be at the expense of the *bona fide* victim. The post-modernists are anti-individuals. They do not care who you are. Their only concern is your group identity. Diversity consultants do this on a professional basis. They claim to find systemic bias and determine that these biases are the product of socialisation, for they believe we are born as 'blank slates'.

Post-modernists are an intellectual mob with a power-seeking proclivity. They seek power, but dress it up in the cuddly language of compassion. They tell us that they are on the side of the oppressed. Everything is a struggle for power, and the evil is always elsewhere. We cannot inform privileged students that they are victims of society. It is firstly factually preposterous, and second it is a take on the world that is unaccountable and irresponsible. Post-modernism does not in anyway address the ills of the planet. It just passes the blame and leaves its students with a wholly negative anthropology. This is the prevailing fundamentalism of the academic world, and it is surely time for a new intellectual archaeology which offers students insights into the world from more diverse political and philosophical perspectives.

The kind of hypersensitivity that we witnessed in the Tim Hunt case (but also Bret Weinstein and many others) is in part a response to the hegemonic politically correct discourse that we find in our 'social justice' empowered institutions of learning. It invites listeners to judge any dissenting opinion using a rather limited, and highly politicised lexicon. Looking at the world of politics, political correctness, until Trump's victory in the United States, was the dogma accepted by almost all the mainstream political parties everywhere in the West. This is why his comments got so much attention, and why he offers hope to those concerned by the developments in our universities. It was not because his comments were necessarily outrageous (although of course some of them were), but because they did not abide to the dogma of the liberal elite. He is a patriot, and wishes to take on the globalists. He thought the 2016 US Presidential Election was going to be rigged. That idea was received with scorn, but it seems electoral irregularities and fraud have happened before in the US as they have in Europe. In the case of the US, we were told that we would only get to hear about Clinton's 30,000 deleted e-mails *after* the election. In Britain, it has been admitted by Sir Eric Pickles, the former Secretary of State for Communities and Local Government, that electoral fraud has taken place in Muslim communities in England, but people dare not speak out about it for reasons of political correctness.[4]

But, in fact Trump is not the aberration that many people think he is. One might assume that he reflects the views of many of those that do not subscribe to the dogma. Building walls to defend borders might sound extreme but it works, as we know from Hungary. When Hungary started telling people the border was closed in 2015, the numbers crossing into Austria through the little town of Spielberg went from 2,000 a day to zero. With more migration crises on the horizon, we might soon face a situation where it will be a case of either build a wall or entertain collapse. Then, a wall does not look like such an extreme measure and we might all be doing it. Borders have to be policed. It is in the interests of everybody, except for people smugglers, criminals and EU bureaucrats with totalitarian aspirations.

Banning entry to the US for citizens that come from states that support terrorism is arguably just common sense in the current terrorist context, and not a reason for outrage. It is only unfortunate that the ban does not extend to Saudi Arabia. If Islamist attacks continue, then European countries may have little choice but to do precisely the same. Recent results in elections across Europe (most notably Italy, Austria, the Czech Republic and Hungary) show that the electorate is getting tired of this cowardice, and that things are beginning to swing towards more anti-globalist thinking.

The speech codes and political correctness that we have been discussing comprise a 'new cultural grammar' that generates connotative messages (Eco, 1970: 553-54). It is a grammar because there are rules, but just as grammar is no longer taught in our schools, this new 'cultural grammar'

---

4   Available at: http://www.telegraph.co.uk/news/2016/08/11/election-fraud-allowed-to-take-place-in-muslim-communities-becau/

is also not taught, but it will be frowned upon if one gets it wrong. It is a covert set of rules with an unwritten ideology that govern the behaviour and belief systems of a given society. These rules have a nihilistic purpose as they serve to redefine the basic social structures and ethos of our communities; theirs is a grammar that undermines our own culture. As with the hate-speech laws (to be discussed subsequently), Islam is a leading beneficiary of this new cultural grammar propagated by the West because it is totally excluded from this orthodoxy of nihilism. Hate-speech legislation works hand-in-hand with this cultural grammar. Weighed down by this masochistic social syntax, the inner life of the Western psyche is no longer the expansive, Faustian character that Spengler (1918) portrayed, a spirit and 'adamantine will' that was constantly trying to transcend the limits of existence; it is instead the rootless, Godless and feeble, untranscendental soul that Evola (1961) had in mind.

Political correctness is designed to restrict thought processes — an assault on the freedom of the mind. It is part of a cultural code that rapidly becomes stifling. The impact of this cultural grammar is entirely negative because it imparts a disrespect for the achievements of one's own culture. But, just as the hate-speech laws are flawed because they will not actually have the desired effect, so is the objective of political correctness. It is of course a fallacy to assume that this lexical obfuscation will determine the way people think. Political correctness does not kill thought, it suppresses it and bigotry will only flourish in the vacuum that it creates. As in the Soviet Union, totalitarian mind control does not work completely. However, if it is felt that the suppressed thought cannot be expressed, then we are just left with the ballot box.

Prejudices are natural: 'they are divinations of the order of the whole of things' (Bloom, 1987: 43). We cannot think in any other terms, even if we are banned from expressing it. We can only pretend to speak with a disembodied voice of authority. There is probably prejudice in every society, and there always will be. We cannot expunge our preconceptions, and we must have the confidence to think logically about our inherited beliefs. Even if a word is delegitimised for a notion, we are still able to conceptualise it.

Fettered with this new cultural grammar, taking offence has become a veto on the speech that the 'offended' see as somehow threatening. In the context of this emerging public psychosis, many think it is just safer to keep quiet, and indeed increasingly this is the advice given by parents to children. It is 'best not to rock the boat', even if the changes to our society are absolutely fundamental. One can no longer ruffle feathers.

This public psychosis appears to be becoming irrational: over half a million Britons signed a petition requesting that Donald Trump be banned from entering the UK for his comment that he would prevent Muslims from countries with a history of terrorism entering the US. The petition triggered a three-hour debate in the UK Parliament. There is currently a petition in the UK to ban Steve Bannon from entering the country, but Islamists who call for the death of Christians are welcome. Societies in the West appear more willing than ever to accept infringements on free speech. It is known at least that the EU has been trying to suppress it for years. In 2001, the European Court of Justice ruled that the European Union could suppress criticism of its institutions and leaders.[5] The Establishment does not seem to condemn such extraordinary actions, but is instead content sleepwalking into this kind of bureaucratic authoritarianism.

Suddenly, oversensitised liberals are insulted by anything that does not adhere to the politically correct dogma. Any opinion that opposes the State sanctioned politically correct one is dismissed in the manner of a totalitarian regime. A coalition of cultural nihilists, feminists, gay activists, ethnic minorities and Islamic apologists have achieved hegemony in the public sphere by effectively creating a restrictive political climate which censors any views that do not conform to the politically correct orthodoxy which they have defined themselves. This hegemony is making our societies increasingly balkanised and atomistic. It is a powerful rhetorical tool and discursive practice used by the media and intelligentsia to silence the dissenting political opinion. It is this marginalisation which President Trump is constantly trying to push back against.

The word 'racist' is overused to such a degree it has become almost semantically vacuous, a kind of slur to reprehend anything that could be perceived as offensive in this oversensitised Western world that we live in.

---

5   Available at: http://www.telegraph.co.uk/news/worldnews/1325398/Euro-court-outlaws-criticism-of-EU.html

Those that succumb to such language are trying to short-circuit fruitful discussion by using slanderous labels that they think nullifies the need for debate. Debate and open minds are needed, not false absolutes and the secularised Christianity of human rights and Marxism. But, both privately and publicly, there seems to be little discussion in Sweden about the topics that really matter. The lively discussions that can take place in the British pub, the Greek restaurant, the Italian café, the Icelandic hot-tub just do not seem to occur in Sweden. Consensus is both the ideal and the social imperative; debates tend to be triggered by outsiders.

The contemporary intellectual culture is so quick to condemn anybody who strays from the orthodoxy — the prescribed commodity of ideas — as 'bigots', that it threatens not only freedom of expression but also any form of creative thinking. What ever happened to the opera of the mind, the battlefield of ideas and its cabaret of expressions? How can we turn back the clock to didactic thinking, the theatre of Stalinism?

In most of the political debates in Sweden, the use of the word 'racism' is little more than a trite slogan to close down argument, a means to ensure the multiculturalist ideology is free of criticism. Unlike America, Sweden does not have a long history of racialised structures of inequality. And yet, criticism of immigration policy will leave one at risk of losing one's job for one will have proven oneself morally deviant. One will have shown that one falls foul of *Jantelagen*, the idea that those who stand out as achievers or as norm-violators should be punished because success is due to the collective and not the individual. The *Jantelag* underpins arguably much of the egalitarianism in Sweden, and reads like the Ten Commandments. It is said that it goes back to Viking times. The essence of it is that if one is successful in life, it should not be assumed that this is because one worked hard or because one is 'better' than anybody else. It is ironic that this ancient maxim still has cultural currency in a country where billionaire wealth as a percentage of GDP is higher than in any other west European country (Sharma, 2016: 108).

The *Jantelag* states that the reason for one's success is because one was given the best opportunities. We are all in fact equal (apparently). Swedish students at school no longer go back to the old Viking manuscripts for their code of ethics, but are instead brought up on the thinking of the

Soviet psychologist, Lev Vygotsky. After the Russian Revolution, Vygotsky and others wanted to build a new 'socialist human being'. Vygotsky writes about how it is the community that 'makes meaning', not the individual. Individual development cannot be understood without reference to the social and cultural context within which it is embedded. Higher mental processes in the individual have their origin in social processes. Growing up under revolutionary Russia, Vygotsky wrote in the context of child development about the relationship between language and thought. Little did he know that after his premature death, his country would be enveloped in a totalitarian regime where his speculations on language and thought would play out in a rather dramatic fashion. Vygostsky (1987: 243-87) spoke of private, egocentric inner speech, and how it can go underground as it takes on a self-regulating function. It becomes a monologic speech form. In Soviet Russia, this kind of private, inner speech must have festered just as it does today in the West in a context of oppressive political correctness and groupthink.

It is consensus that matters, even if it is a false one. Such suffocating social conformity is not questioned, even if the future of the nation is at stake. The price of violating the sacred taboos and going beyond the *åsiktskorridor* (the 'corridor of opinions' that one cannot move out of) can be extremely high. Even asking about the feasibility of integrating 160,000 asylum-seekers in one year would put one beyond the *åsiktskorridor* and risk an accusation of racism. In an environment of intense conditioning, political correctness acts as a form of middle class identity marking in Sweden. Its adherents are the new priesthood in a country where Christianity is almost dead. Political correctness is the new gospel, and public institutions across the country act as the pseudo-Church, policing the groupthink.

Swedes like to maintain a balance and preserve a pleasant, consensual ambience. Private thoughts are almost by definition deviant ones since the level of supposed consensus is such that everybody knows more or less what everybody else is thinking, and therefore there is little point in articulating something. Or at least, that is how Sweden used to operate when it was a homogeneous society, and there was perhaps less reason to voice strong, controversial opinions. Social collectivism was the unquestionable norm. But striving for constant consensus becomes problematic when at least 20 per cent of the population are not ethnic Swedes.

For a country that is more safety-conscious and less risk-taking in many respects than any other I know (it is law to have your car headlights on all the time throughout the year, and it is frowned upon if one goes for the shortest of walks without wearing a high visibility reflective running bib; what is more, the car engines in some taxis cannot start until the taxi driver has blown into the breathalyser mounted on the dash board and proved that he has not consumed any alcohol), Sweden has taken the most almighty risk with precious little discussion or debate. The norm in Swedish companies is for everybody to be involved in discussions, and for the discussion to continue until complete consensus has been achieved. Not so, it seems, when it comes to the most fundamental question of all — the future demographic and ethnic make-up of the country.

A faux consensus-oriented society (to some extent it must be so, otherwise SD [*Sverigedemokraterna*], the anti-mass immigration party, would not be polling on 21 per cent) is a disaster in times of crisis because the national groupthink will lead to the wrong actions being taken. But, it is also dangerous. Violence can ensue when opinions are not aired because it is felt they do not conform to the groupthink. This might be the context in which mass shootings now occur in the US on a regular basis.

The logic of the *Volksgemeinschaft* is that if one's opinions do not fit into the liberal consensus, then one is *persona non grata*. There is a fear of being different in Sweden. Contrary voices are mocked and marginalised. If one is not actively promoting diversity (and its metonymic relationship with race which liberals are invariably anxious to forge), then one must be against it. If one is not pro-mass immigration, one must be a racist or Islamophobic. These are pre-programmed reactions, and prevent rational dialogue. This is the fallacy of false correspondences where erroneous conclusions relating to the central beliefs of an ideology are drawn, even if they do not correspond in any way to what was actually said. Such red herrings or false correspondences always relate to divisive issues.

The discussion of illegal immigrants in Sweden, if one ever arises, has been polarised between the anti-mass immigration party and the naïve do-gooders with their culture of sentimentality and self-righteous hatred for those who do not share their moralising views — views which must be expressed at every opportunity. This kind of political polarisation is now being witnessed right across Europe. A Swedish society of ultra-liberal values has become nihilistic and self-destructive in nature. But, even more disturbing is the complete intolerance of any opposition to the ultra-liberal propaganda that is heard through all the media channels, as we will see. The resulting intellectual gloop goes hand-in-hand with a collapse of objective political analysis in Sweden. Surely, at some point such a society has to break down. Political correctness was meant to unite different social and ethnic groups. Instead, it silently divides them. It is perhaps in this respect that a multiculturalist ideology embedded in political correctness feels most totalitarian: the opposition is wrong-footed, because to speak the truth might not fall within the limits of acceptable discourse. But also because political correctness is not just a question of stating that one should use one word instead of another. One might argue that it has become moreover the basis for social relations more generally in the West.

Political correctness acts like a virus because it creates the problem it claims it is trying to prevent, and so it requires more of itself. Political correctness comes before factual correctness. The 'tolerant' ideology that promotes multiculturalism does not 'tolerate' free speech, criticism of Islam or minorities or any opinion independent of its own stifling ideology. It is a conversation strategy that always supports the minority or the alleged marginalised, be it the refugee or the ethnic minority; a form of pervasive sanctioning that threatens creativity and expression. It creates mental barriers resulting in thinking and speaking framed in perversely different ways. What is spoken is the parroted opinions of commoditised groupthink, what is thought is a chain of free associations. If the latter slips into the former, one is rebuked. In this respect, political correctness acts as a form of group-speech. For the liberal-left elite, autonomy has become heteronomy whilst heterodoxy has become orthodoxy. A politically incorrect argument is null and void in an environment of linguistic cleansing. Political correctness has become tyrannical because it aims to banish ideas which do not conform to the ideology. It is an attempt at a form of cultural conditioning, but it results in specious, politically correct statements of no intellectual value.

Those who object to the dictates of this political correctness are sent for diversity training, a form of re-education to free them from the apparently pernicious white, male hegemonic discourse. Many universities are now employing lawyers to give diversity training to Freshers. Nothing has changed over the years: the behaviour of male rugby and football teams is absolutely no different today from twenty years ago. What has changed is that young people live now in an age where they have been encouraged to become oversensitised to language, to see themselves as the perennial victim. Today, we live in a culture of victimhood where advertisements on television, radio and in the Press constantly invite people to consider whether they may be a 'victim' of some kind of scam or other, and thus eligible for a payout. We are thus invited to become not only overly sensitive to language, but also to actions. Suddenly, all kinds of actions should be perceived as 'harassment'. In this *Brave New World*, language is sanitised, actions are regulated and opinions are sanctioned by a powerful, but vicious social media who will force through nasty, spiteful language the resignations of any high profile figures who question the orthodoxy.

The consequence of political correctness is that people feel as if they cannot speak out against certain events and cannot act on their beliefs. This can be seen in the response to non-terrorist incidents on British soil. When the police tried to deal with the cases of the grooming of young girls by Asian men in Oxford, Rochdale, Rotherham, Derby and Bradford, they were accused of institutional racism. Commentators on the Left did everything possible to blur the facts, claiming completely implausibly that it had nothing to do with ethnicity and religion. Indifferent to the torture that over a thousand British girls were faced with, they ran to defend the perpetrators (all of whom happened to be Muslim) in a despicable display of betrayal. In certain circles, the case was barely mentioned because it muddled their perverse ideology. It is widely approved of to make films about paedophilia in the Roman Catholic Church, but it would be politically incorrect to make a film (or perhaps even make mention of) the same abuse handed out to children by grooming gangs.

Over a thousand British girls were abused and nothing was done about it in part because of the oppressive culture of political correctness. Western societies are falling over backwards to accommodate the multiculturalists' vision, even if it means turning a blind eye to the most appalling abuse.

British children were abused, raped and tortured by gangs of Pakistani men. The Oxford *imam*, commenting on the abuse and rape of white girls, said: 'race and religion were inextricably linked to the recent spate of grooming rings in which Muslim men have targeted under-age white girls'.[6] This ever so obvious conclusion can be made by an Asian, but not by a white Briton. Immigrant group social behaviour cannot be considered beyond criticism. Laughing at the culture of political correctness, the groomers acted as if they were above the law, as if they had *carte blanche* to disseminate their evil knowing that the Leftist media and key members of the Labour Party (and no doubt one or two other ennobled, pro-Islam *éminence grises*) would rush to defend them.

The same happened after large groups of girls in Sweden were molested by migrants from the Middle East and North Africa at various music festivals in 2016. Our fear of racism has led to a dangerous culture of self-censorship, not being able to act when one knows something is wrong. We are losing reasoned argument. It creates a sense of unease when in one's homeland the ancient tradition of fox hunting is banned, but not *halal* meat, where, in accordance with Islamic law, the jugular vein is cut and the animal is left to bleed to death. In 2012, a France2 television documentary revealed that all of the slaughterhouses in the greater Paris metropolitan area are now producing all of their meat in accordance with Islamic *shari'ah* law.[7] The meat is not marked as such. Such developments indicate that society's norms are increasingly dictated to us by an unassailable minority. It might be argued that *halal* is a way to impose aspects of *shari'ah* law on a non-Muslim majority.

If we were on a level playing field, surely both fox hunting and *halal* meat should be banned on the grounds of barbarism. Combining such liberalism with an open door policy to radically different cultures has resulted in a muddled sense of priorities and values. There is something very wrong here, as the non-immigrant population feel extremely awkward

---

6   Available at: http://www.telegraph.co.uk/news/uknews/crime/10061217/Imams-promote-grooming-rings-Muslim-leader-claims.html

7   Available at: http://www.reuters.com/article/uk-france-election-halal-idUSLNE81K01820120221

taking a stand in their own country. It is this PC culture, an Orwellian threat which regulates free thinking and leads to ambiguous one-way conversations, that has led indirectly to a basket of social problems which are increasingly unmanageable. There is a chasm, a jarring disconnect between an all-pervasive public dogma and private thinking. The lack of response to the political correctness agenda is an insidious part of our cultural grammar that has been institutionalised right across the public sector. Attempts to enforce consensus have meant that we have lost certain essential freedoms. What we can communicate and are allowed to believe is increasingly monitored. Leaders of the West are more concerned to condemn what they believe is Islamophobia than Islamist zealotry. The relentless accusation of Islamophobia is often little more than a muzzle on free speech, an effective shield against criticism of any kind. Europe is sometimes unwilling to recognise the real threat of Islamic terrorism, and instead the sentiment is more often an accommodationist one.

The word 'Islamophobic' is used to scare people into silence. The constant recycling of this kind of language against opponents of multiculturalism amounts to a secular *fatwa* because it acts as a pseudo-ruling against free speech, a form of psychological terrorism. It is a means of intimidation, and so-called 'liberals' are increasingly managing to enshrine these bogus accusations into the legal system. Hate-speech laws should protect our *own* cultural values or norms (and, yes, we have our own: we have not yet become the Leftist blank slate that cultural and historical revisionists aspire to). Instead, step-by-step, we are moving conceptually closer to a system of *shariah* law, and that means irrevocable change as the nation is founded on the notion of a secular law. A nation which has conflicting (and not shared) conceptions of justice will unsurprisingly in the long-term become a troubled one. In the face of this threat, relativism is not the answer. Relativism has no values to defend.

A rhetoric of alleged victimhood and the moral superiority that comes with it has brought about a form of disappropriation on behalf of the ethnic Briton, usurping the moral and cultural infrastructure of the West. It is an insidious ideology and to tackle it, our thinking will need to be urgently reprioritised as our cultural heritage and basic system of values are being undermined. The integuments of Western societies are at stake. This is not turning the cultural clock back to the 1950s. It is putting faith and trust in a system and model that has worked for centuries, and not an ill-conceived dictatorial project with a multiculturalist agenda.

* * *

It is my belief that our sense of values is being turned upside down by a spurious idiom of universal human rights which has become inflationary and is invoked every time a minority chooses to disregard his host culture. In the secular societies that we in the West live in today, human rights have been sacralised and mobilised as an ideological tool. The universal human rights idiom sits at the centre of the hegemonic politically correct liberal groupthink, and works to prioritise universality and the abstract over an established, concrete life and stable conceptions of identity based on security and community. The airy-fairy objective of universality ends up impinging on the freedom of the settled community, and contradicting the relativist cause that the human rights advocates have been told they must not question. Ideological imperialism can only end in disaster. It always does. Human rights discourse is synonymous with ideological and legislative protection for any minority group. If legislation is continuously put in place that might potentially offend the majority, then an avoidable conflict might be escalated even if the original idea was a well-intentioned one.

Human rights and its subjective rhetoric of 'making amends' should not be allowed to trample all over religious beliefs, traditional morality and people's sense of belonging. If a country wishes to prioritise spiritual values over human rights, then that choice should be respected. If another nation wishes to question the self-evident doctrines of the Church of universal human rights, then, as intelligent beings, we should at least listen to them. Surely, relativism would insist on that, and surely a real democracy would give a hearing to the majority as well as the minority. But it should really be obvious that there are no truly universal human rights, otherwise there would not be multiple permutations of the 1948 Universal Declaration of Human Rights. As de Benoist (2011: 61) points out, if human rights are so obviously universal, then why have we just decided this over the last fifty years? Ostensibly, there can be nothing inherent in its universality. There is a contradiction between the 'historical contingency that presided at its elaboration and the demand of universality which it intends to affirm' (de Benoist, 2011: 61). The universality they appeal to is the liberal, secularised Western societies based on mass consumption (de Benoist, 2011: 16).

It is difficult to even question the rationale of universal human rights in a consensus society like Sweden without rapidly being labelled a 'fascist'. As de Benoist (2001: 9) observes, 'it is as blasphemous and shocking to criticise the ideology of human rights as it once was to doubt the existence of God'. Religion and liberal ideology have swapped roles. Liberal ideology is now treated like the word of God, and religion is a topic of public ridicule (amongst liberal intellectuals at least). It is a remarkable *volte-face*, and some might say the crowning achievement of secularism.

The whole subjective question of human rights is another example of the intolerance of the Leftist ideologues. It cannot be debated, for it is treated as absolute dogma. Christian dogma is more likely to be discussed than the universality of human rights. It sits at the centre of the liberal creed, a cocktail of contradictions that stipulates human rights as an anthropological universal but at the same time endorses a relativist perspective. However, many of the cultures which we are told to embrace under the multiculturalist umbrella are unambiguous in their rebuttal of Western values which are packaged by the relativists as 'universal'. The common truth of the universality of human rights is completely erroneous. It is the stuff of satire and caricature, an assault on the phenomenology of the human fact.

For the ideologues, it is unsettling that some people might want to escape liberal *aporias* and might not share these values, this overinflated sense of responsibility, hysterical moral zeal or 'hypermorality' (Gehlen, 1969) that the migrants have been so quick to manipulate and cash in on. And, therefore human rights can operate as a pseudo-ideology, a social pathology because it dogmatically stipulates that every individual from the Middle East headed to Sweden is a victimised refugee, even if that is a statistical lie. It plays into this naïve optimistic universalism that the Left is constantly seeking to embrace, and has become something akin to a societal compulsive disorder. Many hope that the migrants to Sweden will constitute cheap labour for an ageing economy. Instead, segregation of the sort that has been witnessed in Sweden the last five years or so might result in urban caliphates and Wahabist nests.

Reflecting on human rights and political correctness, Lacanian Žižek has something useful to say when he states that 'political correctness is indeed paradigmatic of a form of modern totalitarianism'.[8] Many will think this is nothing but populist fear-mongering, as totalitarianism is rightly associated with mass, state-endorsed violence and that is thankfully not the case here, but political correctness along with groupthink was originally a feature of totalitarianism. It has its roots in cultural Marxism and the Frankfurt School whose aim was to unleash a cultural revolution on Western society, but the term political correctness comes in fact from Soviet times when it referred to the extension of political control to ethics, behaviour and education. Political correctness was there to ensure that all aspects of life were consistent with ideological orthodoxy, and that is more or less its function today. However, it is important to understand that *ab initio* political correctness was through cultural Marxism at least explicitly a mode of anti-Western thinking.

Political correctness is of course not totalitarian in the conventional sense as we are not talking about the State controlling every aspect of our lives, but when used as multiculturalist propaganda it is conducive to a totalitarianism of the mind because only the politically correct viewpoint can be the legitimate one. This is characteristic of Goldberg's (2009) 'liberal fascism'; a term which is not oxymoronic in any way, but an accurate portrayal of the current state of affairs in parts of Western Europe. However, Goldberg in his book at least uses the term in a different context. He argues that fascist movements were and are left-wing, and states the case for liberalism having its doctrinal roots in European fascism.

As it is a form of totalitarianism that defines itself paradoxically in terms of 'liberal goodness', political correctness is especially difficult to disagree with. If one were to disagree with it, one would *a priori* not be compassionate, which in a society like Sweden would be reason for being ostracised. But, it is a form of totalitarianism nonetheless. It is a paradoxical form of totalitarianism practised by a group who might be Christian in their actions, but most likely atheistic in their beliefs. All those who believe in freedom (wherever they sit on the political spectrum) must surely reject

---

8   Available at: http://bigthink.com/videos/slavoj-zizek-political-correctness-is-fake

political correctness because, if nothing else, it represents a constraint on ideological choice.

In Sweden, intolerant conformists acting in accordance with the politically correct orthodoxy wish to depolarise gender identities. Sweden is consistently setting new lows for political correctness as feminists (women *and* men who define themselves as such) are given *carte blanche* to create a gender-neutral society on the grounds that gender is an obstacle to participation in a liberal democracy. There should be an effort to push back against these pressures because the nature of nature is polarity. There are only two genders. Sweden is trying to turn sexual norms completely upside down in accordance with the latest dogma. There are genderless schools (for example, Egalia School in Stockholm) where the teachers are not allowed to use the pronoun 'him' or 'her'. This kind of social engineering has been rolled out on a national level. Sweden, and increasingly other countries in the West, is trying to educate young children to think about issues of gender when they are still at an age when this is no proper concern of theirs.

Propagandistic travesty comes before common sense and reason. It is reasonable to assume that this ultra-feminist and well-resourced massaging of the psyche might do long-term psychological damage to the next generation of children. They might be left simply confused as to who they are. That is what normally happens if one redefines ingrained concepts. This extremist thinking is to be found everywhere in Sweden. If it continues as the State ideology, then it might succeed in destroying the conventional family as a social construct. The dissolution of gender differences is the next stage in the incessant trend to constantly create new categories and permutations of pan-sexual union. If historical conventions are not being questioned, then it cannot be 'progress'. Without family, one is left with nothing but the totalitarian State as the support network. The ideology of any totalitarian regime has as its end goal to make its citizens depend on the state for everything. It is therefore perhaps not so surprising that State ultra-feminism has become the ideological cornerstone. In Sweden, the State with its secularist ideology has become *de facto* God, and the State has become the family as well. This kind of thinking has long ceased to be part of the egalitarian project, whose objectives were achieved many years ago. It looks increasingly like a project in State control.

These initiatives chime with the suggested amendments made to the Swedish Constitution in 2009 (*En reformerad grundlag*, 2009: 83) which would make the language 'gender neutral' (*könsneutralt*). Many Swedes seem to subscribe to the strange anti-essentialist fantasy that gender and sexuality are purely social constructs, whatever people choose to make of them, which can be constructed to achieve different political goals. And thus they believe language should reflect that.

It might be old-fashioned to assume that gender is a binary notion with so-called 'gender-outlaws' demanding recognition for a range of gender identities. The whole bear-trap of gender and sexuality has become neither fish nor fowl apparently. There is an attempt to capture the political space by couching arguments in terms that are thought to be too sensitive to deconstruct. Frame something in liberal groupthink terms, no matter how absurd, and few will refute it, as it would 'out them' for not belonging to the liberal hegemony. Total relativism undermines even the basic fundamentals of human society, and thus everything is up for liberal reanalysis.

Back in Stockholm, the books at school have been carefully selected to avoid traditional portrayals of gender and parenting roles. There are 'gender officers' in some schools to make sure this sort of thing is done correctly, and to ensure for instance that boys are given the chance to play with dolls. Sleeping Beauty and Cinderella are not acceptable as they may be deemed sexist. Instead, pre-school children might be given a book where two male giraffes adopt an abandoned crocodile. Other schools have gender-neutral changing rooms for those uncomfortable with the label 'male' and 'female'. In this regard, they are just following the norm set by universities in the West. In Norway, NRK (the Norwegian Broadcasting Company) changed the names of the characters in the extremely popular children's story of *Pippi Longstocking* by Astrid Lindgren. In the original story, the main character's father is absent. This is because he is a *negerkonge* ('negro king') on a tropical island. The NRK version has him being a *sydhavskonge* ('southern sea king').[9] The ideologues that fuss over these things are like stray dogs.

---

9 Available at: https://www.nrk.no/kultur/svenskene-fjerner-pippi-rasisme-1.11957512

They recognise no boundaries, no master, and wander around aimlessly, defecating on the metaphorical pavements.

At the Swedish Parliament, a baroque painting of a woman bearing her breasts was removed as it was thought it would cause offence to apparently both women and Muslims.[10] On that basis, previous exhibitions of baroque paintings at the National Museum in Stockholm, such as the one in 2014 or the Rubens exhibition in 2010, would have to have been banned. All kinds of statues would have to be covered up. Elsewhere, Swedish books are being removed from library shelves for containing 'stereotypical depictions of other cultures'.[11]

It is crucial that a response is found to counter this conditioned consciousness because it is profoundly irrational, inimical to common sense and is leading to the 'politics of folly' (Tuchman, 1984). Political correctness is intolerant bigotry — the very thing that it is meant to oppose. Had the political correctness been put aside and an open, democratic discussion been possible, a solution might have been found earlier to the inflammatory social problems of modern Sweden: the explosion in rape statistics and the gang-style shootings in the major cities that we seldom hear about in the Swedish Press. This has been but one of the costs of unshared idealism. The moralistic ideology of the liberal elite comprising politicians, journalists, academics and judges has closed down the debate completely. There is little point having an open society if minds are closed. In such an environment, any extremist ideology such as militant Islam can only prosper.

To speak out against these developments in Sweden would leave one being described as 'unenlightened'. No society has ever done this before. This is an attempt to create a society of rootless people, denying their history, culture and now gender. A society which has been told it has no culture, that neither race nor gender exist, might encounter a militant Islamist ideology for which these issues have profound, theological significance. Chaos will ensue as the increasingly secular democracies are left supine before the zeal of radicalism.

---

10 Available at: http://www.zerohedge.com/news/2016-05-22/swedens-holy-war-childrens-books

11 Available at: http://www.zerohedge.com/news/2016-05-22/swedens-holy-war-childrens-books

Categories are necessary. The ultra-liberal can try and do away with them, believing, because he has been sufficiently ideologised, that their inherent prejudices are offensive, but he will just recreate subsequent permutations of them. With the current obsessions of 'equality' and 'tolerance', he has arguably already done so. No society has ever lived without some system of categories or classification, because man is a social animal.[12] It is the same with stereotypes: we can pretend they do not exist, that they are erroneous or inherently racist, but they will always be there. They will reemerge if expunged because group identities, professions and social differences cannot be completely erased. In a complex world, the mind needs to resort to perceptions of group identity to simplify the information and create some kind of social order.

Political correctness might be seen as an authoritarian thought-code that claims to stand for tolerance, but is in fact 'fascist'. As Orwell (1944) himself said, 'fascism' has become 'an almost entirely meaningless word', but is synonymous with bullying; and political correctness can indeed be seen as a form of bullying. Political correctness is an attempt to enforce and sometimes legalise certain kinds of behaviour, and thus has no place in a 'free' society. Anything that falls foul of 'enforcing stereotypes' is politically incorrect, and thus unacceptable. The implications of political correctness are therefore profound, because its advocates are looking to sanctify a certain kind of life and mould a certain kind of person. They seek to create clones of themselves: a *mêlée* of technocratic zombies devoid of vim. Political correctness is much more than just words. It is a 'way of belonging' as well as a 'way of speaking'. If one can speak and think uncritically about all the liberal universalist notions, then one truly 'belongs' in the global village. By accepting the liberalist ideology that one does not belong to anything, one has finally found somewhat paradoxically that one belongs to something universal, even if it is wholly abstract.

In this *Brave New World* without stereotypes, conversation must be neutral, carefully packaged in a sanitised vocabulary as every vestige of identity is stripped or concealed: it is to live in a world of countermanded

---

12 Howell (1982) describes a Chewong forest community characterised by an extreme lack of categories.

Ball tickets, a world without religion, class, gender, race, sexuality and political opinion where people are of equal ability. It is not an attempt at creating inclusiveness, it is an attempt at creating a homogeneous universe without colour, personality, flair, detail or mischief of any kind (a sort of ethnographic nightmare). This in itself is rather ironic as political correctness advocates are meant to be advocating 'diversity' *über alles*.

There has to be space for self-irony and mockery. Always. We must be free to shock, and play with life and especially words: small parcels of magic to be treated like little nuggets of gold. This stifling wind is blowing down hypnotic, endless roads where the traveller is meant to rationalise who he is and why he is not better than who he is. It implies an impaired contact with reality, a form of cultural neurosis. Every age has its own collective neurosis, and this is ours. But, it must also have its own psychotherapy to deal with its neurosis. Political correctness is therefore a kind of psychosis where self-obsessed careerists navigate unthinkingly a false reality. It is only those that speak out against it that have not succumbed to this collective psychosis.

Political correctness at universities across the UK has now almost reached the epidemic proportions that it has in America. Political correctness is crying out for affirmative action, but academics give in to these demands without fail because, once again, any response to political correctness is considered politically incorrect. Humour is really the best strategy to deal with inanity; flippancy is the finest armour-plating against the enemy. One should aim to bring an air of persiflage to the proceedings.

'Enforcing stereotypes' is universally the platform for comedy. If we are not able to talk in terms of stereotypes and not able to be critical, then comedy really is dead since all humour is critical in some way. Humour and laughter is surely an important function of every gathering, every society. If nothing else, it operates, as Bergson (1975: 76) pointed out, as a control mechanism for deviant behaviour, and as a social means of recognising an absurdity. It creates an arena for the examination of controversial social issues, and a means of connecting across boundaries. In the absence of this social corrective, if criticism is not allowed, and there is no humour, who is to say that one is not living in a totalitarian state? Who is to say whether our future will be neither democratic nor free, but instead totalitarian masquerading as democratic and free?

Cultural relativism is the principle that an individual's human beliefs and activities should be understood by others in terms of that individual's own culture. It purports to be a mode of thinking where there are no objective truths that transcend individual and cultural perspectives. In practice, it has been employed as a tool of unrelenting intellectual assault for a politically correct, moralistic ideology. This is the *Lebenswelt* that we are meant to all share. The form of cultural relativism practised by the liberal elite is effectively spiritual entropy with a masochistic distaste for its own culture; a secular heresy of Christianity and a pernicious lie. It is implausibly over-permissive, and is an attempt at mobilising a rather perverse imagination. Cultural relativism might be acceptable as a principle if its adherence and normative advocacy were universal. But *shari'ah* law for instance is explicit in its institutionalisation of inferior status for non-Muslims; the *jizya*, the poll tax on non-Muslims is the cornerstone of an entire system of humiliating regulations for non-believers. *Shari'ah* 'is a complete way of life based on a submission to God alone' (Qutb, 1964: 82). It crowds out anything non-Islamic.

As Qutb, the former leading member of the Muslim Brotherhood, says in *Ma'alim fi al-Tariq* (Milestones), 'anyone who serves someone other than God'— be that someone (or something) a priest, president, a parliament, or a legal statute of a secular state — 'is outside God's religion, although he may claim to profess this religion' (1964: 60). The Kantian categorical imperative — the maxim that nobody should act on a principle that he would not wish to be universal — an idea that is so central to thinking in the West since the Enlightenment, would be incomprehensible to the Islamic culture which centralises the notion of 'honour'.

This might become the context in which the liberal West is preaching the benefits of cultural relativism. Its result is that there is no measure of truth or morality. On the one hand, we are saying we will turn a blind eye to a Muslim uncle who removes his niece's clitoris with a knife because it is their traditional culture (there has never been a single FGM conviction in the UK, but we know the practice is widespread), but on the other hand certain representatives of the incoming Islamic culture (but also Western politicians) are telling us we should convert our churches to mosques (the demand made recently in Sweden).[13] It is doubly feeble: respecting others even if their values are completely alien to our own, but at the same time letting our own values be subjugated by other, ill-intentioned ones. Only a confused nation that has lost its purpose, forgotten its historical trajectory could be ambivalent to such developments. There is at least no chance of Sweden falling into the Thucydidean trap.

The West is prioritising a vacuous system of beliefs based on a fallacious cultural relativist principle. If everybody should tolerate everybody else's beliefs and cultural practices, then relativism becomes a trans-cultural moral principle and relativism is false since it would be disregarding the diversity of cultural beliefs. We are asking people to be tolerant of intolerance in another culture, but not in our own.[14] The relativist has a worldview of their own, one that they exempt from their relativism to make their own pronouncements about no one belief being universally true. It is structurally self-confuting. Individually, how can we not be ethnocentric when cultural prejudice is innate? Diversity is a pernicious ideology because it assumes that everybody of a certain ethnicity thinks exactly the same. The basis for the philosophy is that the way somebody thinks is inextricably tied to their group identity. That is what the racists think. This is precisely the biological essentialism that the post-modernists are always complaining about.

And yet the same people on the Left who rush to denounce so-called imperialists often fully hypocritically support the EU and its previous accession talks with Turkey, a country bordering on a dictatorship after the failed coup in July 2016, and one which sports an appalling human rights record. When the EU attempts to go beyond what is normally defined as the geography of Europe, it is clear in fact that the imperial fantasy is not dead.

In the spirit of this blanket cultural relativism, Swedish Integration Minister Erik Ullenberg's justification for removing the word 'race' from Swedish

---

13 Available at: http://www.bbc.co.uk/news/uk-37364079. According to David Cameron, there were 4,000 cases of FGM in Britain in 2014 alone. See: http://www.independent.co.uk/news/uk/politics/david-cameron-extremism-speech-read-the-transcript-in-full-10401948.html

14 It is at least pleasing to see the anthropologist James Laidlaw (2013) question the validity and relevance of cultural relativism.

legislation was that he was concerned some might infer that a certain race is 'better' than an other.[15] He wanted to deny the concept of race, but could not formulate the denial without using the word 'race', and so demonstrated the meaninglessness of his project. Such initiatives suggest that Sweden has officially endorsed cultural Marxism. Swedish liberal politicians and journalists harbour a curious wish to create a society of rootless people. Journalists always entice SD members to talk about 'Swedish values'. Once the SD politician has listed them, they then quickly follow it up with the assertion that the stated values are not in fact Swedish, but 'international'.

Their perennial intention is apparently to convince people that Sweden does not stand for anything. This is the contemporary *doxa* amongst Leftist thinkers. If the Swedish people are not rooted to anything, then there can be no objection to allowing in so many people with roots that belong elsewhere because there is no cultural content to dilute. Note that the same politicians and journalists talk all the time of 'integration', but if Swedes are rootless and a Swedish value system is a myth, then one might rightly question what one is trying to integrate them into. The idea that Sweden needs to be created *ex nihilo* is both false and ludicrous, and is engineered so that the cultural nihilists can appeal to their tiresome universalist principles as the basis of society. But there is no reason to assume that liberal democracy will reign supreme in the future. The new Chinese middle class will not be living in a liberal democracy. Turkey and Russia have turned authoritarian. There are potentially millions of young radicalised Arab males, many of whom have come to Europe. They have not grown up under liberal democracy.

But there *are* of course Swedish values and there is such a thing as society. It is not a random assembly of individuals. There is a Swedish cultural ethos based on centuries of heritage, solidarity and bonds of trust between people who do not know one another but share an identity. Nationality means many things, but it is not about owning the right document or certificate.

Migration should be a contractual arrangement. Surely, even the multiculturalist can see that the Swedish way should be based on 'a certain idea of living together' (to quote the European Court of Human Rights in their

---

15 Available at: http://www.thelocal.se/20140731/race-to-be-scrapped-from-swedish-legislation

upholding of the French *burqa* ban).¹⁶ Sadly, for many of the 'new Swedes', welfare support is often their only modality of belonging to Sweden. Some are conspicuous aliens who have made sometimes little effort to be part of their host country. Many of these people belong first and foremost to the exiled *ummah*. They are 'clients' of the Swedish welfare system. They are housed in one of the suburban ghettos, given enough money to live off, but no opportunities to move into mainstream society. Not ever mastering the language, some tend to turn inwards to the Muslim community where they have been sent, and many of them remain there for the rest of their lives. They are not 'outsiders' there. It is not difficult to see why integration works better in the UK than in the Scandinavian countries.

As Scruton (2015: 238) notes, 'relativist beliefs exist because they sustain a community — the new ummah of the rootless' — the globalists who wish to expunge all social identity markers perhaps, but who will end up with a society where public order does not work because the sense of loyalty and allegiance has been erased. But, it is our rootedness in our surroundings that creates unknowingly an existential framework which governs large parts of our lives and our overall philosophy. To belong somewhere is to be part of the collective consciousness that defines the community, that community which is the permanent and perpetual condition of things. As a member of a community, one belongs to an organic reality. It is not clear what can be gained from constantly trying to undermine such parameters of belonging and idioms of social association. The notion of 'belonging' should conjure up positive feelings of intimacy and attachment, not negative ones inspired by the neurotic relativist dogma.

Relativism and political correctness are perhaps nowhere more suffocating than in the American education system. In the US in particular, but also increasingly in the UK, education is turning into some kind of strange therapy. Some universities in the UK have dissent-free 'safe spaces' where coddled students can be free of banter or any kind of language that might somehow be perceived to be sexist, racist or any other *-ist*. Only speech that stigmatises the opponent and conforms to the feminist, anti-racist ideology

---

16   Available at: https://www.theguardian.com/world/2014/jul/01/france-burqa-ban-upheld-human-rights-court

is acceptable. This silencing of the opposition is to be found in all totalitarian regimes, as it serves to underpin the crucial distinction between 'us' and 'them'.

As a sign of the depressing globalisation of American university norms, Edinburgh University for instance operates a 'safe space' policy where there is a zero tolerance policy towards discrimination based on: age, class, disability, gender and gender identity, marriage and civil partnership, political affiliation, pregnancy and maternity, race and ethnicity, religion, belief and sexual orientation.[17] It is difficult to know how this works in practice. The policy also includes a clause which states that it does not discriminate against anybody on the grounds that they are a sex worker (whorephobia). Goldsmiths, London adds biphobia, transphobia, disablism, nationality, gender presentation and language ability amongst others to the endless list of reasons for which somebody might take offence.[18] Our corporatised universities are beginning to look like something out of a Monty Python skit, with the causes of the cultural Marxists resembling a malignant self-parody, with their over-concern for minor detail. Sadly, this is not a case of surreal humour or hyperbolic absurdity, but one of a plethora of examples of despotic university bureaucrats trying to turn a dynamic environment into a sterile one through attempts at policing thought.

Universities are becoming oppressive breeding grounds of dogmatism with the multiculturalist, anti-racist ideology that lecturers are passing onto their students. It is not fascist to defend one's culture and history, or to attempt to preserve the prevailing social ecology. It *is* fascist to close down debate through threatened violence and thuggery. Students should be taught that they can be proud (and not guilty) of what their grandparents did, for they were defenders of freedom. We cannot educate people in self-hatred. They should understand that culture and intellect are not objects of resentment, and that it is both good and correct to celebrate achievement. Instead, students nowadays constantly crave some kind of moral superiority by declaring war on the past, by attempting to remove statues of Cecil Rhodes for instance

---

17   Available at: https://www.eusa.ed.ac.uk/eusapolicy/internal/safespaceupdate/
18   Available at: https://www.goldsmithssu.org/pageassets/yourunion/governance/policies/Safe-Space-Policy.pdf

in the manner of the Taliban blowing up Buddhist monuments. They desire a propagandistic mutability of the past whereby the past can be modified or massaged to match the ideologised vision of the present—another feature of totalitarianism.

This kind of guilt and self-contempt is absolutely key to the liberal ideologisation of the individual. As Žižek (1984: 41) correctly observes, the reason why the KGB recruited so many people from Cambridge in the 1920s and 1930s was because a section of the well-connected upper class felt a great sense of guilt. Around them, there was economic chaos and misery, and yet they were living a great life of privilege. It is for this reason that communism had such appeal. The KGB made hay whilst the sun shone within the Oxbridge Colleges. Eighty years later, things are slightly different. Students at Canadian universities are now encouraged to report their 'white privilege'. This kind of discrimination and vilification of white men borders on abuse. Notably, class is never on the list of privileges, and thus the biggest losers of such a perverse project are exactly the group that need most help: white, working class males. The post-modernists are attacking knowledge and creating an ethos of institutional atrophy at the heart of our universities. Nowadays, those who are white and have a whiff of privilege about them are made to feel guilty about any perceived superiority, and thus some of them choose to feign the habits and speech of the working classes. We saw this with many members of the previous Cabinet in the UK Government who went out of their way to even change the way they spoke. George Osborne, the Chancellor of the Exchequer was well known for peppering his speech with glottal stops to make him sound like a yob, but then even the Prime Minister at the time (David Cameron) started doing it, desperate for some covert prestige. 'Call me Dave' seemed to be the only way, except for those that know him or are related to him of course. This guilt complex is a Western syndrome and has reached levels of paranoia. The same people that are telling us that race does not exist imply that one should somehow feel a specious sense of guilt for being 'white'. Such flaccid, bourgeois liberalism, riddled with such contradictions, is trying to corrupt our social consciousness. Fortunately, there is something of a backlash against this disingenuous behaviour, and many people in the UK irrespective of their political position warm to the Conservative Backbencher, Jacob Rees-Mogg MP simply because he does not try to be somebody else. He is posh, and is the first to admit it. He is also a brilliant polymath and the most effective backbencher of my generation.

For the multiculturalist nihilist, the problem with white males appears to be that they have been historically the dominant group, and this feeds into the Foucaultian 'economy of power relations' (Foucault, 1983: 208-26). The multiculturalists are thus correcting the ideology of the other by enforcing their own dominating ideology, and therefore once again are the epitome of hypocrisy with their double-standards moral fervour. They wish to destroy one alleged hegemony, and then create their own. This moral bullying is often indicative of the atheistic multiculturalist who has forgotten that dogmatic atheism culminates in the paradoxical conclusion that religion is the only thing that counts. The multiculturalist believes that the migrant who assaults German women and children is rebelling against German power structures, and that Germans who criticise such assaults are racists. The German media became unambiguously an enemy of its own people when it tried to defend and make excuses for the Afghan, ISIS-flag-carrying axe murderer who came to Germany in 2016 claiming that he was a refugee.[19] We are living in surreal times where we absolutely cannot trust our own liberal media to support the ethnic majority.

Even if Western culture has given us Mozart, Shakespeare, Bach and Pushkin, it is considered inherently flawed, because this genius has come almost exclusively from Western white males. And therefore, it is better to live in a dissolute world, to indulge in an effete, self-critical culture without freethinking iconoclasts. We live in a world where Stockholm University removes all the pictures of white male Professors (so-called DWEMs — Dead White European Males) from the walls for no other reason than because they are 'white and male'.[20] Paradoxically, this was done apparently in the name of 'diversity and tolerance'. Hertford College, Oxford did the same, and then the trend caught on in a number of the other Oxford colleges. In such a context, the incoming culture thus rapidly be-

---

19 Available at: https://www.theguardian.com/world/2016/jul/19/germany-train-attack-could-prompt-rethink-of-counter-terrorism-policy

20 Available at: http://culturalmarxism.net/ridiculous-swedish-university-removes-all-portraits-and-busts-of-white-male-professors-in-the-name-of-diversity/

comes the strong culture, as we have been so busy denying and repudiating our own. Multiculturalist dogma in practice is therefore a much more sinister notion than simply respecting other cultures, a notion which few could disagree with. This vainglorious experiment risks creating cultural apartheid, a mosaic of conflicting identities. It employs a speech code that amounts to a form of Wittgensteinian verbal imprisonment: an obsessively homogenising, neutral language that is based on the systematic shunning of stereotypes devoid of judgement and opinions, but anxious to employ cuddly euphemisms. Such language makes it easy to forget that liberalism is authoritarian and concerned with control and power, even if it is not as brutal as the real totalitarian regimes of the twentieth century.

Language that 'locks up thought' fences in ideas that can only be expressed in a private arena, and so thinking and prejudice is privatised and open debate is shunted from the regulated public space to the unregulated Internet — the memic abyss. If thinking about the 'big topics' is internalised *en masse*, then a section of society risks being pushed towards a shadowy periphery. There are legal limits to expression, but not yet legal limits to thinking. With the policing of public debate, one should surely expect radicalisation to continue to flourish. Equality legislation will have had totally the wrong effect, and might with retrospect be seen as a mistake, as it will have disaffected a significant percentage of the population whose voice has been silenced by the law.

In part, this explains the pervasive malice and nastiness that is to be found on both left- and right-wing oriented Internet chat forums, often written by people who, when not sitting in front of their PC, are perfectly decent and well-mannered. This dichotomy of pseudo-totalitarian, over-regulated socio-cultural spheres and cornered thinking will create many more problems for our Western societies in the future, if it is not addressed. The countries that the liberals blanket-label as 'racist' such as Russia have other authoritarian issues of their own, but they do not have this problem, because speech is not policed for political correctness (it might be policed for other things). The narrative of political correctness is quite rightly irrelevant.

In such a context, cursing under one's breath or sacrosanct silence becomes an active force, something more than a sign of introspection in an age of anxiety. Increasingly, some people refuse to voice any political opinion; an air of intimidation lingers when the daylight is dim and the shadows are tawny. The gathering clouds look increasingly autocratic in moments of Socratic doubt. Ways of speaking and the symbolic patterns of language have been redefined by liberal norms which are in fact illiberal. Spoken language is constantly screened by liberals for evidence of 'sexism' or 'racism', not understanding that language evolves in a context of complex, intertwined language contact and social processes. Language is not auto-telic; it does not have its own agenda in the way that 'liberal fascists' seems to think it does.

Sweden, and indeed much of the West, is suffocating in political correctness: a secularised, pseudo-religion that requires unthinking support and demands absolute loyalty amongst the groupthink apparatchiks. Ironically, these are often the same liberals that fought in the 1960s to free us from dogma. And in a further ironic twist, they typically comprise anti-Christian activists who put the rather Christian virtue of 'pity' at the centre of our society. Some might claim that a society run on Christian virtues is a 'weak' one; a society run on Christian virtues by atheists is a perverse, ideologically and morally confused one. Life is and always will be essentially unfair because the strong thrive and the weak suffer. Society can attempt to mitigate some of this, sometimes quite successfully so, and this is to be applauded. However, we cannot deny the fact entirely, because it is a reflection of human nature.

Today, those in denial are often demagogues of a fraudulent diversity, hypocrites who represent a complex, illogical consciousness, an *affaire fatale*, which is rapidly eroding individualism. They might hail the end to 'whiteness' with their paeans of multiculturalist openness, but would not dream of sending their children to schools with large numbers of students from ethnic minorities. They want to be relativists, but their curious repudiation of the West and their cosmopolitan contempt for embedded identity shows them to be anything but relativists. This is an attempt to package some very 'unprogressive' thinking as 'progressive' and its proponents have been accurately described as the 'Regressive Left' (Nawaz, 2012).

As we have seen, Leftist thinking is often anti-Enlightenment, but it is the Enlightenment that espoused values such as equality that they apparently care so much about.

What matters in society now is not the objective truth, but the anti-knowledge which is wrapped up in a manufactured set of politicised emotions. Anything that does not fall within these boundaries is an unwelcome truth or stereotype, and thus we have an information war between the ideologised liberal mainstream media and the Internet where the facts can be obtained (as well as many unpleasant rants). Both sources engage in fake news too. Such a culture of falsity has become intimidating in academia where the tendency to self-censorship is particularly prevalent, and the weight of the PC culture can be burdensome. If you speak your mind, you risk rejection from your colleagues. It is that simple.

The truth cannot be constantly blurred. Otherwise, society's problems cannot be addressed, or worse still the finger will be pointed at the wrong group. Not just political correctness, but liberal groupthink has rendered it taboo to make ever so obvious connections about the repercussions of the changes taking place in our society. A small nation such as Sweden cannot be allowed to descend *vers la boue*, to move silently towards an unspoken catafalque in the name of politicised charity, so laden with ideology. And newcomers cannot perhaps be expected to give up the ultimate exigencies in their lives: their identity. We are living in times of complex entanglement and subverted reticulations. We will not be able to 'progress' until the institutional culture of silence and intimidation has been dismantled.

III

Freedom of Speech

> Just living is not enough. [...] One must have sunshine, freedom and a little flower.
>
> — Hans Christian Andersen

FREEDOM OF SPEECH MUST SURELY be the foundation of liberal democracy. No country can have absolute freedom of speech. Otherwise, it would not be able to have an intelligence service or an Official Secrets Act. But we must have the right to offend, and the right to uphold the tradition of satire. As Tallentyre (1906: 198) wrote in a maxim that is often erroneously ascribed to Voltaire: 'I disapprove of what you say, but I will defend to the death your right to say it'.

It is never wrong in and of itself to discuss a topic, no matter how sensitive it might be. *Parrhesia*, the right to speak one's mind without fear or restraint, must be the prerogative. *Parrhesia* is intrinsic to freedom. Someone is said to use *parrhesia* if he *risks* telling the truth. This takes us to the crux of the problem in all of these essays: the cultural context in which telling the truth has been problematised; the courage required to 'speak out'.

As Foucault (1983: 1-4) describes it, in the Greek context it was believed that to tell the truth one needed certain moral qualities, but also a sense of the 'culture of the self'. This takes us back to the Socratic principle of 'knowing yourself'. Foucault speaks of a '*parrhesiastic* game' which presupposes that the *parrhesiaste* has the moral qualities which are required to know and tell the truth. Typically, the *parrhesiaste* will voice an opinion that other people would not dare to express, perhaps because they just believe it is wrong or because of a culture of oppressive groupthink they feel as if they dare not talk about it. To be outspoken and 'take the risk' is to embody authenticity. Today, we are playing a *parrhesiastic* game between the truth-teller and the liberal groupthink interlocutor. The game might have terrifying consequences. The secular multiculturalists assume they are the embodiment of these moral qualities and thus apparently know the truth. Armed with the truth, they believe they are vindicated in potentially destabilising European nations like Sweden through mass immigration from Muslim countries. Paradoxically, they aspire to moral superiority, but seem to believe in nothing except for feminism and multiculturalism. Their supposed moral superiority has no legitimate foundations. They mock Christianity, but apparently like to 'do good'. It is these people that sit at the axis of power in Brussels alongside Macron and Merkel.

The modern-day *parrhesiaste* such as, say, Trump, Wilders or Farage, challenges the 'mass' received opinions of our age, speaks with splendid autonomy, is silenced, scorned and called a '[…]-ist' for speaking the unspeakable truth in these troubled, ambiguous times. It is those who risk speaking out that tell the truth. Telling the truth in such an oppressive context is representative of a certain manner of being, a certain *je ne sais quoi*.

As Foucault (1983: 4) says: 'parrhesia comes from below, as it were, and is directed towards above. […] In parrhesia, the speaker uses his freedom and chooses frankness instead of persuasion, truth instead of falsehood or silence, the risk of death instead of life and security, criticism instead of flattery, and moral duty instead of self-interest and moral apathy'. It is a modality of truth-telling, and should be the social imperative of our times. *Parrhesia* is criticising the majority. The mass-think participants, the silent majority are not *parrhesiastes*; they are not taking *any* risks. They are not detaching the search for truth from the ruling cultural hegemony. It is better to be a truth-teller and take the risk than indulging in the normative, self-denying falsehood and *canard* that surrounds the *agora*.

He who wishes to silence debate because the topic itself is in some way 'controversial' is surely little more than an anti-free speech totalitarian.

There must always be some limits to the freedom of speech, but it should at least be an inalienable right to express an opinion. Freedom of speech was once the 'line in the sand'. After all, that was the struggle of the twentieth century after the totalitarianism of Nazism and Stalinism. It cost us millions of twentieth-century lives to salvage them, but our freedoms in the West are being eroded bit by bit. Freedom of speech is being eroded by the Islamists and oversensitised Leftists; freedom of national Governments and their sovereignty are being chiselled away by the increasingly dictatorial European Union.

We are losing freedom of speech through two channels: directly through hate-speech legislation, which is blurring a most important distinction between the legal and civic prohibition, and indirectly through a pervasive culture of political correctness, self-censorship and liberal groupthink. The former pertains to Western Europe, the latter to the West generally, and especially so in the United States. By restricting rhetorical freedom through these means, liberalism and its culture of political correctness is violating its own principles. Freedom of speech has been sacrificed at the anti-racism altar. But the former is far more important. Freedom of speech in the West seems to mean nowadays freedom to support globalist liberalism. But it might be argued in fact that anti-racism itself is a form of covert racism, since it condescendingly treats Pakistanis in Britain or Somalis in Sweden, say, as morally inferior human beings who require some kind of State shielding.

As for hate-speech, it is a subjective undertaking of course to determine what constitutes and what does not constitute hate-speech, and national legislative definitions vary (although not by very much). The fact that it is so subjective probably means the legislation should not exist in the first place. Much of contemporary rap is arguably little more than hate-speech with its fiery rhetoric promoting violence in chaotic syntax; the repellent invectives are just ignored, or worse still often embraced by young women who are often the object of their abuse. It is important to embrace it because the offending lyrics play presumably into oppressive power structures against ethnic minorities. Some of rap is the cornerstone of an anti-culture that celebrates scoundrels who in questionable grammar glorify rape, physical assault and sometimes rebuke the nations that have supported them.

A cursory glance at European hate-speech legislation shows how respective Governments have attempted to criminalise free speech, anxious to control the thoughts expressed in the presence of others. One country after another has simply copied and incorporated hate-speech legislation with more or less the same wording. Perhaps aided by social media, packaged opinions on such topics as hate-speech can quickly spread and gather momentum to the point it is inevitable that they are accepted, and often with little discussion. We have witnessed this with same-sex marriage legislation. Hate-speech and hate-crime have become rapidly part of the liberal vocabulary, but these words are often used synonymously with the word 'insult': an alarming trend.

A wave of oversensitised liberalism has come crashing down on our vulnerable shores, leaving people to negotiate the insanity of a panoply of universalising potential hate-crimes. For example, wolf-whistling is now considered hate-crime by the Nottinghamshire police in Britain because it is categorised as 'misogynistic abuse'.[1] Approaching an unknown woman in a flirtatious manner might fall under the same category, and potentially be a criminal offence. Potential victims are strongly encouraged to contact the police 'without hesitation'. Wolf-whistling is an extreme example of political correctness because it takes a gesture which whilst sexist has always been used to show appreciation, and classifies it as 'hate'. It is no longer just about legislating against prejudice, but has gone a step further, beyond political correctness. Our Western societies are now being policed for any behaviour that deviates beyond the norm of the neutralised character of liberal managerialism, and as such are rapidly losing their appeal for anybody who has not been blinded by the ideology.

Sec. 18(1) of the UK Public Order Act of 1986 (POA) states that 'a

---

1   Available at: https://www.theguardian.com/lifeandstyle/2016/jul/13/nottinghamshire-police-count-wolf-whistling-hate-crime

person who uses threatening, abusive, or insulting words or behaviour, or displays any written material which is threatening, abusive, or insulting, is guilty of an offence if: a) he intends to thereby stir up racial hatred, or; b) having regard to all the circumstances racial hatred is likely to be stirred up thereby'. Section 5 of the POA states that it is a crime to use or display threatening, abusive, or insulting words 'within the hearing or sight of a person likely to be caused harassment, alarm, or distress thereby'. Harry Taylor, an atheist who placed drawings satirising Christianity and Islam in an airport prayer room, was convicted in April 2010 under Section 5 and given a six-month prison sentence.[2] The Racial and Religious Hatred Act of 2006 amended the Public Order Act of 1986 by adding Part 3A. This Part states: 'A person who uses threatening words or behaviour, or displays any written material which is threatening, is guilty of an offence if he intends thereby to stir up religious hatred'. Lauren Southern and two other activists were recently permanently banned from the UK after being arrested under schedule 7 of the Terrorism Act 2000 for distributing leaflets entitled 'Allah is Gay'. The UK now uses terrorist legislation to arrest young girls distributing silly leaflets, but at the same time welcomes home hundreds of ISIS jihadists who have committed rape and murder in Syria.

However, when it comes to minorities, hate-speech legislation and actual events on the ground seem at times to have little to say to one another. As an example of this, we may wish to remind ourselves of the response to the Mohammed cartoons.

On February 3rd 2006, at the demonstrations outside the Danish Embassy in London following the publication of the Muhammed Cartoons in an obscure Danish newspaper, hundreds of Islamists expressed their allegiance to terrorism.

Thick crowds of bearded men, clad in thobes and *taqiyahs* wave black flags and shout frantic abuse into megaphones. Their dark eyes are full of hatred and revenge. Film footage on www.youtube.com shows furious Muslims screaming and holding up placards saying: 'Annihilate those who

---

2 Available at: http://news.bbc.co.uk/1/hi/england/merseyside/8549613.stm

insult Islam'; 'Jihad in the name of Allah''; 'May Allah bomb you'; 'May Osama Bin Laden bomb you'; 'May we bomb Denmark, so we can invade their country and take their wives as war booty'; 'Take lessons from Theo van Gogh [the Dutch film maker who was assassinated for criticising Islam] for you will pay with your blood'. The whole crowd shouts: 'bomb, bomb Denmark, bomb, bomb France, bomb, bomb Spain'.[3] The British police did nothing for six weeks even though the written material displayed was unambiguously in breach of the Public Order Act, as described above. Eventually, after much political pressure from Conservative MPs, a handful of men were charged and all except two were released on bail.

In Denmark, the *imam* Mohamed Al-Khaled Samha at the Odense mosque in October 2014 called Jews the 'offspring of apes and pigs', but no charges were made.[4] And yet a Dane who described the 'ideology of Islam' as 'oppressive' and 'as misanthropic as Nazism' on a Facebook post was fined for hate-speech.[5] No charges were made either by the Danish police against another *imam*, Abu Bilal Ismail from the Grimshøj mosque, who in July 2014 prayed for the death of Jews at a sermon in a Berlin mosque. 'Oh Allah, destroy the Zionist Jews. They are no challenge for you. Count them and kill them to the very last one. Don't spare a single one of them,' Ismail said.[6]

And yet, in June 2010, the Danish crown prosecutor sought to lift MP Jesper Langballe's parliamentary immunity so that he could face charges under Article 266(b) for publishing an article about the creeping 'Islamisation of Europe' and the subjugated status of Muslim women.[7] Similarly,

---

3 Available at: https://www.youtube.com/watch?v=qoMeUcC_M20
4 Available at: http://www.thelocal.dk/20141014/video-danish-imam-calls-jews-apes-and-pigs
5 Available at: https://globalfreedomofexpression.columbia.edu/updates/2016/02/somethings-rotten-denmark-criminalizing-blasphemy-hate-speech-law/
6 Available at: http://www.independent.co.uk/news/world/europe/danish-government-denmark-radical-imams-citizenship-aarhus-mosque-islam-extremism-a6949651.html
7 Available at: http://politiken.dk/newsinenglish/ECE989953/case-against-mp-for-racist-remarks/

in Germany, a twenty-seven year old man and his wife were recently sentenced to ten months in prison and fined 1,200 Euros because he voiced concerns about the refugee crisis on Facebook.[8] Somebody in Lübeck contacted the police about the chat group with its 900 members which he found offensive. He also contacted Facebook, but Facebook confirmed that the group did not breach its rules. But it seems criticism of German immigration policy might fall foul of German hate-speech legislation (*Volksverhetzung*). The description of this crime reads like a satire, particularly as the *Volksverhetzung* legislation has normally been used for Holocaust denial. Legislators seem to be putting rather innocuous comments made on a webpage on the same footing as denial of the largest genocide ever recorded. With disproportionate responses like this, we risk creating a culture of totalitarian fear and silence, and that is perhaps the objective.

The hegemony of Leftist thinking (now written into such laws) claims to have a monopoly on the ultimate truth. Like all totalitarian states, they have to use oppression to impose their worldview. Such incidents represent authoritarian liberalism at its worst, and are cause for great concern. It is the ultimate paradox. As Popper (1945) tells us, totalitarian ideologies were meant to be the enemy of open societies, but the society that describes itself as 'open' is now open to using the same authoritarian ideologies. Without borders, they are certainly open in one sense, but they are no longer 'free'. Sweden prohibits hate-speech, and defines it as:

> Den som i uttalande eller i annat meddelande som sprids hotar eller uttrycker missaktning för folkgrupp eller annan sådan grupp av personer med anspelning på ras, hudfärg, nationellt eller etniskt urpsrung, tros bekännelse eller sexuell läggning, döms för hets mot folkgrupp till fängelse i högst två år eller om brottet är ringa, til böter. (*Brotttsbalkan*, 'The Swedish Penal Code', Chapter 16, Section 8)

Those who publicly or in some other form threaten or make statements that

---

8   Available at: http://www.sueddeutsche.de/muenchen/dachau/dachau-bewaehrungsstrafe-wegen-volksverhetzung-1.3066010

threaten or express disrespect for an ethnic group or similar group regarding their race, skin colour, national or ethnic origin, faith or sexual orientation may be charged for inciting group hatred and face up to a two year prison sentence or a fine.

This Swedish law was passed in 2002, and appears in fact to contravene Article 9 of the European Convention on Human Rights which provides a right to freedom of thought, conscience and religion.[9] The law is extraordinary for its use of the word *missaktning* ('disrespect'). *Missaktning* could refer to almost anything. There is no objective standard for identifying 'disrespect'. It is not difficult to show disrespect in a pluralistic society where values are not shared by all. If enforced, one could indeed imagine that Kafkaesque totalitarian nightmare of a police state where acting in accordance with one's own Western culture could be interpreted as being 'disrespectful' to another group, so that one is subsequently charged and sentenced. Surrounded by meaninglessness, we are no longer sure what we should fear. It is a moment of critical self-awareness, an understanding of where we sit in the new existential order where everything is politicised and where friendships have to be forged with great care.

Pastor Åke Green was prosecuted (but acquitted) under this Swedish hate-speech law. He held a sermon at Borgholm on the 20th of July, 2003 where he explained at length why he felt homosexuality was incompatible with Christianity. He did this with reference to various Biblical texts (Genesis 1:27-8; Hebrews 13:4; Genesis 19:1-5; Romans 1:21-8; Leviticus 18:22-30; Matthew 15:18; Ephesians 5:3-6 etc.).[10] The Supreme Court ruled that the constitutionally guaranteed freedom of expression did not protect him. However, it was conceded in the appeal that the freedom of expression provided by the European Convention on Human Rights which is superior to Swedish law did give him protection. For once, Europe got it right.

In a not dissimilar incident in 2015, Pastor McConnell faced charges in

---

9   See European Convention on Human Rights: http://www.echr.coe.int/Documents/Convention_ENG.pdf
10 Available at: http://www.svd.se/svensk-lag-hade-fallt-green

Belfast for holding a sermon where he described Islam as 'satanic'.[11] Also in the UK, Paul Weston, Chairman of Liberty GB was arrested in 2014 on suspicion of religious harassment for reading a passage from Winston Churchill's book *The River War* (1899) about Islam.[12] Whilst living in the Sudan, Churchill described Islam as a 'militant faith'. The interesting point here is Weston was arrested because he was standing in front of the Winchester Crown Court reading out a passage and a passerby heard the word Islam, and called the police. He was not subsequently charged because he had not broken any laws, and was in no way guilty of hate-speech. But a passerby assumed that a white person holding a Tannoy in public talking about Islam must amount to hate-speech. This is how far our public paranoia of any kind of commentary on Islam has gone. If we are going to legislate against the freedom of speech, one would have thought somebody calling for the elimination of a country, as the group of men did outside the Danish Embassy in London in 2005, would be more likely to be charged than somebody describing a religion as 'satanic'. In the Weston case, there is a pathological fear of an individual's rights here; a sinister anti-freedom development that appears to be spreading rapidly in our societies. Had Paul Weston been talking about Christianity, the passerby would have just assumed he was a harmless happy-clappy evangelical. Thus, this is as much a commentary on the culture that is developing as it is on the legislation.

The logic of hate-speech legislation plays into a therapeutic culture of emotional correctness where every issue has to be judged in emotive terms. The problem of cultural vulnerability is constantly inflated, and any exposure to adversity might be potentially troublesome. The offended (there must be somebody) should be eked out. It is an obsessive mollycoddling of minorities, and the protected group is ethnically defined. This is explicitly the case: the white minorities of Leicester, Slough and Luton have not acquired victim status. Minority status is defined by ethnicity

---

11 Available at: http://www.bbc.co.uk/news/uk-35232068
12 Available at: http://www.bbc.co.uk/news/uk-england-hampshire-27186573

and a miscellany of other variables, but not class and not by being a statistical minority alone.

Christian morality as written in the Bible might be unacceptable in Sweden, but the Islamic characterisation of non-believers as 'infidels' is apparently not problematic. Islam enjoys a degree of immunity from criticism, or even comment. An immunity that Christianity has lost, and Judaism never had. We are witnessing therefore a nihilistic assessment of our own historical values, and an unwillingness to stand up for our own customs and mores, which have defined us for centuries.

With a socialist minority coalition Government, Sweden is anxious to silence all opposition to what seems to be a rather explicit pro-Islam and feminist agenda. Members of the *Miljöpartiet* (party to the current coalition Government in Sweden) seem incapable of speaking about anything but extremism and gay rights, but judging by the friends they keep apparently have no problem with Islamic extremism (surely the greatest enemy to the gay rights platform).[13] A bonfire of incompatibilities. The leader of the party described 9/11 on live Swedish television as an *olycka* ('accident') and many leading members have been caught displaying hand gestures associated with the Muslim Brotherhood.[14] Following the Åke Green case, church sermons in Sweden were monitored carefully by gay activists with the hope that parties such as this on the Left could effectively couple Church attendance with bigotry and homophobia. Such developments explain the obviously atheistic bias of the Swedish state media which takes its instructions from such ideologues.

Freedom of speech is one thing, but now freedom of opinion and expression seems threatened too. It is no longer the case that people have the right to express their own views, and if they do so, there will be consequences. With actions like this, it seems the current paradigm is

---

13 Available at: https://www.theguardian.com/world/2016/apr/18/swedens-housing-minister-resigns-amid-extremist-links-row

14 Available at: http://www.svt.se/nyheter/inrikes/har-vagrar-romson-svara-pa-varfor-kaplan-fick-ga

simply one where one must either sign up to the increasingly totalitarian liberalist agenda, or else one's career is jeopardised.

An objective outsider would surely conclude that hate-speech legislation has been drafted with a view to discriminate against the ethnic Swede or Briton, and to somewhat explicitly favour minorities. As a corollary to this, cartoons depicting Muhammed led to violence perpetrated by Muslims all over the world and resulted in the death of at least 200 people, but cartoons showing the gassing of a Swedish anti-mass immigration politician were ignored and apparently totally acceptable.

The leader of the Swedish anti-mass-immigration party (*Sverigedemokraterna*), Jimmie Åkesson, was portrayed by journalists in *Länstidningen*, a social democratic newspaper in Östersund as a cockroach that needs gassing.[15] A disproportionately large cockroach with the SD party emblem blazoned on its thorax is about to gobble up the party leader. His neck and caricatured head can be seen stemming from the creature's mouth. Behind it stands a pest controller dressed in boiler suit and wearing a gas mask. The gas tank has all the emblems of the other Swedish political parties stuck to it. The pest controller is moving in and Jimmie is about to be exterminated.

The symbolism could not be clearer. The SD is a political party that is made up of part humans, part insects. The whole image feeds into the Nazi imagery used in Hitler's speeches when referring to the Jews as animals that should be exterminated. In a classic dehumanisation of political foes, dissidents to the Leftist agenda are to be exterminated. The only archetypes the cartoon can be associated with are the Nazi hate pictures of Jews in the 1930s. Those images paved the way for the gas chambers at Auschwitz, Sobi Bor and Bergen-Belsen and the execution of millions of Jews, as well as the mentally ill and other groups.

There is increasingly a ban on satire, but once again only if the satire involves ideologically protected immigrant groups. A number of leading French intellectuals have been convicted of incitement to racial hatred

---

15 Available at: http://www.ltz.se/

for satirising or simply telling the truth about Muslim immigration: Renaud Camus (one of *les nouveaux réactionnaries*) faced charges and was ordered to pay 4,000 euros for saying that local French populations will be replaced by newcomers who produce faster.[16] One might indeed argue that France's sovereignty is under threat from Arab immigration, and that the French are living in a context of censorship. This is a fact, but as Pamela Geller always reminds us: 'truth is the new hate-speech'.[17] A French intellectual is unable to tell the truth, even in a way that could in no way be seen as racist, but female Arab immigrants break French law on a daily basis by wearing the *niqab*, the cloth that covers the face as part of sartorial *hijab*, which the Sarkozy Government banned. If caught, they are cautioned but never charged.

When hate-speech laws are drafted in such a way as to ensure legal protection for 'minority groups', an Islamic fundamentalist promoting *jihad* on Swedish soil might not be charged, but an ethnic Swede denouncing militant Islam may be culpable. Hate-speech laws were introduced in a context of macroscopic, rising Islamic terrorism. As the law stands at the moment, they serve potentially to victimise the ethnic Swede. Their purpose appears to be to suppress the views that the illiberals cannot tolerate. The effect is precisely the opposite to what they should have been intended for. Depending on how they are implemented, hate-speech laws in Sweden might result in the loss of freedom of speech in public spheres, unless one is part of a minority. This is perverse (perhaps in the rhetoric of liberal groupthink a form of 'racism' against its own people, sometimes known as 'reverse racism') and is nothing but the 'politics of folly'. In this respect, America has the advantage of the First Amendment to the United States Constitution, which prohibits the making of any law that abridges the freedom of speech.

In some cases, legislation appears to suggest that there can be only one

---

16   Available at: http://www.lemonde.fr/societe/article/2014/04/10/l-ecrivain-renaud-camus-condamne-pour-provocation-a-la-haine-contre-les-musulmans_4399551_3224.html

17   Available at: https://www.youtube.com/watch?v=XLzlQ7WrvfQ

permitted opinion, that of the *islamogauchistes* where religion is concerned. The Government wants to do the thinking for us, and it is therefore a regime that is increasingly tyrannical. The right to disagree is inherent in democracy; in certain west European states such as Sweden, that right is fading further in the public domain at least, and thus it is fair to assume that democracy is in danger. The acceptable discourse has become so narrow, it represents more or less the mono-perspective of barefaced propaganda, a propaganda which is supported, as we shall see in the essay 'What is going on in Sweden?', by all the State-subsidised national newspapers.

Sweden appears to be unique in that it does not have a single national newspaper that will report anything tackling the anti-racist propaganda. It is an intellectual dishonesty of staggering proportions. The population has been to some degree socially engineered to put concepts such as 'racism' and 'social justice' before 'reason' and 'logic'. Individual, critical thinking is frowned upon because by definition it would be 'deviant', as it would not follow the State propaganda. In the Soviet Union, this kind of totalitarianism pushed intellectuals underground to form resistance groups, secret meetings and discussion groups etc. In Sweden, they have not so much gone underground as just left the country. The only people that speak out about the statist groupthink are the foreigners and a handful of exiles. In some respects, it is the bureaucratic totalitarian's dream because people do not question it.

It is important not to legislate against 'offence being taken', because racist or sexist opinions will not go away just because we forbid their expression. We have a moral duty to laugh at fundamentalists of all kinds, but it has become dangerous to do so. There can be no immunity from mockery. Indeed, it is becoming difficult to articulate any judgement that is not in the favour of a minority. To suggest that one taste, religion or belief is 'better' than another might be perceived as 'elitist' and thus an offence to equality. But notice it is only the liberal elite themselves that hypocritically pass such judgement. The notions of feminism, equality and diversity are of no concern to the average woman on the street. They are too busy just surviving from day to day to dwell on such things.

If we remove judgement of this kind, we will become the 'robots' that some American students furnished with campus hate-speech regulations, racial micro-aggression paranoia (on some American campuses such as the University of Minnesota, asking: 'Where are you from?' or saying 'You people...' or 'You are so articulate' is considered micro-aggression), gender-inclusive language and sexual harassment guidelines have already turned into.[18] The University of California has an infantilising micro-aggression policy where such questions and statements (taken from their policy document) are not permissible and 'legally actionable' as: 'I believe the most qualified person should get the job'; 'America is the land of opportunity'; 'I don't believe in race'.[19] Such statements apparently represent 'one form of systemic everyday racism'. Elsewhere at Purdue University, describing America as a 'melting-pot' is considered micro-aggression.[20] It is difficult to imagine a more uptight country than one that enacts linguistic codes which forbid interpersonal offence; such nonsense has a cartoon quality to it but it is spreading fast. Untenured academics, such as the armies of exploited adjuncts in America, will feel as if they have no choice but to abide by this post-Orwellian speech code laid down for them by these sclerotic institutions, for they know they will not get tenure if an authoritarian liberal could claim they are racist.

On prestigious American University campuses such as Yale, students have signed petitions to repeal the First Amendment.[21] At Harvard, they have dropped the title 'Master' because the students made the case that it evokes slavery.[22] American Professors at UCLA have been accused of

---

18 Available at: http://sph.umn.edu/site/docs/hewg/microaggressions.pdf

19 The University of California's microaggression policy is adapted from Sue (2010) *Microagressions in Everyday Life: Race, Gender and Sexual Orientation*.

20 Available at: http://www.dailywire.com/news/4965/purdue-university-if-you-call-america-melting-pot-pardes-seleh

21 Available at: http://www.dailywire.com/news/4965/purdue-university-if-you-call-america-melting-pot-pardes-seleh

22 Available at: http://www.bbc.co.uk/news/education-35659685

racial aggression for correcting students' grammar.[23] Students believed that grammar correction meant they were having an ideology imposed on them. This is the extent of ultra-liberal ideologising in these American factories of conformity. Similar stories can be found right across America. It is the ultimate hypocrisy: a generation of students who describe themselves as 'tolerant' embracing a culture of censorship. Universities should prepare students for life. By embracing such a mollycoddling culture, they are failing miserably in their task.

Academia is no longer the place for open minds and free exchange of ideas that it should be. With these developments in North America at least, it looks more like a 'closed shop' which attempts to politicise every aspect of social life. North American (and increasingly European) universities operate under perverse belief systems that centre on victomological practices such as micro-aggression, safe-spaces, BRTs (Bias Response Teams) and no-platforming. More than 100 US universities have BRTs which aim to foster a 'safe and inclusive environment' by offering support to anyone 'who has experienced an incident of bias'. A bias incident can occur whether the act is intentional or unintentional. So, no more jokes or irony. Language is being policed systematically in US universities and the result is a culture of silence. Nobody dares express an opinion in case it might be thought to convey a bias. Students are encouraged to report 'biased' speech to BRTs. All these universities employ the same vacuous, totalitarian speech code. They act like a homogeneous blob in their demands for heterogeneity. We provide a 'safe and inclusive space', they will insist. By psychological safety, they mean freedom from offence, which in itself is absurd. It is more or less impossible not to offend somebody at some point. Thus a safe environment is a silent one where there is no risk of any bias being expressed. When you have silence, you can run your ideological bull-dozer right over the masses. Shaming into silence is the antithesis of psychological safety. It creates instead a culture of fear and

---

23 Available at: http://dailycaller.com/2013/11/26/prof-corrects-minority-students-capitalization-is-accused-of-racism/

paranoia. The notion of 'safety' has become one of the most peculiar institutional sacred cows. The irony is that they think they are addressing the perennial post-modernist oppression, but instead have created through authoritarian means a truly oppressive environment. But that was perhaps intentional. Either way, it is a great pity for the generation of students going to university now. At university, you should not have to take yourself off to a quiet corner of the pub for an earnest chat.

Dissenters, if there are any, are shamed into silence or in fact frequently removed from their posts. The politically correct monoculture is a rigid orthodoxy. As well as 'safe', institutions that use this speech code have to be 'inclusive'. There is nothing inclusive about alienating everybody that does not subscribe to the totalitarian speech code. That is obviously exclusive. It is the antithesis of inclusivity. And so the virtue-signalling is entirely fake: a 'safe' and 'inclusive' institution is more probably an alienating, authoritarian monoculture that nurtures a psychological paranoia. Adjectives such as 'safe' and 'inclusive' are therefore institutional double-speak, but are an important part of the new political correctness, the social justice warrior (SJW) ideology, the new pseudo-'progressive' authoritarianism.

The *parrhesiastes* employ this speech code of safety, inclusion, social justice etc. and wrap all their talk in terms of the Obama discourse of 'values' to make their discourse appear innocuous and well-intentioned, but they are in fact pursuing an insidious political ideology that is founded on intolerance. In a UK context, they like to think they are 'inclusive', but Brexiteers must stay away. 'Values' are once again part of the oratorically persuasive means to make an ideological position sacrosanct. It is a means of making a political statement, but dressing it up in semantic cotton wool. As with political correctness and 'progress', to object to values risks making one appear morally inferior. It is a form of moral totalitarianism that perversely uses morals as part of its propaganda warfare. In a totalitarian society, you don't have the freedom to disagree. And this is more or less the case now.

The people that use this speech code are on the whole post-modernists who like to frame every argument in terms of power relations and complain of oppression, and yet the entire purpose of discoursal practices such as these ideological speech codes is to sustain power relations, form group identities and create a peculiarly oppressive environment where dissent is not only socially awkward but where infringements on free speech may actually be considered hate-crime.

By using words with positive connotations such as 'values', 'justice' and 'progress', the liberal-left have managed to make SJW a 'naturalised' ideology, i.e. it has for many won acceptance as non-ideological 'common sense'. The word 'values' gives the impression that it is independent of ideological determination. It has become opaque, and is therefore no longer visible as an ideology, but appears instead as more of a social idiom. Since it does not appear ideological and since its reference terms seem morally positive, it is able to quickly become hegemonic at an institutional level. If everyone and every institution subscribes to these values, then they rapidly become meaningless. They are nothing more than 'just-so' statements. But in a way, this seems the point of the exercise in documenting the 'values' in the first place. It is to confirm that such and such institution has signed up to the erroneous worldview that one moral code is being declared 'objectively true'.

But 'social justice' is of course a misnomer. It is a clever attempt to take a term whose apparently good intentions one could hardly question. It is a 'value' after all. If 'social justice' meant helping the poor that would be fine, but it is in fact a blurry cover-term for everything from transgender rights to Islamophobia. It is a form of activism based on deeply polarising identity politics. The liberal-Left have corrupted the language before the conservatives could get a look in. We are 'progressive, inclusive, safe and fight for social justice'. Who could possibly disagree with that? As Althusser reminds us, ideology works by disguising its ideological nature. Every totalitarian ideology needs a speech code, and this is the contemporary one. The ideology is amorphous with no fixed doctrine, but will seek to fetishise any 'marginalised' identity. In a world of proliferating gender identities, potentially new forms of marginalisation can appear all the time and they will be covered by the social justice rhetoric.

American university campuses have become inquisitorial snow-flake havens for extremists whose actions are Talibanic. A climate of fear has descended on these indoctrination mills. Clinton Committees were set up at American universities to persuade all students to vote Clinton. Attendance at the Clinton Committee was obligatory for Faculty members. The Committee was used to report on students suspected of having voted for Trump. Some American academics have to attend workshops where they are informed students must be free to select their gender and race.

In America and now in the UK, if you diverge from the nameless totalitarian agenda which acts almost as a secular religion, you will not be given tenure and certainly not be hired. Some universities in the West are beginning to resemble Orwellian nightmares where colleagues spy on one another, with managers reading colleagues' e-mails (legally under the Prevent legislation in the UK) to see if anybody is challenging the orthodoxy. Orthodox views are strongly held, but weakly supported. In certain parts of the Humanities and Social Sciences, conservative thinkers are non-existent. It is simple: if you are a conservative, you are not going to be hired. Students are unable to defend the orthodox views because they have never been challenged on them. If they are ever challenged, they will claim that 'you are invalidating my existence'. If universities are not wedded to Mill's principles ('He who knows only his side of the case knows little of that'), then the whole future of knowledge is threatened.

Causing offence in this environment could be a hate-crime. But now we are seeing these belief systems move from the university to society generally. This is the current trend. Not just students, but all of us are now being encouraged to be hyper-sensitive, to embrace this culture of blame where so-called oppressions such as racism and sexism have been wildly exaggerated. The West has embraced cultural nihilism: a pathological distaste for its own culture. And in order to implement the nihilistic agenda of multiculturalism, it has introduced hate-speech legislation, censorship of mainstream and social media. Censorship is spreading rapidly from the universities through the channels of our societies and in the UK is openly supported by the Leader of the Opposition, Jeremy Corbyn. Spain has banned the use of social media to call for protests, and the former British Secretary of State for Education and Minister for Women and Equalities, Nicky Morgan, announced a plan to force teachers to report children who disapprove of homosexuality to police and social services under the guise of 'fighting extremism'.[24]

There are countless more examples of attempts to close down free speech with social media being forced into censorship through the likes of the new German hate-speech legislation (NetzDG). Social media companies can now be fined 50mln Euros for not removing 'offensive' material within twenty-four hours. Twitter hands out temporary bans to users who post offensive material which could be anything perceived to be critical of Islam. Infowars, run by the explosive Alex Jones, has recently been given a temporary ban by Twitter. Infowars has nearly half a million followers on Twitter. Unsurprisingly, its numbers of users is now falling. If language is policed systematically, the whole purpose of social media becomes somewhat questionable.

Freedom and 'free speech' are the solution to the problem of how to respond to Islamism, but instead it was the first casualty of the migration crisis. To be anti-*jihad* and a freedom of speech activist is not a banal expression of bigotry. We will not find the right solution if we allow the moralistic censors to legislate against the discussion or delegitimise it. Hate-speech laws, as they are currently drafted and implemented, do not result in social harmony, but instead create a miasma of fear and trepidation, a dangerous cocktail of unaired, suppressed views.

As we have seen, in academic circles it is just assumed that one endorses the ultra-liberal agenda and its propagandistic and omnipresent speech code (the 'happy talk' of tolerance, social justice, inclusion and diversity). This speech code, this moral imperative for the masses, is the equivalent of an incipient intellectual totalitarianism and is leading to social apartheid. It is a single, totalising orthodoxy that tolerates no opposition. It does not even pretend to enforce dichotomies. It is so totalising that every conversation ensues in a manner that implies there *can* be no opposition. It assumes

---

24 Available at: http://www.bbc.co.uk/news/education-33325654

a mass uncompromising adherence by not even bothering to identify the opposition, but by just pretending that it does not exist. In the days of the aftermath of the Brexit vote, staff at Oxford University and at universities all over the UK received patronising e-mails from Vice Chancellors and Heads of Department apologising for the apparent intellectual scar that was Brexit. The e-mails were worded in such a way that the Vice-Chancellors just assumed they were speaking for all of us. After all, it would surely be unthinkable to be an academic and wish to leave the European Union. On the day after the referendum, the Vice-Chancellor of Oxford's e-mail spoke of 'how we will all always remember where we were when we heard the news', as if it were an event on par with the Kennedy assassination in terms of tragic impact. This kind of intellectual patronisation was to be seen again after the 2016 US Presidential Election. E-mails were sent out asking people to attend Chapel services where they would pray for the 'unsettled world' that Trump would surely bring about, 'giving voice to fears and concerns at world developments, and remind ourselves of the common need for love and inclusivity'. For weeks and months afterwards, university sermons would continue to conjure up a 'fragile world of morally corrupt values'.

University departments felt the curious need to remind us how committed they were to 'diversity', implying that Brexiteers were all narrow-minded doctrinaires. The idea that there was a Brexiteer amongst them was not even entertained. Oxford College chaplains would shake their heads in disbelief and label the apparently invisible opposition as 'the new ISIS living in thatched cottages'. Their partisan sermons and prayers had missed the target, entertained false dichotomies. Living in their liberal cocoons, some of the Bremainers thought the result was impossible. It seems they had been living in a false reality. They thought they had created a world just as they wanted it.

Through groupthink and Newspeak whose purpose just as in *Nineteen Eighty-Four* is to make certain modes of thought impossible and is thus the literal expression of linguistic determinism, the Left builds an ideological wall, protecting themselves from anybody who holds opposing views. The new Newspeak of the hyper liberal-progressives is used to veil reality. But to those not blinded by the propaganda, it does little more than satirise reality. It blurs the connection between words and concepts, muddling the intrinsic constitution of linguistic signs by recycling sloganistic words.

We self-censor in order not to breach institutional equality and diversity policies, and the repressive speech code operates as a verbal landmine fuelled by paranoia, demonology and social intimidation. An innocuous comment could explode in one's face because an invisible, virtual party finds it offensive, or pretends to find it offensive, because they know such a response would be beneficial. With increasingly universalised speech codes and mass thinking, communication and dialogue in the West may never be the same again because freedom of speech is becoming synonymous with 'inoffensive' speech. This rather indirect, but sometimes violent intimidation must of course be eschewed. Now that more or less everybody in the West is armed with audio and video-enabled Smartphones, every minutiae of potentially 'inoffensive' speech can reach through social media — the digital panopticon which turns private experiences into public ones and which nowadays amounts to an electronic copy of the Self made *de facto* public property — an audience of millions in just seconds.

But, it is difficult to articulate anything without offending somebody in a world where so many are trying to play the victim. Since it is socially unacceptable not to observe the stifling speech code, those 'liberals' who spearhead this agenda, these so-called social justice warriors, rise to the top in the public sector. If one side of the discussion is politically correct, the other side is axiomatically incorrect. All that is left are a set of moralised points that cannot be contested without running the risk of being charged with political incorrectness. It also results in an expectation to conform to a culture through language. Thus, within liberal circles, one is expected to use the word 'partner' and not husband, wife, boyfriend or girlfriend. To do otherwise, one might run the risk of being accused of being 'sexist' (or perhaps more correctly, 'sexualist', but not in the botanical sense of the word of course) for assuming the individual is heterosexual. But, 'partner' is the default term for homosexual couples (and not heterosexual ones) and this lack of neutrality makes it problematic if a single, heterosexual man is asked about his 'partner'. In a minoritocracy, it is the discourse of the minority that must take priority.

Its proponents have thus weaponised social pressure, and used it to their advantage to climb the career ladder. By conforming to this methodology, they have shown that they are pioneers of diversity, equality and anti-discrimination. It would seem that they are pursuing authoritarian means to implement an anti-fascist agenda. At the moment, the force of political and social coercion is such that almost everybody is conforming to the agenda.

This is the atmosphere in which academics, politicians and many in the public sector in the West work today. Thinking aloud is therefore checked in the 'age of unenlightenment' (Powers, 2015). In accordance with this speech code, criticism of Islam in particular is becoming not only socially unacceptable, but criminalised through hate-speech laws. If one cannot tell the truth for fear of being accused of hate-speech, then we are indeed living in a dangerous Orwellian world. Dangerous because speaking one's mind risks isolation, and potentially far worse. Those who have spoken up for our freedom and have simply told the truth about *jihad* (Wilders, Rushdie, Hedegaard and Geller for instance) live under a constant daily death threat from Islamic radicals. Some of them such as Wilders and Geller have been banned entry to the UK. We have closed the door to freedom-fighters who wish to protect our interests if their views do not conform to the State ideology: multiculturalism.

After having spoken out against Islam, Wilders has lived for over ten years under constant police protection, returning to a heavily guarded prison-like basement flat in the Netherlands every evening. This alone surely tells us everything we need to know about the threat facing us. A man who has dedicated his life to preserve freedom and democracy is marked for death. If we chip away at our own liberty in this fashion, we will eventually lose it.

The divinity of speech and freedom is what our culture is predicated on. The highest faculty of the human being is articulated speech. Language is power and influence of the best sort. We must use it to offer a more positive and enriching discourse than the tired blame-game of dead French philosophers.

IV

Losing Those Essential Connections

> Destroying rainforest for economic gain is like burning a Renaissance painting to cook a meal.
>
> — Edward O. Wilson

VAPORISED WORDS LINGER IN ARID self-interrogation. There is an extended silence, a short sonata of raised eyebrows and then a meaningful grin. Ibbi, an Inuit hunter, sits in my freezing hut, patting his firm bulk full of seal meat. Implausible palindromes are whispered over black coffee, and jokes are shared about his *embonpoint*. Thin jokes, admittedly. Here we sit hour after hour, pensive and introspective, during the interstices of everyday life. As is so often the case in this remote, bewitching place, our thoughts turn to the urban sprawl-sopped lands beneath us, to those living in choked cities that we call 'civilised'. For Ibbi, living without industry is an ideal, swerving 'progress' and 'development' and thus living without fumes and noisy *spiel*. He would prefer to live in a cosmos with a transcendental dimension. He shakes his head, 'we, *hamani* ["down there"], are the prisoners of monotony'. 'You do not hunt, you do not live in nature', he says. We have chosen a less holistic reality.

With a deep, earthy voice, he tells me how *hamani*, there is just this mixed up, globalised world, *inuit pa.pa.pa...* ('so many people, so many people'). 'There is no connection to the place, the land, the spirits that inhabit the land and now the people. You are losing your connections with one another', he continues. An explosion in the world's population has crowded out wildlife all over the planet. We are living in denial about the biggest problem of all. Many journalists only dare to talk about the problem of ageing populations, never the unsettling truth that the line for population growth is almost vertical on the chart. With the ice melting, the barrier to the outside world — the frozen buffer —, both metaphorical and physical, is disappearing. A time of privileged isolation is coming to an end, and Ibbi is well aware of this. The world of *hamani* is coming closer and closer, impinging on the indigenous lifestyle, diet and traditional cosmologies. Isolated from the outside world for so long, mining prospectors, Government officials, scientists and environmentalists are now entering this melting corner of the Arctic.

Ibbi does not dream of any 'elsewhere'. His *Lebenswelt* is his *nuna*, the settled land of connections, a universe of kin, family and traditions — the more obvious presuppositions. This is where he *belongs*. He has seen and fears the 'other', the *Mitsein* of nihilistic drift and Western, atomistic individualism. A place where surrounded by thick crowds of *takornaqtoq* ('strangers', literally: 'he who has not been seen before'), he becomes the stranger himself. 'How can you be happy if surrounded by strangers?' he asks. It is of course true that we live in a society of strangers, but up until now it has been a society where strangers can meet face-to-face and enjoy the spirit of free cooperation and shared beliefs. That is now under threat, for we live increasingly in the hullabaloo of the circus, the spittled zoo of globalisation. The hubbub, hurry-scurry and helter-skelter of the minutiae of modern life renders our lives topsy-turvy and convoluted, torn apart from the basic modes of existence. Nature is no longer the *living* cosmos; we have forgotten its inherent meaning. 'You are living in a *disconnected* world', he sighs.

To lose these connections would be the greatest fear for the Polar Eskimo; it would be to live in an ontological vacuum without a soul (*tarneq*). But for us, we prefer to discard the ambiguities of the spiritual world, and fill the emptiness of the wild places with the stigmata of suburban housing estates. In the spirit of epistemological anti-foundationalism and excessive cultural relativism, we are being told that we do not need these connections of place, family, religion, customs, cultural identity and faith any longer. Globalist liberalism is the ideology that imparts this falsehood, that promotes a way of life that breaks these bonds, connections and ties. It is liberalism that will leave you alone, apparently in a secularist nirvana, but in fact wallowing in a consumerist frenzy of disconnectedness.

Since 1991, liberalism has become the sole, dominant ideology of almost the entire world (North Korea and Iran are obvious exceptions). It is at least the operational system of Western civilisation, colouring even conventional wisdom. When I speak of liberalism, I am concerned with 'a state of mind which, in certain circumstances, can become universal and infect opponents as well as defenders' (Eliot, 1939: 16). Liberalism used to concern itself with individual interests and freethinking, but it has morphed into something remorsefully other. Ironically, liberalism that started as anti-totalitarian has become quasi-totalitarian itself as it attempts to control society in accordance with a matrix of 'ideal principles', and 'denies the ontological space in which alone we can operate in a truly human fashion' (Milbank and Pabst, 2016: 253). The dialectic of liberalism has become a mordant paradox. It began as an anti-colonialist project, but ended up as US imperialism. Although it is notoriously difficult to define, the aspiration of socio-cultural liberalism in the West is to create an atomistic individual without culture, religion, sexuality or identity who lives in a world where commercial value has been turned into the essence of all life. Kalb (2008: 40) sees it as a form of secularised Christianity because both are unassuming and humble, and tell us not to make claims we cannot substantiate. It pretends to embody the dominant ideology of modernity. It has become something of a meta-ideology, a doctrinal tsunami that obliterates alternative thinking.

There is an implicit assumption that liberalism's intentions are better and more high-minded than conservatism's, and as such it purports to be as much a moral doctrine as a political doctrine. But liberalism is a destructive ideological hegemony that has become authoritarian, almost messianic in nature. We have allowed the dogma of liberalism to subvert cultural values. Liberal thinking threatens to destroy the shared values that underpin the countries of Western Europe, and in doing so will destroy the post-modern liberalism which they all stand for. It will be this self-defeating.

One of liberalism's diktats states that it is axiomatic in Western society that minorities are unquestionably persecuted in some way. Our ideologies are framed in the negative; they seek legitimacy by trying to appear to resolve some injustice or other. Implicit in this is of course an anti-elitist element. Liberalism is thus a negative anthropology which holds that man's social constructs are malevolent and biased. Liberalism prioritises vice over virtue at a time when what is needed is a revitalising *esprit de corps*. The assumption is that we are self-interested, fearful and greedy. Human virtue is dismissed, and negative freedom defines liberal thought. Liberalism betrays itself as the best option in a world of evil. It rules our plurality and posits itself at the end of history. Ultimately, liberalism represents therefore anthropological and ontological pessimism and yet always tries to position itself as *the* meta-narrative.

This ideology is in fact self-annihilating, for it is an anti-Western ideology perpetuated by Western intellectuals and journalists. As we have seen, the ideology prevents any kind of negative commentary on another culture and in this sense pretends to represent a form of positivity; it is a kind of blind, extreme cultural relativism: a normative claim which forgoes the possibility of any moral judgement. To deny cultural relativism is no doubt to court the accusation of racism, but cultural relativism has become a form of absolutism of its own. However, it is always 'culture' and not race or any other construct that dictates that young girls should have their genitals mutilated, that infidels (i.e. non-Muslims) should be butchered, that it is a sin to listen to music or watch television etc.

The liberal ideology is centred on an ill-defined, putative guilt for Western cultural domination, a notion that has an irreducible position in current political discourse in the West. A quagmire of moral guilt has impinged on Germany most obviously, but also large parts of Western Europe where ironically none of the guilt can be correctly ascribed. Here, the liberal psyche much prefers guilt to responsibility. Liberals like to cynically calculate how they can appear noble by helping minorities. But, if one compares the indifference that liberals showed to African genocide (Rwanda, 1994, Burundi 1972 and 1993), the Mao-Mao terror of Kenya (1952-1960), the Angolan Revolution (1961), the 300,000 slaughtered by Idi Amin (1971-79) or the Nigerian Civil War (1967-1970) where blacks were killing blacks, to colonialism or any conflict which pitches the European against the African or the Arab, it is obvious their main concern is their own guilt, and not conflict *per se*. In the civil conflicts mentioned (and in many others), infinitely more people were killed and atrocities committed than in African conflicts involving Europeans. Is there ever discussion about the Arab or African slave trade which trafficked more than the Western variant? It was Europe that stopped the slave trade. Let us not forget that Saudi Arabia declared the slave trade illegal in 1962, Mauritania in just 1980 and Niger in 2003. Those who rail unthinkingly against colonialism will not talk about the Chinese land and resources grab right across Africa, or the way poor South American countries such as Ecuador have become mortgaged to China. They will not want you to watch David MacDougall's award-winning ethnographic film, *To Live with Herds* (1972), where the Jie of Uganda talk about how they miss the colonial days. They will certainly not want you to hear about ethnic tribal racism in Africa, the racist policies implemented in 1970s Uganda that targeted the Asian population or the ethnic cleansing against white Zimbabwean communities. At the time of writing, South Africa has abandoned the rule of law and allowed blacks to legally seize land from white farmers without financial recompense. Several months after the vote the BBC has still not reported on the story. The mainstream media has ignored it because it does not conform to their cultural nihilistic agenda.

Instead, the liberal mind is always trying to develop projects to address inequality in accordance with their narrow definition, many of which make no difference at all. Sometimes, as in the case of many international aid schemes to African countries run by corrupt dictatorships, they can make matters even worse (Burnham, 1964). The liberal must try to cure the evil even if it has no knowledge of the suitable medicine. They never ask what these people can do for themselves. We should be suspicious about moral actions which claim to have no personal motive. Of course they serve a self-interest. But to say such a thing no doubt makes me a 'bad character' with antithetical values.

Liberalism thrives off division and can only couch its shaky premises in what it sees as the ills of Western society. The differences of opinion on this topic have been described as 'culture wars' (Hunter, 1991), but I see no war (in Western Europe at least). There is neither a viable alternative to secular modernity in Western Europe, nor is there opposition in academia to the multicultural animus. If it exists, it is silent and hiding, disenfranchised by the manipulated slogans that have been tossed at it. It is hoped that the silent conservative cohort can now emerge from the counter-ideology shadow. The multicultural imperative, which in its current politicised mandate might amount ironically to the complete undermining of Western liberal values in favour of sexual oppression, racial exploitation and potentially radical Islam, is not being challenged effectively in the West. That is because of the cultural grammar that has been imposed on us, and to which I have referred to previously. The fact that this organised mendacity is going unchecked is of some concern.

The basis for a 'persecuted' identity is now predominantly 'race' and 'sexual identity'. If one is an ethnic minority or a homosexual and one lives in one of the 'freest' societies in the world, then it is assumed one is somehow 'persecuted'. As the 'persecuted' person, one will be subject to openly positive discrimination, especially so in the public sector. This obsession with allegedly persecuted minorities is part of a multiculturalist project spearheaded by the post-modern Left to deconstruct the nation-state with its institutions and to delegitimise a national identity which is incorrectly assumed to be somehow fascist or elitist. These faux ideals have formed the basis for the establishment of political parties which masquerade as something else. The Green Movement in particular seems to be more interested in the Gay Games than saving the planet, more focused on linking an LGBTQ identity to environmental values than doing anything at all to preserve the wild places left on Earth.

The multiculturalists, the gay-green movement and EU federalists are keen to give up national sovereignty for spurious reasons, and do not hesitate to support giving powers to a super-elite of European Commissioners who look totalitarian in their ambitions for a European superstate. Merkel speaks of the 'European Unification project' by which she means another empire run by Germany. She speaks as if she were the leader of the entire European Union, telling Italy what it can and cannot do to stimulate its economy and inviting an extraordinary 1.2 million refugees into Germany without consulting the electorate. Surely, if there is one question that concerns a nation's citizens, it is *who* is the *Wir*. This unprecedented move is one of the most flagrant abuses of democratic legitimation I can think of. The behaviour of the odious woman bearing the permanent U-shaped grimace is bordering on dictatorial.

Whenever the concept of the nation is undermined, it is clear that democratic constructs come undone. And that, I believe, is the objective here: to create a totalitarian European state by stealth. An unholy union that works all the time, one that does not give people the say. When one gives them the say, they vote to escape, as we saw with Brexit. The apparently enlightened and universalist EU jurisdiction might prove to be as nightmarish as the experiences of totalitarianism of the twentieth century, a subject that we will return to in the 'The Globalists in Brussels' essay.

The egalitarianism that is always invoked by the liberal-Left is a powerful symbol because it conveys the all-important inclusiveness which virtually every public institution in the UK felt the need to remind us they symbolised, after the Brexit referendum. Egalitarianism means conformism, and is thus creativity-denying. And, let me say it plainly, without metaphor and in the manner of a good *parrhesiaste*, we are not all equal and it is not morally wrong to say so: there is hierarchy in every group of individuals, and in a hierarchical society everybody has a purpose. There is also a difference in the innate qualities between a man and a woman; men and women are different and attracted to quite different things (not least different careers) which is why the gender-pay gap obsession in the UK is such a nonsense. Just look at beauty. Are we all equal? Hardly. For the common man, the belief that all men are equal is simply a consolation for the qualities that they envy in others. Imagine for a moment if it were true; self-improvement would be impossible. Neither individuals nor groups are equal, but are instead characterised by an inequality of competence and moral character. Our traits are inherited, and thus inequality is mostly genetic. If we were all equal, our hierarchical social structures would presumably not perpetuate. Egalitarianism is a fabrication, and can only be achieved by holding those back that strive for excellence. If all things are equally good, they are equally indifferent. In practice, egalitarianism means in contemporary Western society at least, that everybody has to stoop down to the lowest common denominator.

Our society has made it socially problematic to rise above this egalitarian lie, but it is doubtful whether we will still insist on equality when our overcrowded planet has run out of resources, and we are living in a state of permanent conflict as the Inuit hunters believe will happen.[1] Writing in 1958, Huxley tells us how concerned he was at how prescient his book had become, particularly with regard to overpopulation. Then, there were 2.8 billion people on the planet. One doubts he could have possibly imagined that less than sixty years later, that figure would have risen nearly three times to over 7.3 billion. Huxley said the coming age will not be the 'Space Age', it will be the 'Age of Overpopulation'. More and more people will be fighting over scarce resources; ethnic and tribal conflicts will open up across Africa leading to a form of perpetual civil war, as the population of some African countries such as Uganda is expected to increase five-fold within the next thirty years. The population explosion in Africa will inevitably lead to even larger numbers seeking to come into Europe. Mass migration was not a 2015 problem, but will be an existential challenge of enormous proportions for the future.

Liberal environmentalism over the last fifty years has completely failed to address any of these problems: the world's population has multiplied, the

---

1   It is intriguing that equality as the primary motivating factor for governmental actions appears time and again in the dystopian literature (Ayn Rand's *Altas Shrugged*; Huxley's *Brave New World*; Vonnegut's *Harrison Bergeron*) which describe totalitarian, over-regulated societies.

planet's finite resources are quickly depleting and our air and water have become toxic. One must remember, this is what we call 'progress'. The Chinese choking to death in the fumes of their own 'progress'; the unprecedented loss in biodiversity because humans are crowding out wildlife all over the world. The problems are caused by incessant human expansion. The future will be an overpopulated planet fighting over finite resources, and in such a world there will be no place for liberalism.

Wishy-washy liberalism does its best to 'raise awareness', but is incapable of saying 'no' and is therefore the worst possible approach to tackling environmental problems. As Scruton (2012) has argued, environmentalism should be a conservative issue. The ecological crisis should force conservative thinkers to reconceptualise their guiding assumptions and principles. It would then become conservationism, and would make drastic, but essential measures. Working through local NGOs, as much land as possible should be bought up and set aside as wilderness, totally untouched by humans. In theory, this would limit population growth as it would now be the humans (and not the animals) that are hemmed in. It would create a carbon sink to absorb and filter the pollution. It would allow wildlife to thrive and give a permanent home to endangered species. We are not talking about evicting indigenous groups to make way for national parks. These will not be national parks, but pure wilderness areas. Liberals would no doubt deem that to be eco-colonialism, but it saves the environment from rapacious developers, mining companies and corrupt local Governments, and will go much further to help the planet than recycling plastic bags. If only the green liberals could be a little braver.

Liberalism and equality sit therefore rather awkwardly with the environmental reality. One might argue that we need less equality, and more equity. Equity would require everyone to do what their abilities allow them to do. Everyone is given equal opportunities to succeed, but because our abilities range enormously, only some can deliver on those opportunities. The remarkable paradox is that the liberals, those purveyors of inclusiveness, who speak incessantly of tolerance and equality and who all readily sign up to the EU causes do not seem aware that this body is interested first and foremost in taking away their rights as citizens of sovereign states with its attempts to remove decision-making from their nationally elected MPs. Some draft legislation even attempts to criminalise banter. They think they are signing up to some kind of transnational, borderless, liberal dream, but instead get a high-handed centralisation of power led by angry individuals such as Schulz who bangs his fist on the table in a Hitlerian manner when he does not get his way (as commented on by Silvio Berlusconi when he visited the European Parliament). The EU is a scam, masquerading as something that it is not.[2]

Post-modern liberalism and radical Islam are both closed systems of thought with very different cues: one is extremely violent and based on aggressive religious domination, the other claims to be pacifist and based on a sense of self-loathing, ideological aggrievement in a society that is characterised as iniquitous. They are both quasi-totalitarian, have universalist ambitions and tolerate no opposition. Both radical Islam and contemporary liberalism assume that their appeal is so universal that they cannot be considered as ideologies, and yet they are both systems which make a claim on the truth. Unlike with radical Islam, in the case of liberalism, there is a misrecognition of its own presumptions.

Both of them destroy the souls of communities. Post-modern liberalism has its roots in the French Enlightenment and the work of Jean-Jacques Rousseau. Its central belief is that man is good, and that civilised society is the problem. If somebody commits a crime, we should not blame the criminal, for it is society that is at fault. The other central belief of post-modern liberalism is that utopia is achievable through social progress. This is the inhuman doctrine, a revolt against reason, that has infiltrated our institutions and that has a stranglehold on academia in particular. Instead of Enlightenment idealism, Edmund Burke (1790) insisted that the real rights of man are rooted in tradition and faith, and he questioned the dubious pursuit of equality and the socialist maxim *ni dieu, ni*

---

2   Available at: https://www.youtube.com/watch?v=0bPqaqGJ5Js&t=65s

maître. It is his ideas that still inspire conservatives today. In accordance with this thinking, we should be able to question the view that dramatic cultural change is both necessary and inevitable.

In parts of Scandinavia, liberalism is the backbone of the judiciary and legislative system. This liberalism which believes there is nothing ineradicably evil in human nature shows a complete disregard of a history of centuries of warfare, torture and evil. And it has become hegemonic because its advocates believe this is the only acceptable cultural framework for any society. Liberalism considers itself the sole principle that constitutes human reality, and any country that falls foul of its criteria, say Russia or China, are by definition not 'developed' to the same degree for the simple reason the cultural thinking of these countries is not theirs, and thus illegitimate. This is how liberalism is hegemonic.

Left liberalism, as practiced in Sweden with its overwhelming emphasis on diversity and empowerment for minorities, is not equipped to meet any of the challenges, environmental or otherwise, that face the West in the twenty-first century. As practicsed in Sweden, it is a negative, nihilistic ideology that threatens to destroy the best things in that society and undermines its cultural wealth. It is time that we stopped rejecting our spirit; time that we discarded the pathos of repudiation, aspired to anti-nihilism and became once again comfortable taking our side of the fight. We need a less liberalist 'emancipatory' teleological view of society, and should be able going forward to challenge the nihilistic tendencies inherent in this ideology. Otherwise, we will be just left to drift in a tide of liberalist fancy towards the beach of disconnectedness.

V

What is going on in Sweden?

The deal with multiculturalism is that the only culture you're allowed to disapprove of is your own.

— Martin Amis

THE SUN DIPS AT JUST before 3pm, and amidst the pantry twilight my thoughts and preoccupations turn inwards as they tend to do at this time of the day. Such a light and glowing hearth with its quivering flame suit well the contemplative mind. Upon the wall hangs a faded photograph of the Queen Mother falling out of a barouche after one too many pink Gins. In the adjacent photo, a group of young gentlemen, grinning like Cheshire Cats, sporting pink *pantalons* and spats, looking as if they have cadged an invitation to the polo. Luncheon complete, I draw the red, velvet curtains and turn the radio on. The forceful, vibrant sounds of the Somali language penetrate the cool air of the living room. It is P2, a Swedish public radio channel, (the equivalent of Radio 3 in the UK more or less) that broadcasts in Somali for two hours every day. I turn the Roberts radio chrome tuning dial knob, hoping to find the news in Swedish, but the next audible frequency is instead a discussion programme in Arabic: raised voices, extended overlapping speech and discursive violence. A few more rotations of the chrome dial, and then finally an extended news programme in Swedish. There has been a major terrorist attack in Paris: earlier in the morning, a group of Islamic fundamentalists representing Al-Qaeda entered the premises of a French satirical newspaper, *Charlie Hebdo*, and killed, execution-style, the entire editorial board of the newspaper. Several related attacks occurred in the Paris region immediately after.

After the horrendous details of the *Charlie Hebdo* terrorist attack have been digested, there ensues on the radio a discussion of what has occurred. Swedish journalists (newspaper editors and reporters) and politicians are invited to give their views. Instead of condemning the terrorist attack for what it is, a hideous act of savagery, one after the other calls in to give his or her analysis of the motivation for the shootings. A consensus rapidly forms: the tragic events occurred because the assailants had been 'excluded' from society. Before knowing anything at all about the terrorists, it is assumed that they came from difficult backgrounds and had been denied certain opportunities in life. Society had somehow failed them. Back to Rousseau-esque post-modernism. They had not been integrated. The overall message was clear: the executioners were the 'victims', not the journalists who wished to promote the freedom of speech and whose blood-soaked bodies laid sprawled across the meeting room floor in central Paris.

The remarkable thing about the response to this and other terrorist incidents is the repeated empty rhetoric about multicultural diversity and mutual respect that is expressed by the Western leaders, and more conspicuously the near-silence from the rapidly growing Muslim community in the West (where were France's six million Muslims in the *Charlie Hebdo* memorial marches in Paris?). In 2015, a young Danish filmmaker Finn Nørgård was gunned down at a debate on blasphemy in central Copenhagen. A demonstration of solidarity and inter-faith dialogue was held after his murder and attended by over 40,000 people but there was not a single head-scarf in sight. Even the more moderate Muslims (and at no point is one suggesting *tout court* that all Muslims are enemies of the West) often see little reason to condemn the events, perhaps because some see *jihad* as fundamental to the Islamic faith and its theology. But where are these moderates? One cannot hear them, and according to the Turkish President, they do not exist (2013).[1] European leaders constantly tell us that the

---

1 The one very clear and welcome exception is the Moroccan-born Mayor of Rotterdam. He has told the Muslim immigrants in no uncertain terms: 'Stop seeing yourselves as the victims, and if you don't want to integrate, leave'. He has received death threats from local Muslim leaders.

terrorist attacks have nothing to do with Islam, but it is not the Christians slamming planes into skyscrapers, blowing up underground trains and driving trucks into crowds of revellers.

In this essay, I want to focus on Sweden and describe some of the events I have witnessed these last five years in particular. It was during the 2014 Swedish General Election campaign that I realised there might be something wrong. Election posters and placards were everywhere to be seen. But *Sverigedemokraterna* (SD) — the anti-mass immigration party — their placards had been removed or vandalised. The third largest party was curiously invisible. Postmen had refused to distribute their literature, the party website was hacked, the party election hut had been burnt down. The list goes on. One might quite reasonably ask whether any of these actions belong in a genuine democracy, and indeed whether it is time to have election observers in Sweden. If the UK's third largest political party's headquarters were attacked and newspapers refused to advertise the party, it would be a major scandal. But not in Sweden. It is thus legitimate to ask whether Swedish elections are in fact free and democratic. In 2010, three of the major Danish political parties (*Dansk Folkeparti*, *Venstre* and *Det Konservative Folkeparti*) issued a statement urging that the Council of Europe send election observers to Sweden to monitor 'violations of democracy' regarding the treatment of SD.[2] These are not minor Danish political parties; these are parties that are either in Government now or that have been in governing coalitions previously. Once again, things are perhaps not what they seem.

Before the General Election in 2014, Danish parliamentarians became in fact sufficiently concerned by the Swedish immigration policy that they raised the issue of closing the bridge that connects Denmark with Sweden. Having gained Swedish residence permits, asylum seekers are free to enter Denmark. Leading Danish politicians have described the Swedish immigration policy as a 'liability'.[3] More recently, their other neighbour

---

2   Available at: http://www.thelocal.se/20100831/28680
3   Pia Kjærsgaard, the former leader of *Dansk Folkeparti* and current speaker of the *Folketing* in an interview in January 2013.

to the West, Norway, said that if Sweden collapses (because of its open-doors immigration policy), it will contravene the Geneva Convention and will secure the border completely, preventing the chaos from spreading. Sweden's neighbours are then preparing for its collapse.[4]

The thought of election observers in Sweden is perhaps not as outrageous as it might initially appear. It is undoubtedly the case that election observers are already needed elsewhere. In May of 2016, Nobert Hofer of the Freedom Party of Austria took 51.9 per cent of the vote in a run-off against the green Socialist Van der Bellen, but then lost the election as the postal votes apparently went against these results. The election had to be embarrassingly rerun because of electoral fraud.

Parties on the Left in Sweden speak of the 'Swedish Dream' which means omnipresent multiculturalism, or more accurately Muslim-only communities. The *Miljöpartiet* policies must remain a 'dream' as complete open immigration would rapidly become impossible to finance, and the infamous welfare system would collapse in no time. Indeed, the 'dream' did not last long. By the end of 2015, the numbers of migrants from the Middle East and North Africa moving to Sweden was completely out of control. Heaving mobs of young, angry Arab and Pakistani men waving Pakistani flags, shouting *Allahu Akbar* were to be seen piling up on the Macedonian and Hungarian borders.[5]

Not a single woman can be seen in the footage. The images were caught on drones, but not shown on mainstream television, which instead tried to compile images of people who bore some resemblance to refugees, and not Islamic activists.

At the height of the crisis, the Swedish Government looked like inept amateurs. Crying in public, they looked as pathetic as the Germans who applauded the 'refugees' arriving in streams only to discover subsequently that

---

4   Available at: http://www.zerohedge.com/news/2016-02-24/norway-warns-sweden-will-collapse-pm-will-defy-geneva-convention-protect-border

5   Available at: https://www.youtube.com/watch?v=kGezwC68BMs and https://www.youtube.com/watch?v=S4K4okVa7dU

some of them were illegal immigrants and gangs of radical mobs looking to rape and pillage. Germany let in over a million people and today hosts the most iconic of culture clashes as young Muslims shouting *Allahu Akbar* harass nature-loving FKK nudists grilling *Bratwurst* on the beaches of the former East Germany.[6] It might be a scene out of Monty Python, but this is the reality of the present and a glimpse of the future that a Merkel-defaced Germany is going to have to deal with.

The result of these enormous changes in both Germany and Sweden is that today in some Swedish towns, 50 per cent of the population are refugees from Syria and Iraq.[7] What has happened in Syria is undoubtedly a tragedy of epic proportions, but ultra-liberal politicians in Sweden have embraced this tragedy in a way that has changed the face of their country forever. To facilitate the 'multicultural dream', an airline, Refugee Air, was set up in 2015 by a migrant to Sweden, Emad Zand, to fly directly as many refugees from North Africa into the country as possible.[8] Zand claimed that there was no reason why Syrians could not fly to Sweden. It is not illegal. He intended to fly them in for free. Once in Sweden, it is difficult to send them back.

This kind of thinking is surely guided by the naïve philosophy of the Swedish state media which dictates that if we remove the concept of nationhood, we will all be the same and the world will be free of conflict. If only it were that simple. It is the ultra-liberal politicians, and not the silent Christian minority, that believe in fairies. The *Miljöpartiet* comprising secular extremists wishes to do away with religious holidays, as well as school grades and national borders, and holds to any number of other pie-in-the-sky policies. Like the radical Left, the high priests of the secular intelligentsia, these politicians are cultural Marxists following Gramsci's lead in trying to 'liberate' us from Western civilisation and the Christian

---

6   Available at: http://www.dailywire.com/news/7877/men-shouting-allahu-akbar-invade-nudist-pool-michael-qazvini

7   Available at: http://www.ibtimes.com/syrian-iraqi-refugees-are-half-population-swedish-city-1619232

8   Available at: http://refugeeair.org/

soul.⁹ In doing so, they wish to present a dualistic vision of the world, the good and the evil. Those who share the falsified moral high ground with them are the 'good'; the rest are by definition 'evil'. It is like listening to a sermon, but without the religion. 'Dump the Christianity and keep the liberal ethics', as Iris Murdoch said. Journalists and politicians on the Left seem to regard themselves as a liberal, intellectual elite in a country that is meant to be classless and beyond religion.

SD has been ruthlessly condemned, silenced and spurned by the Swedish media, this self-arrogated liberal elite and voice of leftist propaganda. The other political parties have worked with the media to stigmatise and denigrate SD at every opportunity. SD candidates have been physically attacked, and had bricks thrown through their windows, but one will not hear about it on the radio.¹⁰ The headquarters of Sweden's third largest party is hidden in a Stockholm garage with no signs on the building. This is a sad indictment of a country that sets itself forth as the model democracy.

The norms of egalitarianism, democracy, the *trygghet* ('sense of security') of the welfare benefit system and gender equality that underpin the Swedish model are perceived to be entirely non-negotiable. Sweden is a one norm society, and norm violation is considered unorthodox behaviour. These norms represent a negation of the Faustian ethic, an almost anti-stoic approach without any sense of individual accountability. This demonisation of stoicism is part of the imaginary form of Swedish nationality propagated by politicians and journalists. SD are portrayed, if mention is made of them at all, as 'norm violators'. This is the ritual of Swedish politics. It is clear that SD has reality on its side, but perhaps one has to be an outsider, somebody sheltered from the propaganda to understand that. It is just a question of how much longer the Swedish electorate

---

9   Gramsci also understood the importance of cultural unity. It is this that preserves the identity of a group and enables them to defend themselves as a group against an unwanted foreign body. Gramsci understood the dangers of altering primary self-identification.

10 Available at: http://www.thelocal.se/20140908/sweden-democrat-candidateattacked

wishes to deny the reality. At this point in 2018, it is clear that things are beginning to give.

There is a 'democratic crisis' in Sweden, but it has nothing to do with the rise of SD as the media will have one believe. It is a crisis because in an 'open democracy', there must be freedom to discuss and debate the key issues, however sensitive they are. Discussions of immigrants and integration policies in Sweden are characterised by bland, empty and frequently mendacious rhetoric. Media types rush to call mass immigration critics 'fascists', but will not call an Islamist an Islamist. Attempts to prevent freedom of speech create a totalitarian ethos; complete obfuscation of the opposition party belongs in a 'flawed' democracy. SD, a party that is frequently criticised for being 'nationalist', has been branded as 'un-Swedish', and is therefore somehow 'illegitimate'. It is not entirely clear how a party can be 'nationalist' and 'un-Swedish' at the same time, unless one has been duped into believing that Sweden does not stand for anything. Those that claim this tend to contradict themselves by insisting that Sweden stands for egalitarianism and feminism, and thus there *are* Swedish values.

Anti-mass-immigration sentiment in Sweden is considered anomalous and aberrant. Swedes do not speak out about the obfuscation of the issue even when their communities are changing so rapidly. Just as the East Germans let the Berlin Wall be built, Swedes do not object. The fact that there is no objection at all to State control on so many different levels suggests that Swedes are already living in a pseudo-totalitarian society, but one where the living standards are high.

The media frames SD as the 'evil' party because they are the only party who are seen to *not* support the group that is perceived to be the 'victims'. This is the ideology. The truth is that the victims might also be considered the elderly Swedes whose benefits are reduced to subsidise the mass immigration of migrants. But the people that make up this group are ineligible as *bona fide* victims, since they are entirely 'ethnic Swedes'. In order to benefit from the system, it is essential again to be able to receive ideological (and sometimes judicial) protection, and this is reserved for certain ethnic groups. In return, this group will be safe from public scrutiny.

If the numbers of Muslim immigrants continue at the present rate, ethnic Swedes will be a minority in their country by 2050. Sweden might risk transitioning from being the most tolerant, liberal society to a society run on quite a different values system. A liberal ideology gone wrong will have undermined a nation. Left-wing politicians will have irrevocably changed one of the safest, happiest societies in the world in the space of just fifty years, and left behind what many thought was an infinite *bien-être*. The weak, tolerant Swede not only welcomes mass immigration, he blames himself when it goes wrong. The Swedes were not tolerant enough, apparently. The naïve plan to create a 'multicultural utopia' risks becoming dystopia within just a few generations. When the ethnic Swede is the minority, it is unlikely that he will be able to claim 'victim' status and thus be on the receiving end of the same positive discrimination.

It is this Nietzschean 'imperative of herd timidity' (2003: 124) that has smashed the European consciousness, and left us like sitting ducks for a 'strong' Islamic culture based on honour, conformity and total submission. This will supersede a guilt-based culture. Honour-based cultures centre on something greater than the individual; it is based on the entire group. With mass immigration from the Middle East and North Africa to Europe, a holistic, communitarian culture based on honour comes into contact with an anti-honour culture festering in an environment of political polarisation. In the former, the moral status of the victim is at its nadir, in the latter it is at its zenith. We must learn again to rise above this; we must regain our sense of honour, the ethos of social honour. If we can admire Islam for one thing, it is for its sense of honour (but not for its honour killings). Arab societies honour strength, and can have no compassion for the kind of weakness that the West has enveloped itself in. The *mise-en-scène* is that of a naïve herd, ensnared in a morality that it thinks is universal, ambling through a self-destructive modernity to the cultural abattoir.

Some of the immigrants to Sweden, particularly those from Somalia have created their own entirely separate, asymmetrical communities and very distinct *oikos*. As such, Sweden and other European nations are rapidly becoming places where incomers who have gained citizenship do not share the same commitment to place as the ethnic group. Indeed, many of the countries from which the migrants come have little or no notion of citizenship. In places like Afghanistan, community membership is based on tribe or faith rather than political obedience. These people want to retain their culture and identity based on quite different modalities, but equally want to benefit from the welfare state. Multiculturalists typically allege at this point that this is either an ethnocentric opinion (and therefore illegitimate), or that Sweden is now a secular, multicultural state (their ultimate objective), and that there is no 'one' host culture. Such a concept would be laughable to most nations beyond the West. It might even be politically incorrect to suggest this. But, it is also the case that Sweden is an extremely difficult country to integrate into. For those that bring with them an alien culture and for whom sociality is practiced in an entirely different way, it will be a difficult task. Half of Swedes live on their own, and many die on their own. This notion alone would be unthinkable in any of the countries where the migrants come from, where the family networks are far denser.

When the 'we' becomes confused or even conflicting in this manner, social disintegration and unrest normally ensues at some point. Secularism as a State ideology is unlikely to have any staying power because one cannot live with a neutral view towards values without creating a vacuum that will be filled. Secularism is often presented as the *de facto* ideal every society should aspire to, but it just creates an institutionalised void which is filled by the next, stronger incoming culture or religion.

In Sweden, it is not a 'clash of civilisations': it is voluntary cultural redundancy on the part of some Swedes. It is an extreme form of cultural repudiation imbued with anti-patriotism, a schizophrenic self-denigration which amounts to a masochistic distaste for their own culture. It is cultural suicide comparable to that undergone by Islam after the dissolution of the Ottoman Empire. Sweden, France, the Netherlands and other European countries are institutionalising separatism and difference in their own societies, and then demonising the former indigenous majority for not being tolerant enough when the new paradigm fails. This process is especially acute in Sweden. Sometimes, attempts are then made to traumatise anybody for trying to represent a majority identity or for speaking out against this. Such a set of ideas is inimical to our social and cultural identity. Many would recognise this, but claim that it is inevitable, irreversible and that nothing very positive ever came from nationhood. It is almost as if there is some kind of 'invisible hand' at work here.

To label opponents of mass Muslim immigration as Nazis, as is done in Sweden, is another means of preventing debate, akin to the no-platforming that is happening in our universities. The Nazis killed perhaps as many as ten million people. SD (and the new *Alternative för Sverige* political party) is a political party that is voicing an opinion. The supposedly implacable enemy that the Left constantly invokes is fictitious. The use of such labels creates a distorted image of their antagonist, whom they can then scold. Hundreds of millions of people have died under left-wing ideology and terror, but being right-wing is unacceptable. Extremism can only apply to right-wing thinking apparently even when militant socialist thugs such as the *Antifascistisk Aktion* and *Revolutionära Fronten* promote violence and anti-semitism. The media is trying to create a false, and very skewed perception of reality, and Swedes are struggling to see through the anti-racist, irrational propaganda, even if of course not everybody is conditioned in this way.

It has been claimed by SD supporters that Sweden is a 'dictatorship'. Peter Fleischer, Google's global privacy counsel, also likened Sweden to more dictatorial countries in 2007 when commenting on the wiretapping measures to be introduced by the Swedish Government.[11]

It is not a dictatorship. There is no one demagogue; there is instead an extreme 'liberal' machine which operates in conjunction with a propagandised media. Many have boycotted State media because of its bias, but also

---

11 Available at: http://news.bbc.co.uk/1/hi/world/europe/7463333.stm. Google said it would not place any servers in the country if the wire-tapping law was passed.

because, as we shall see, it simply does not cover the main issues. Cleverly, it ensures that there is a broad discussion on a narrow politicised range of topics, giving the impression of an open democracy whereas all that is happening is that the presuppositions of the extreme liberal ideology are being enforced by a liberal in-group. The State media sets the agenda for the public consciousness: racial and sexual discrimination (something that is nigh impossible to encounter in Sweden), the plight of the 'refugees', homosexuality and environmental awareness.

The intolerance of those on the Left who peddle this ideology is worrying. The longer the obfuscation regarding the most important issue continues, the more powerful SD will become. SD's policy is to reduce the current number of immigrants by about 90 per cent, which would bring Sweden in line with its neighbour, Finland. The other parties see this as a 'fascist', xenophobic agenda, and thus all the other political parties 'act in concert' and refuse to form a Government with SD. This *cordon sanitaire* is looking less and less viable, and the correlation between SD votes and Muslim immigration to Sweden is almost perfect.

The media is complicit in what can only be described as a 'silent revolution'. It is 'silent' because irreversible changes are happening to society without any meaningful discussion or consultation with the electorate. As part of this process, the media is being 'controlled' by Governments, and not just in Sweden. Editors of leading newspapers are not reporting on issues that challenge the State multiculturalist ideology, even if they would sell significantly more newspapers by doing so. That must be because editors are being 'controlled' to some degree; journalists are being told they cannot report on certain issues. Facebook and Twitter accounts are being constantly censored; most alt-right online activists report that large numbers of their followers have suddenly just disappeared.[12] We are no longer living in free societies. That time has long passed; we are now edging toward a new kind of techno-authoritarianism whose diktats are governed by the identity politics movement. Journalists investigating the

---

12 Available at: https://www.rt.com/viral/346494-facebook-reddit-censor-orlando/

Orlando massacre were told they were not to use the term 'radical Islam', they were not to go to a local mosque where a guest *imam* in Central Florida told the Congregation 'to kill gays'. The haunting, soft-spoken *imam* appeared on TV saying that 'we kill homosexuals out of compassion. Out of compassion, let's get rid of them now. Death is the sentence. There is nothing to be embarrassed about this'.[13] The transcripts of the killer's 911 calls were edited to remove references to Islam and ISIS.[14]

The real news stories such as Germany flying in refugees on illegal night flights seldom make the news.[15] In August 2016, shortly after the coup in Turkey and at a time when tourism in Turkey had virtually collapsed, there were on some nights eleven flights arriving into Cologne alone between the hours of 1am and 6am.[16] They land, lines of buses collect the refugees and then the planes take off again. When they leave, it says on the destination panel 'unknown'. Officially, there are no flights at these hours: 'es gibt keine Nachtflüge'. Sure, just as 'there is no jihad in France'. To conceal it from the public, some of the planes land at military airbases such as Wunstorf (in the district of Hannover). Merkel is fulfilling the arch-plutocrat Soros' dream of mass immigration and the break-up of the national consciousness such as it is. When one hears of such events, one wonders whether Merkel has agreed to a secret deal with Erdoğan, the man who claims that Turkey was fighting ISIS but who in actual fact was bombing the Kurds who were fighting ISIS.

The 'refugee night-flights' should have been a major scandal, one printed on the front page of every newspaper as the leader of Germany indulges in State-sponsored people smuggling in order to apparently destabilise her own nation. But, instead there was nothing. The Government is colluding with the media to conceal what is happening, running on an anti-racism

---

13   Available at: https://www.youtube.com/watch?v=Vev-OzHQy94

14   Available at: http://edition.cnn.com/2016/06/20/us/orlando-nightclub-shooting/

15   Available at: http://www.express.co.uk/news/world/698766/Germany-migrant-secret-flights-planes-Syria-Merkel

16   Available at: https://jungefreiheit.de/debatte/interview/2016/eine-nacht-auf-dem-flughafen-koelnbonn/

ticket. Tommy Robinson, a UK activist, was arrested and imprisoned in May 2018 for a 'breach of the peace' which meant that the police did not approve of his journalistic coverage of the British child-grooming scandal. But no action was taken against a Pakistani man who was videoed whipping people with a stick at a Hyde Park Corner free speech rally two weeks previously. There was a media gagging order on Robinson's arrest. Cultural nihilism is now leading to politically motivated arrests. In a world where everybody has the latest digital media technology in his or her pocket, one cannot conceal the truth for long. With the refugee night-flights, there is of course an analogy here with the CIA rendition flights which were a major scandal involving planes flown in during the night under similar circumstances. That was front-page news, and rightly so, even if comparatively speaking the numbers were tiny. When thousands of refugees are flown in, there is just silence.

With rather wide-ranging censorship and a selective, partisan media that are prepared to overlook such extraordinary events, we are rapidly creating a toxic atmosphere of paranoia, fear and anxiety for free speech supporters. These are very sinister developments indeed when such actions are taken using clandestine methods. We know that Brussels, the *de facto* capital of the European Union and current European refuge for Islamist militants operates in the same fashion if it gets a chance. In 2016 for instance, it was proposed that a new EU authority should control all Schengen national borders.[17] Germany and France wanted to push this through as quickly as possible without debate. It is a familiar situation. The EU uses a crisis to consolidate its power, reducing the influence and sovereignty of nation-states, and tries to introduce the most significant reforms at a time when they are least likely to be noticed.

Sensitive topics cannot be discussed because they have been made taboo by the media, and in Sweden by the consensus-based society that has been established following decades of Social Democrats' welfare politics.

---

17 Available at: http://frontex.europa.eu/news/european-border-and-coast-guard-agency-launches-today-CHIYAp

In the case of Sweden, 'revolution' may seem like a hyperbolic description since there is no civil or military uprising. But a revolution it is because it is bringing about the biggest demographic and cultural change the country has ever known. However, it is being done by stealth, as immigration has been rendered a taboo topic. The efforts to silence debate such as restrictions on freedom of speech; the blatant harassment and violence shown to journalists who tell the truth; the abuse of mass surveillance to track down critics of immigration policy; the rewriting of legislation to remove any references to 'race'; the demonisation of the only political party that dares give the facts on mass immigration can only be described as 'extremist'.

The politicians and journalists work together to hide the facts, and thus the politicians' ultra-liberal propaganda is unencumbered. Not questioning this, the generous Swede believes he has given prosperity to the 'refugee', even when the refugee is not a refugee: a kind of institutional Christianity in a country that is no longer Church-going for the most part, and where Christenings are increasingly being replaced by secular *namngivningsceremonier* ('name giving ceremonies'). Record numbers of Swedes have been leaving the Church in recent years, and certain members of the Muslim community now want the empty churches to be turned into mosques.[18]

According to the Swedish Integration Board (2005), two-thirds of Swedes question whether expansionist Islam is compatible with Western society, but this issue is simply not open for *public* discussion. Anybody who mentions something beyond the so-called 'Overton Window' (a range of ideas considered currently politically acceptable) will be marked out as a fascist.[19] It is in fact striking how the same survey across Europe has produced the same result; but mainstream parties refuse to respond to public opinion. Something has to give, and indeed it already has. Anti-Establishment parties are on the rise throughout Europe, but Brussels still

---

18 Available at: https://sweden.se/society/10-fundamentals-of-religion-in-sweden/
19 Named after Joseph P. Overton who coined the term.

will not listen. Swedish politicians talk all the time of integration, but few, one suspects, really want it. Integration must surely mean integration into a shared culture, but there is little evidence of that taking place in Sweden. If the newcomers were being integrated, they would be taught for instance that religion belongs in the private sphere. Instead, it seems that Swedish politicians would prefer to create separate, conflicting communities, and just hope somehow that they will not bother them.

And according to various studies such as the UN Human Development Index (2013), Sweden was until very recently considered more or less the closest thing to what one might call the 'perfect' society. Its citizens enjoyed the highest standard of living in the world, with Sweden ranked first in the world in terms of human development: Swedes benefited from a very supportive welfare system, excellent education standards and very minimal crime and corruption. Sweden was a safe, secure place: an essential notion for the Swedish identity bound up in the word *trygghet* which is the slogan for every political party. The political objective has to be to maximise *trygghet*, ('feeling of security'); i.e. control every aspect of people's lives, and then they will be 'secure'.

Sweden was considered the ultimate multi-party functional democracy, the fetish of the Western modern world. But as the 'December agreement' shows, coalition politics in Sweden can be anti-democratic.[20] To prevent SD from voting down the Government's budget and triggering a constitutional crisis and possibly an election, the Governing coalition entered into an agreement in December 2014, just three months after the election with the Alliance (the opposition block excluding SD). The agreement stated that the minority coalition government is to be given free reign to govern without any opposition. It was a desperate attempt to prevent SD from having any political influence, and was meant to run for eight years, but lasted for just under one year before the Christian Democrats decided to leave it. This is the state of democracy in Sweden.

---

20 Available at: http://www.wsj.com/articles/prospect-of-early-elections-looms-again-in-sweden-1445000982

This is effectively Sweden enacting Mussolini's Acerbo Law where a party in fascist Italy that received the largest number of votes was guaranteed a two-thirds majority.[21]

It will not happen, but if SD were to hypothetically win outright the forthcoming General Election in 2018, then it is not unreasonable to assume that the entire democratic process would be unravelled in Sweden. Emergency legislation might be passed and the party would be blocked from forming a Government, perhaps on the grounds that they represent a threat to liberal democracy. In 2004 in Belgium, it looked as if the anti-immigration party, *Vlaams Blok*, could win outright. Indeed in that year, they became the largest single party in the Flemish Parliament election. The party was accused of falling foul of a 1981 anti-racism law, funding to the party was cut off and the party was effectively closed down.[22] A party supported by one in four of the Flemish electorate was shut down. This is the state of democracy in continental Europe. It is reasonable to assume something similar would happen in Sweden.

Sweden was in fact an extremely homogeneous society up until at least the mid-1970s when a decision was taken to make it a 'multicultural society'. From the 1990s onwards, Sweden started to take in refugees from the Balkans. Over the last ten years, Sweden has accepted refugees primarily from war zones in the Middle East and North Africa: Syria, Iraq, Somalia and Afghanistan. For years, Sweden has taken in 'refugees' from peaceful, but autocratic Eritrea. These are young men who do not want to serve in the army. More recently, Sweden has taken in disproportionate numbers of asylum seekers, in some years accepting more refugees per capita than any other country in the world. The numbers are extraordinary: nearly 100,000 refugees came to Sweden (many from Syria) in 2014 for a population of just 9.6 million people, and in 2015, the figure was as high as 160,000.

---

21 Source: https://www.britannica.com/topic/Acerbo-Law
22 Source: http://www.economist.com/node/3379882

If the UK were to receive a proportionate number of refugees to Sweden, that would mean we would see over 650,000 refugees from war zones coming to its shores every year. Or to put it another way, the UK would require every year a new city the size of Leeds to house the newcomers. Cracks are beginning to appear and in just one year, Sweden had according to the UN 2015 Human Development Report fallen out of the top ten countries ranked in terms of human development.[23]

Sweden received more unaccompanied minor asylum seekers than any other country in 2015. Over 35,000 child migrants came to Sweden in 2015: three times as many as went to Germany. Seventy per cent of them came from Afghanistan, i.e. not a war-zone. The cost of caring for children is much higher than for adults. Children who are not placed in foster homes are hosted in asylum centres that cost the State SEK 1900 (US$ 225) a day per child. That is more than what a business traveller would spend to stay at the Sheraton Hotel, Stockholm.[24] Sweden spent US$2.5 billion in 2016 housing children from Afghanistan, and its overall spending on refugees in 2016 surpassed its entire defence budget.[25] Sweden has lost touch with reality. To spend such disproportionate amounts of money on dependents from another country surely implies that there is a much broader agenda here.

Sweden is rapidly becoming a completely 'other' country — unrecognisable to Swedes of the previous generation. Outsiders have never looked so out-of-place as crowds of miserable looking Arab men, wrapped in scarves, stand and shiver on the snowy streets in the winter months. Women covered head to toe in the beetle black *burqa* walk the aisles of the secular supermarket with active piety. It is the 'mother of incompatibility'. Sweden's response to the ISIS Caliphate was to open her doors to cultures whose values are diametrically opposed to her own in every sense. It has

---

23 Source: http://hdr.undp.org/en/composite/HDI
24 Source: http://www.bloomberg.com/news/articles/2016-03-13/why-are-so-many-child-migrants-turning-up-at-sweden-s-borders
25 Source: http://www.bloomberg.com/news/features/2016-03-17/too-generous-for-its-own-good-sweden-s-welcome-mat-in-tatters

done so without a thought for the potentially baleful consequences. As we have seen, Sweden prides herself on human rights, fairness, tolerance, democracy and gender equality — values which are continuously evoked by politicians across the political spectrum and which the average Swede wishes to identify with. Few would dispute that Swedes should blindly follow the UN Convention on Refugees and Asylum — legislation written in an entirely different era and in a context of a Europe with border controls — and that an infinite amount of asylum seekers should have a non-negotiable, subsidised existence the moment they arrive. It is extremely unlikely that the same 144 nations would sign up to this legislation today, knowing that it is openly abused by hundreds of thousands of people. It is clear that the right of asylum needs to be rethought. Granting asylum to somebody who has made it to a nation's shores just ensures that dozens behind him will drown trying to live out the same fantasy.

There is nothing to stop an Eritrean man pretending he is homosexual, and claiming asylum in Sweden on the grounds of 'fearing persecution'. In an oversensitised world, it is rather easy to be afflicted by the 'fear of persecution'. Certainly, any conservative academic in a Humanities department might surely be vulnerable to persecution as a multiculturalist defines it. In a world of open borders and mass mobility, such transnational legislation as the UN Convention on Refugees and Asylum and the *European Convention on Human Rights* could end up 'sinking' countries, unless they withdraw from such legislation or replace it with something more practical for the twenty-first century.

Feminism is ingrained in the language of Swedish morality, but the idea that a woman could be equal to a man in many of these conservative Muslim societies whence the refugees come is in no way realistic. These patriarchal communities remain entangled in the Gordian knot of misogyny. The feminists have run up against what they erroneously perceive to be a white patriarchy, but have no problems with the incoming migrant patriarchy. All of these values mentioned above define Sweden today, but are quite incompatible with Islamic religious doctrine, irrespective of how 'radical' the Muslim refugee is. The fact of the matter is that the way of life of the average Swede is in some way blasphemous or injurious to many of the incoming migrants. Instead of integration, tolerance and peace, one should expect tension, violence and potentially war. The latter outcome, the worst-case scenario, must of course be avoided at all costs and is very unlikely: pacifist Swedes are much more likely to give in to Islam than to form any kind of defensive *testudo*.

One cannot reconcile feminism with mass immigration from the Middle East and North Africa. If these new migrants become the ethnic majority, then the feminist project will be finished. It will be totally decimated. The ferocious feminists who try to ruin their ideological opposition under the false pretence of being the protectors of women will be disenfranchised. If they were real protectors of women, they might have something to say about female genital mutilation practiced in many of the asylum seekers' countries.

Ironically, female opponents to the militant, virago feminists are frequently attacked in the most demeaning and sexist ways. Some of these ultra-feminists would no doubt happily criminalise the practice of women staying at home with their young children. And men are not considered legitimate discussants for issues that affect women. Through character assassination, men are sometimes excluded from any debate on women. In fact, all the opponents are excluded, leaving just a tired monologue. These techniques are used time and time again because their users know they work.

Many feminist writers refused to condemn Boko Haram when they kidnapped hundreds of Nigerian girls because they were concerned it might be perceived as imperialist, Islamophobic or against cultural relativism. Feminists seem more eager to smear the critics of *jihadism* as 'Islamophobes' than to stand up for women's most basic rights. When it comes to deploring brutal repression, the Left cannot be so selective. Otherwise, they will just look like they are bereft of any moral compass. Feminism was a legitimate movement that wanted to achieve equal rights for men and women. That has been achieved in Sweden, and most other Western countries. This ideology has been written into legal codes, leading to new understandings of sexuality and family. It is now a power struggle of women over men (straight white men at least).

The naïve response to the issue of the potential demise of feminism in the light of Muslim majority countries in Europe is of course that the new migrants — the collective victimhood — will have Swedish values (even if they have insisted previously that Sweden does not stand for anything), but that is unrealistic. It is more likely that they will grow up in segregated communities which will not share any of the values the multiculturalists are anxious to promote. One cannot compare Somalis who grew up in 'closed' Islamist societies ruled by Al-Shabab and *shari'ah* law to the better educated European Bosnians who came to Sweden in the 1990s and who practiced a moderate form of Islam. The idea that the Somalis and Afghans coming to Sweden are going to preserve Western values and culture is more likely putting hope before experience.

Swedish politicians alongside EU bureaucrats claim that refugees are needed because Sweden is an ageing society (and thus contradict their claim that they are refugees, when it is clear many are migrants), and in order to continue the generous welfare benefit system, more immigrant workers will be required. However, this is a thoroughly flawed argument. The idea that Sweden needs constantly more young people to look after an ageing population is the logic of a Ponzi scheme. Ponzi demography is a policy which tries to increase profits for a small group of people at the top of the pyramid by adding more and more people to the bottom of the pyramid. Everything seems fine, but when population growth stalls, the economy goes into decline, high debt crushes consumption and the people at the top take their profits leaving those at the bottom potentially without work and in debt. The whole model is dependent on constant population growth which ultimately can only end in environmental degradation, and thus be a cost to an economy that does not properly account for externalities. As we have seen, the politicians that advocate these policies call themselves 'green', but one would never know it.

Our models and economic philosophies are based on constant expansion. The ultimate result would be that our economies end up like

Japan's: at the end of the road; 125 million people living on a cluster of small islands. With nowhere to grow, the bubble of the late 1980s burst and the economy just slowly declined for the next thirty years. It plays into the fallacy of believing that perpetual, exponential growth should be an economic and demographic objective in a world with finite resources. If immigrants were needed, it would surely be more sensible to operate an immigration policy based on common sense (as the Australians do) where people are allowed in when certain skills are required, to fulfil gaps in the job market.

However, Sweden apparently only wishes to welcome the least qualified, and yet at the same time appeals to a self-image as the utopia of modernity. The wave of refugees that came in 2015 and 2016 will become an unsustainable burden on the Swedish taxpayer for years and years because many do not (or are unable to) work. The already over-taxed Swedes will soon have to pay even more taxes to support hundreds of thousands of migrants. The problems of integration have not even begun to be tackled. The Yazidis who came to Sweden were asked why they came to Sweden, and they responded that 'they could not live with Muslims'.[26] Little do they realise that Sweden has a significant Muslim population, and that their fate once again will be to live amongst Muslims.

The idea that refugees will fund an ageing population is just naïve, and not backed up by a single fact. Refugees wish to come to Sweden (as opposed to say its neighbour, Finland) in such overwhelming numbers in order to benefit from its extremely generous social security system and because their extended families are already there and can vouch for its unconditional generosity.[27] Most Swedish politicians (the SD party excluded) refuse to recognise this obvious truth even when the refugees articulate it themselves. According to Swedish Government statistics, over

---

26 Source: http://foreignpolicy.com/2016/02/10/the-death-of-the-most-generous-nation-on-earth-sweden-syria-refugee-europe/

27 Large numbers of videos can be found on www.youtube.com where male migrants from Syria explain clearly their rationale for going to Sweden. Here is one: https://www.youtube.com/watch?v=EmqbtyfQ3f8

seventy per cent of those that arrived in 2015 are young, healthy men, men who have travelled right across Europe searching for the best deal. Ninety per cent of unaccompanied minors who came to Sweden in the same year were male.

Politicians like Reinfeldt (the previous Prime Minister of Sweden) have waged cultural and demographic terrorism against their own people, and yet Swedes continue to vote for these policies (for the time being at least). The extent of ideologisation in Sweden is truly apparent when Swedes say, 'We are not allowed to vote SD', a comment which one often hears. Sweden appears at times to be run more on a basis of an NGO than a democratic nation-state. One cannot build a country on pity. The mainstream media needs to report what it perceives to be racism less obsessively, and to focus more on the real news stories such as the rape epidemic that has afflicted Sweden since the migration crisis.[28]

The public domain is the province of the State, and the State is pursuing a nihilistic, anti-racist ideology which is effective in serving a psychological function: to make the reader or listener feel good about himself, in the sense of manipulating him to make him feel like a caring citizen who is trying to save the world. As has been stated previously, this is an information war. One side has State media and globalist politicians on their side, and the other simply has an online presence. In a world of universal internet access, ignorance of matters related to the information war has become a 'choice'.

The Swedish media keeps its listeners and readers in the dark about the issues that matter. Voting for the one party that wishes to bring the immigrant situation under control would risk social alienation. But if SD is so 'racist', one might ask why it was that in the last General Election the party was slightly more popular amongst the immigrant vote than with ethnic Swedes. Are the refugees 'racist' too, or having come from a place

---

28 In Norway, a three year old boy was gang-raped by refugees. Swedish and German children have been raped by migrants in all manner of public places; a Swedish woman was raped in central Stockholm. She struggled, so the Somali slit her throat. When the police turned up, he was still raping the corpse. (Source: http://conservativepost.com/sweden-shocked-again-after-woman-raped-to-death-by-somali-immigrant/)

which is definitely not a socialist utopia, can they perhaps just see common sense? The parties on the Left (i.e. all the other political parties except *Alternativ för Sverige*) need to be perhaps more careful about whom they are trying to alienate. The anti-norm is not necessarily the group of people they thought they were.

It will not be reported in the Swedish media, but the repercussions of mass immigration from the Middle East are being felt at various levels of Swedish society. According to the Organisation for Economic Co-operation and Development (OECD), the once admired Swedish education system is rapidly deteriorating. The most recent OECD report stated: 'Student performance on the Programme for International Student Assessment (PISA) has declined dramatically. […] No other country participating in PISA saw a steeper decline than Sweden.' According to the report, nearly half of the children from immigrant backgrounds (48 per cent) failed to make the grade in mathematics. Out of the thirty-four OECD countries, Sweden now ranks twenty-eight in maths (below Lithuania which is in OECD accession talks) and twenty-seventh in reading and science. In 2000, Sweden was ranked tenth for reading and eleventh in science. Sweden's neighbour, Finland, has been consistently ranked in the top five and in 2006 came first for science and second in reading.[29]

Ethnic Swedish children share classrooms with children who are used to writing Arabic, Pashto and Farsi, not speaking and writing Swedish. Swedish children would flounder in the Iraqi or Syrian education system, so it is no surprise that these immigrant children struggle in Swedish schools. Many are not able to cope, and the ethnic Swedes are denied the opportunities they surely deserve. The system is failing both groups of people. In the last election, there was endless talk in the media about the free-fall in Swedish school standards, but with the exception of *Sverigedemokraterna*, every politician refused to make the connection that is so obvious to any objective outsider.

There is much evidence to show that other social structures are under

---

29 Source: https://www.oecd.org/pisa/keyfindings/pisa-2012-results-overview.pdf

relentless pressure. Since Sweden passed the bill on Immigrant and Minority Policy in 1975, effectively paving the way for the transition from a homogeneous to a multicultural society, violent crime has increased astronomically. In 1975, 421 rapes were reported to the police for the entire country. In 2014, the figure had increased to 6,620, and then 7,230 in 2017.[30] In 2015, there were over 18,000 cases of sexual assault reported in Sweden. As elsewhere in the world, this is presumably a small fraction of the overall figures. Recorded interviews (subsequently posted on Twitter) with police officers show that Swedish police are so overwhelmed by reports of rapes that they often do not have time to investigate them, even when young children have been raped. Two generations previously, such crime and on in this scale would have been unthinkable in Sweden.

The former Prime Minister, Tage Erlander, understood perfectly well in 1965 that the success of Sweden was due to its homogeneity when he said:

> *Vi svenskar lever ju i en så oändligt mycket lyckligare lottad situation. Vårt lands befolkning är homogen, inte bara i fråga om rasen utan också i många andra avseenden.* (Source: Valfrihetens samhälle (Tiden 1962), s. 82)

> We Swedes live in an infinitely luckier situation. Our country's population is homogeneous, not only in terms of race, but also in many other respects.

Today, such a comment would undoubtedly be considered 'racist'. It seems by the mid-1970s Sweden was anxious to show to the world that it was a 'tolerant' place, and exploiting the concept of 'tolerance' became a means for the next generation of radical liberal politicians to push through policies that favoured ethnic minorities entering the country. It was the liberal Olaf Palme, the son of a refugee, who wished to pursue the policy of multiculturalism for the reason that he believed the well-being of immigrants was conditional upon the recognition and promotion of their cultures. His words echo strongly in the Sweden of today. It is of course one thing to respect immigrant cultures, but quite another to suggest that

---

30 Source: https://www.bra.se/bra/brott-och-statistik/valdtakt-och-sexualbrott.html

the national culture needs renewal, or better still needs to be subsumed in an incoherent mosaic of immigrant cultures.

One can guess what Erlander might have made of the results of the multiculturalist experiment that has blighted Sweden; a segregated society poised to explode. As the statistics show, in Sweden, rape and violent crime was more or less unheard of until recently. According to the United Nations Office on Drugs and Crime (UNODC) data for 2012, Sweden has now one of the worst rape statistics in the world. More rapes are committed per 100,000 people in Sweden than any other country in the world but Lesotho. Such a statistic must surely shock the average non-Swede. It is certainly true that Sweden has a broader definition of rape and that much care should be taken with comparative data on rape, but it cannot explain away the problem in its entirety.

Neither the mainstream media nor the Government will permit any discussion of these statistics. Similarly, the German Government and media tried to cover up the mass rape and assault cases by Arab men on German women in Cologne on New Year's Eve, 2015. They chose not to mention that the 'refugees' were throwing fireworks at the cathedral. But they could not cover up the reports the assaulted women gave to foreign media when they told them that the Arab men shouted *inshah Allah* as they raped them.[31] Very similar events took place in Sweden, but were covered up by the Media-Government. All of the victims said the rapists were immigrants from the Middle East and North Africa, but they were accused of racism by their own people, the inadvertent apologists of sexual harassment and crime.

The non-immigrant population have been blinded and deafened by the deception of this quasi-totalitarian ideology and power of the new cultural grammar. Reality is being blurred for 'ideology is a dreamlike construction hindering us from seeing the real state of things, reality as such' (Žižek, 1989: 48). Such planned, mass sex attacks are common in the wake of defeat, and the response to these attacks was that of an ideologically defeated nation.

---

31 Source: http://www.express.co.uk/news/world/643129/Algerian-sex-attack-rape-Allah-wills-it-German-student

It is said that police officers on the scene in Germany on that New Year's Eve did nothing, knowing that if they were to act they would be accused of racism or Islamophobia. With instances like this in the West, it seems that ideology is hindering the effective operation of our civic institutions.

The Swedish Government does everything possible to blur the statistics by classifying for instance second generation immigrants as Swedes, but Police Commissioners have confirmed in phone conversations that approximately 80 per cent of the rapes are committed by immigrants from North Africa and the Middle East. Last year, Peter Springare, a veteran police officer in Örebro said that almost all the crimes were committed by migrants from the Middle East. He was investigated twice by state prosecutors for inciting racial hatred. Subsequently, the Swedish Government has done everything possible to silence him. In 1996, a report by the Swedish National Council for Crime Prevention showed that immigrants from North Africa were twenty-three times more likely to commit rape as Swedish men. After that, the Justice Department prevented the Council from publishing data on crime committed by immigrants. If the facts do not support a multiculturalist ideology, then they are erased.

If people wish to stop what they perceive to be Islamophobia and racism, then clearly the onus is on the Government to publish up-to-date crime statistics by ethnicity.[32] Then, we can see who is right, and what is propaganda and what is not. The electorate has a right to visibility on such issues. If the authorities refuse to do this, then it must be because they want to hide the truth. It is understandable that the Government does not want to inflame a sensitive issue, but it cannot point the finger at its own people (as some politicians do) without proving statistically that this is the right thing to do. Swedes must *now* overcome the pathological fear of being labelled Islamophobic, and speak out about these issues. They must challenge the weight of

---

32 On 22nd of August 2018 (just before publication of this book), a researcher gained access to the official statistics and released them. These statistics show that nearly 80 per cent of rapes and attempted rapes over the last five years were committed by non-Swedes who had been in the country for less than a year. The majority of these men came from the Middle East and Africa. Swedes now have access to the truth on this matter at least.

opinion and take an independent stand. Data from other countries suggest it is very unlikely that ethnic Swedes have suddenly started committing all the crime. Running at 116 per cent occupancy rate, it is said that 70 per cent of the prison population in France are Muslims.[33] One might baulk at coupling Islam with terrorism and crime of any sort, but if one looks at who was convicted of terrorist related offences in the UK in the two years after September 2001, every single one of them were Muslims. According to the UK Government, from the years 2001-2013, 71 per cent of people convicted for terrorist offences in the UK were not white.[34]

Cable leaks from August 2008 (cablegatesearch) recognise all of these problems. Indeed, they talk explicitly of Muslim immigrant communities with unemployment of 75 per cent and of violent crime being several times more likely than among 'native Swedes'. These problems are therefore known and recognised by officials, but just not publicly. Cable leaks refer to the tendency not to discuss these issues because they are too divisive. These leaks show that the policy of obfuscation is an attempt to furnish the reader and listener with a diet of lies and misinformation. Wikileaks blew the lid off that can of deception. These cable-leaks talk of the problem of radicalisation, and the complete failure of integrating Muslim communities in Sweden: 'Raised in isolation from the rest of Swedish society, second-generation youth describe a feeling of alienation and a conflict between their Muslim and Swedish identities that make them vulnerable to radicalisation' (Wikileaks, 8th of August, 2008). This was in 2008. Ten years later, the problem of radicalisation in the context of Islamism has become a far more serious issue. After Belgium, more foreign *jihadists* travelled from Sweden to Iraq and Syria to fight for ISIS than from any other European country.[35]

---

33 Source: Institute for Criminal Policy Research, 2014
34 Available at: https://www.gov.uk/government/publications/operation-of-police-powers-under-the-terrorism-act-2000-2012-to-2013/operation-of-police-powers-under-the-terrorism-act-2000-and-subsequent-legislation-arrests-outcomes-and-stop-and-searches-great-britain-2012-to-20
35 Source: International Centre for the Study of Radicalisation and Political Violence (2015).

Certain suburbs of the major Swedish cities, Stockholm, Gothenburg and Malmö, have been described as Islamic ghettos — no-go areas for the police. It is the same in the *banlieues* of France where supremacist *shari'ah* has long trumped *laïcité*. Women are now banned from some Parisian cafés in the suburbs of the city. In the summer of 2015, there were three grenade attacks in one week in Malmö alone (grenade attacks have become an acute problem in Sweden); shootings and violent rape are increasingly common. In March 2015, two masked men, armed with Kalashnikov rifles, entered a Gothenburg bar where people were watching Barcelona play Manchester United and opened fire with automatic weapons on the crowd. Two were killed and over a dozen were injured. The following month, there were more shootings in the same area of the city. Sweden now far outstrips the UK in terms of fire-arm related deaths.[36] But perhaps not for long as gang violence between young black men has made London's homicide rate in 2018 worse than New York's. The mayor of London, Sadiq Khan, just shrugs his shoulders in response. He is more concerned with preventing President Trump from visiting London and with attempting to overturn the democractic result of the Brexit referendum. Khan has become the face of cultural nihilism in London.

One or two Gothenburg suburbs were recruitment grounds of Islamic State fighters. According to some reports, there were possibly 150 Islamic State fighters from Gothenburg alone.[37] ISIS and Al-Qaeda were explicit about their intentions to infiltrate Europe with terrorists. These are people who claim to be refugees, and who have travelled across the Mediterranean as part of the ongoing migrant crisis. These terrorist groups have even published their plans, but still no response from the Swedish Government. The politically correct discourse we have wrapped ourselves in is like a self-imposed gag order.

The Islamic State claims that it smuggled over 4,000 ISIS fighters into Europe, hidden amongst innocent refugees. According to Europol, these

---

36 Source: International firearm injury prevention and policy, 2010.
37 Source: *Foreign Policy* article, February 2016.

figures are correct and could in fact be slightly higher.[38] Many of these must have come to Sweden. Radical Islam is entrenched in Europe, and the *jihadists* are already abusing the generous policy of political asylum which is looking increasingly like a scam as the people given 'refuge' never return home.

One would think the terrifying prospect of ISIS agents entering the country might even deter the most liberal of politicians from continuing this 'extreme' immigration policy. But no, it seems multiculturalism as a policy is still acceptable even if it runs the risk of coddling terrorism. This is happening at a time when Christianity is in sharp decline and actually dying in Sweden. The collapse of Christianity in parts of Western Europe has undoubtedly left a void, an ontological abyss. Many people in the West are walking in a cloud of cultural, epistemological nothingness. They are no longer able to leap from the finite to the infinite, and thus they are unable to rise from the inevitable ruminations of our own despair. They have no belief in anything which is philosophically grounded and appears real to them, and have therefore no strength. Belief is strength, which is why we appear so weak and feeble to the devout Muslims entering our countries.

Perambulating in this cultural chagrin is the former Minister for European Affairs, Birgitta Ohlsson, a member of the *Folkpartiet*, who called for the abolition of the Swedish nation-state (*avskaffa Sverige*) on the National Day of Sweden (June 6th 2001) in the newspaper *Expressen*. Instead, she wants global federalism. Her ambition is to destroy once and for all Sweden's alleged homogeneity by increasing exponentially the number of migrants. This particular politician can be heard talking incessantly about stopping 'extremism', but her views can only be described as 'extremist'. Ohlsson and her fellow-thinkers are iconoclasts, fanatics. She wishes to destroy the wealth of the Swedish nation-state, encourage the building of

---

38 Source: Rob Wainright, Director of Europol. The figure was used in a European Parliament briefing: http://www.europarl.europa.eu/EPRS/EPRS-Briefing-548980-Foreign-fighters-FINAL.pdf

mosques in Sweden, replace national parliaments with a one-world parliament and encourage more Roma to come to Sweden.[39] She is an enemy of the State and an enemy of the Swedish people.

Birgitta Ohlsson co-authors articles with George Soros, who is using his billions to fund extreme liberal politics and left-wing media (Media Matters). Russia was quick to recognise the subversive character of his powerful, well-funded network and has closed it down. The Soros Foundation has now quit Hungary following pressure from the Hungarian Government. Other countries might consider doing the same because he is determined to undermine sovereign European nation-states, and is using his vast wealth to do so. Ohlsson predictably enough couples a sense of national identity with racism, and appears to be living in a strange fantasy world. Fantasists like her believe that by ending differences (racial, cultural etc.), we will all live in peace. She might perhaps try telling that to what is left of ISIS. This enemy is surely the most evil ideology the world has seen since the time of Nazism, and Humpty Dumpty will have ever such a great fall as when *jihad* is launched in Sweden.

Elsewhere, Swedish journalists from *Dagens Nyheter*, such as the editor-in-chief Peter Wolodarski, believe that Putin is the one that blew the cover on the asylum-seeker sex attacks at a music festival in Stockholm. They claimed that he has been using the website *Nyheter i dag* to spread disinformation about the rape epidemic in Sweden (and the multiple incidents of asylum seekers raping boys). With an economy mired in recession due to Western sanctions, one suspects that asylum seekers raping Swedish boys and girls is not exactly Putin's priority. If the rape epidemic is an illusion, one might question why the newly arriving male migrants to Norway and Denmark (coming from the same countries as the migrants to Sweden) were given mandatory training on sexual consent and Western sexual norms. Still, the Swedish Prime Minister insists that the increase in rape has nothing to do with immigration. Political leaders in Germany and Sweden are abusing their democratic rights by destabilising their own nations, and then denying all responsibility for their actions.

---

39 Source: article in the *Östgötakorrespondenten*, the 29th of December, 2009.

They are pursuing 'extremist' policies, and in order to avoid criticism insist on associating extremism with right-wing politics only.

Refugees fleeing from a country with tens of billions of oil reserves (Iraq) were meant to be ciphers for Swedes who could then feel good about themselves. But as the riots and car burnings of 2010, 2013 and the summer of 2018 showed, when migrants set light to scores of cars across Sweden in a social media coordinated attack, the inhabitants of these failed, segregated communities have agency of their own and sometimes extremely violent agendas. One wonders whether this is what the former Swedish European Commissioner for Home Affairs (i.e. a European technocrat), Cecilia Malmström, meant when she spoke of mass Muslim immigration to Sweden as 'cultural enrichment'.

More recently, the Government cleverly changed tack. Once again, in order to ensure that refugees act indeed as ciphers, Sweden decided to manipulate this kindness and focus in particular on 'unaccompanied refugee children' as a group. The Government thinks not unreasonably that it is more likely that people will feel empathy towards a refugee child than an adult. And indeed, that is the case. So, in 2015, up to 1500 refugee children were arriving every month — mainly from Syria. Children were fast-tracked through the process, and once they get residency status they were allowed to invite their whole family, who will also be Swedish residents.

Asylum seekers caught onto this, and put their children forward knowing that it will mean their own asylum applications will be fast-tracked. The chances of receiving permanent residency status are far higher for a child. As we now know, many of these 'minors' were not children at all. They arrived without documents and officials took their word for their age. However, it has in fact been proven that fraud occurred on a very significant scale. Many of the applicants were in fact in their early twenties, and sometimes much older. But staff at the *Migrationsverket* (Immigration Service) were expected to turn a blind eye to the fraud even when a forty-year-old man claimed he was a child. They do not speak out because they fear being called 'racist' and losing their jobs, which is the probable consequence if they break the anti-racist groupthink.

Syrians knew that if they could get to Sweden, they would receive the permanent right to stay. These kinds of policy statements from Löfven and Merkel aggravated the migration crisis further, and gave even more impetus to the people-smuggling migration machine. Indeed, such a policy turned a refugee crisis into a migration crisis which has become a clash of civilisations crisis. This is in part the explanation for why hundreds of thousands of people were headed to Sweden. In the autumn of 2015, every Syrian, Iraqi and Afghan had the magical word 'Sweden' on his lips.

And at the same time, suburbs of the major Swedish cities where the new arrivals are headed have become pressure cookers of discontent—hermetic communities, sometimes operating under their own laws. We are creating an ethos of cultural and linguistic apartheid where cultural loyalty comes way before State loyalty, religious identity before nation. If there is a relationship between the Islamic ghetto and the local political order it is an antagonistic one. The censorious edicts of the *imams* and *mullahs* are being increasingly accepted.

The *Foreign Policy* article 'From the Welfare State to the Caliphate' (February, 2015) describes how Swedish refugees from Chechnya, Syria and Iraq have become Al-Qaeda leaders, and that there are now Swedish *jihadi* brides, most of whom were Somali refugees in Sweden. All of these people benefited for years from Swedish benefits paid for by the ethnic Swedish taxpayer, who after the Danes are subject to the highest rate of taxation in the world (top rate: 60 per cent). Swedish *imams* (one of whom claimed to be a member of ISIS) who have called for the death of infidels have insisted on television that the money they receive from Swedish tax payers is 'Allah's money'. Other *imams* in Germany have called repeatedly in so-called 'sermons' for the Islamification of Europe, declaring modern Europe, 'the ungrateful daughter of Islamic Civilisation'. Alongside a whole bank of interviews, these 'sermons' from screaming, hate-filled *imams* are televised and available on the Internet.[40] In 2011, a Somali

---

40 The Middle East Media Research Institute TV Monitor Project (MEMRI) has a whole library of recordings. Available at: http://www.memritv.org/clip/en/4970.htm

imam living in Sweden said live on Sweden P2's Somali radio programme that all converts from Islam should be killed.[41] The Chancellor of Justice refused to consider this to be hate-speech even if it was an unambiguous incitement to violence, and the *imam* was allowed to continue calling for the death of infidels.[42] Two years later a Swedish woman was imprisoned for two years for making a defamatory comment on Facebook about eight migrants who gang-raped a woman in 2011.

The Swedish Government's response to this extremely alarming situation has been not only to ignore hate-speech from the *imams* invited to their country, but also to increase (not reduce as the politics of common sense would surely dictate) in 2015 the number of refugees from the places where the Swedish *jihadists* headed, i.e. Syria and Iraq. This news was spread amongst the many billions active on social media within seconds, and then Syrian TV channels aired in several countries in the Middle East started to tell people to leave Syria and go to Sweden. From a Swedish perspective at least, common sense seemed to have just evaporated under the summer's evening sun.

And so, the migration crisis got under way: over a million people were on the move in the summer of 2015, spurred on by the idiotic, impeachable Merkel and Löfven, who encouraged asylum seekers to come to Germany and Sweden. Naturally, the Swedish media only aired one side of this crisis. Sweden is facing a media blackout as described by Arnstberg & Sandelin (2013), a Swedish journalist and retired researcher who were brave enough to tell the truth about Swedish immigration statistics, but whose book has been completely ignored by the Swedish media. But the Swedish people really have a right to know the facts. The costs of the refugee policy are borne by the taxpayer, and thus one might assume they have a right to know the truth about Sweden and its refugee policy. Arnstberg & Sandelin provide all the data, and it will not be repeated here, but Swedes should really know that an extraordinary 60 per cent of welfare benefits in Sweden are paid to immigrants.[43]

---

41 Source: http://www.thelocal.se/discuss/lofiversion/index.php/t44886.html

42 Source: http://www.thelocal.se/20111020/36866

43 Source: *Foreign Policy* article, February 2016.

In the UK, there was in the summer of 2015 much debate as to whether such recipients were refugees or migrants. As far as Sweden is concerned at least, this is a migration crisis, and not a refugee crisis. The real refugees are the poor, suffering women and children in Turkey, Lebanon etc. who have fled war to the neighbouring country. Article 1 of the Geneva Convention as amended by the 1967 protocol defines a refugee as follows:

> A person who owing to a well-founded fear of being persecuted for reasons of race, religion, nationality, membership of a particular social group or political opinion, is outside the country of his nationality and is unable or, owing to such fear, is unwilling to avail himself of the protection of that country; or who, not having a nationality and being outside the country of his former habitual residence as a result of such events, is unable or, owing to such fear, is unwilling to return to it.

Refugees are people who flee against their will because of fear for their lives. According to figures available at *Migrationsverket*, since 1980, only one in ten of the people coming from the parts of the Middle East are 'refugees' in accordance with this definition. The next generation of ethnic Swedes, perhaps the last generation, will look back at Sweden's immigration policy with incredulity. They will quite reasonably want to know what motivated this collective psychosis, and how one managed to lose all connection with reality.

Sweden responded to the very significant increase in street begging with the normal platitude about how the Roma have been mistreated for centuries, i.e. they are the victims and thus ideologically protected. But, the plight of the Roma should not be an issue for Sweden. However, Swedes being the masters of expiation, like to eke out victims to fill up its pantheon of losers. The difficulty with these responses is that it does not in any way address the problem. It is a blanket, ideological response, but never a political solution. By taking this standpoint, Sweden is turning a blind eye to the human trafficking that it is promoting by its policy of allowing this to flourish. Most Swedes feel uncomfortable seeing so many beggars in what is meant to be a utopia. The solution is simple: stop giving money to the beggars, and they will go elsewhere.

Even in the totalitarian Soviet Union, people still had a grip on reality. However, talking to ethnic Swedes, it is clear that the proselytising of the mainstream media has been extremely effective, as they appear to have bought wholeheartedly into this radical, anti-racist ideology. This comfortable world of welfare support where every other employee appears to be *sjukskriven* ('on sick leave') and where humanitarian supremacy reigns to the benefit of the *salus* of humanity, is about to be shattered, and the lunacy of thirty years of immigration policy will be revealed.

It is not as if the Syrians happened to be in Sweden when the war broke out, and thus sought asylum. These are people who have been told of a mysterious land in northern Europe that is prepared to offer them asylum and the rights that that entails; they just have to get there. Such a policy has fuelled the industry of people smuggling with groups asking for large sums of money to ensure safe passage to Sweden. Sweden's fanciful policy is leading to the kind of crime that the so-called 'humanitarian superpower' was meant to be stamping out. Sweden should not turn a blind eye to this hypocrisy. It has encouraged very significant numbers of people with fake ID and fabricated asylum stories to be trafficked to Sweden. *Cui bono?* If they end up living in a separate, parallel Swedish society where there are few opportunities for them, one really wonders who is the winner.

It is demeaning for the immigrants who have abandoned their native country to be used as economic pawns in a gigantic game of globalisation, and it is unnerving for the hosts because it imposes brutal modifications on their societies. It should be obvious that the solution to these terrible conflicts and wars in North Africa and the Middle East is *not* major population shifts. That will never address the problem. And with further crises and perhaps warfare over finite natural resources, some countries might be left with a stark choice: police the borders or collapse.

The Swedish morality play has veered far from its script: the liberal as a protagonist has tried to rescue the victim (the refugee or the beggar), but the victim has taken advantage of the liberal's naïvety and constant urge for 'goodness'. There will be an unexpected, but fatal twist in the play: the do-gooder will end up the victim, but there will be nobody to look after him. A disturbing *dénouement*; he might even be an 'infidel' in a country that was once his own. His insistence on pronouncing the multiculturalist sceptics as 'racists' (even if Islam is not a race) will have left him powerless and alone in a society whose vision he should have been questioning, and not 'accommodating'. A morality play might even become a tragedy.

The over-politically correct will no doubt consider this an Islamophobic perspective on the problem of migration, but we are concerned here with belief systems (not people). Let us also not forget that -phobia means 'irrational fear'. There is nothing 'irrational' about the fear of *radical* Islam; it is presented in the atrocities of terrorism all over the world, every week of the year. And there is a difference between being anti-Islam and counter-*jihad*, just as there is between prejudice and postjudice. It is not a question of resorting to prejudices to articulate views on radical Islam, but it is about drawing rational conclusions from postjudices. If we wish to preserve what is good about our societies, then we should all be counter-*jihadists*.

Islam is fundamentally different from Christianity, for it works on the logic of totality; it is an authoritarian religion in the sense that it dictates right down to the finer details how one should live one's life. Given that Swedish cultural values are diametrically opposed to those held by the majority of the migrants, and given the disdain that radical Muslims have for the secular Western life (though that does not stop them coming to the West, which in itself is proof that they have no intention of integrating), it is surely in everybody's interest for the radically minded to stay in the parts of the world where Islam is the dominant religion, i.e. principally North Africa, the Middle East, the Horn of Africa, the Sahel, Central Asia and other parts of Asia such as Pakistan, Malaysia, and Indonesia. This was presumably the thinking behind some of Trump's electoral announcements, and indeed his actions after his election.

If one deems such a critique to be Islamophobic, then one is effectively self-imposing the values of *shari'ah* law which is what communities in the West are actively doing. *Shari'ah* law does not tolerate any criticism of Islam. This might be blasphemy, and the critic might be subject to a *fatwa*. Our own Western societies do not tolerate criticism of Islam either, which is why after an Islamist terror attack, world leaders rush to tell us how 'peaceful' this religion is. Their clownish powerlessness has become frankly embarrassing, and their words have the ring of insults. We must come to terms with the lie of liberal modernity. It is surely time to consider what kind of society defines its own citizens as oppressors when the truth is quite the opposite.

The logical corollary of the policies being pursued is that the domination of the ethnic Swede has to end, and that the future society is for the marginalised and victimised. It is no wonder that so many are rushing to claim victimhood. Victimhood confers identity, but it also fosters moral dependence and leads to the creation of a society divided along lines of moral conflict as people compete for status of victims. This is bordering on a form of totalitarian thinking, as any opposition is considered intolerant, uncompassionate, even 'extreme', and thus illegitimate. They are employing doublespeak, as 'tolerance' according to the Left means accepting everything I tell you about racism, bigotry etc., and disrespecting everything else. This is an attempt at creating a polarising hegemonic mindset based on soft narratives that evoke sentimentality and false values. This well-intentioned totalitarianism is no less dangerous than the violence of communist doublespeak, but is arguably more effective at deceiving the masses because it is couched in cuddly terms.

The difference between this ideological censorship and that of the fascist totalitarian system is that the enemy is the 'in-group' (the ethnic Swedes in the case of Sweden) and not the 'out-group'. This is therefore a perverse, nihilistic ideology based on liberal censoriousness. It is nihilistic because it is based on denial. Liberal censoriousness has meant that we have lost the freedom to discuss things, unless it concerns the liberal triumvirate of 'pieties', the shibboleths of virtue: tolerance, equality and diversity, which nowadays seem far more prominent than the theological virtues of love, faith, hope and charity. One is expected to respect these new pieties absolutely.

These three terms operate as *a priori* categories of understanding, and would typically make up what Nietzsche called the 'slave morality': the response of the weak to their domination by the self-affirming strong. But, this time it is the strong (in an economic sense) that are adhering to the values of the 'slave morality'. It is the 'strong' that embody the impoverished loss of spirit. Guilt and self-loathing is not being instilled in the 'strong' by the priesthood, as Nietzsche would presuppose, but by the political elite and the media in a secular society like Sweden. The hegemony of these values represents a threat to the West because they promote mediocrity and gloss over individual achievement.

As we have seen, the defenders of liberty are styled as fascists while the fanatics are portrayed as victims, as in the Swedish response to *Charlie Hebdo*. Those who revolt against barbarism are themselves accused of barbarism. Sweden is setting itself up for a form of social internal combustion. A form of internal combustion that was entirely unnecessary and avoidable.

It is known that radicalisation is happening in the mosques, the faith schools and the prisons — places which are completely alien to most of us, and yet the legislation introduced to address it (the *Prevent Duty* under The Counter-Terrorism and Security Act 2015 legislation in Britain, for instance) is focusing on the universities. It is easy to be tolerant of something that does not infringe on you and that you cannot see. The problem of radicalisation is brewing away, but we are totally unaware of it until it is too late. In preventing radicalisation, the mosques seem like an obvious place to start, but the Government has its hands tied because the mosques are not public institutions. Instead, it is public institutions like our universities that are monitored and subject to further freedom infringements every time there is a terrorist incident.

By striving to be a leader in humanitarian issues, Sweden has created a troubled, parallel society of plural monoculturalism and internalised divisions. Its political leaders are so infested with anti-Western ideology, they have become morally blind. There are Muslim communities in Sweden where women are little more than serfs in sprawling clans that control their movements, tell them who to marry, and whose actions are governed by *shari'ah* law. This is the reality of the 'multicultural dream' in some Muslim communities in Sweden and elsewhere in Western Europe: rape, honour killings, *jihadism* and a medieval system of law. As shown in a CNN documentary (February, 2013), there are now *shari'ah* patrols modelled on Saudi Arabia's *muttawa* in parts of East London where young British women are told to cover up and wear the *hijab*, homosexuals are harassed and passers-by are stopped and told 'it is a Muslim area' and therefore alcohol is banned.[44] The same happens in Oslo, Copenhagen and Brussels where Muslims are now the largest religious group; and in parts of Spain (Lleida), *shari'ah* patrols have tried to ban pet dogs, even poisoning some of them.

The dynamics of group difference will always exist. One society comprising largely illiberal Muslims who divide the world up into believers and non-believers, and another, a 'liberal', secular society that has lost its faith and put its trust in a utopian, post-Christian multiculturalist paradise. The former will not tolerate the latter, and thus, assuming the status quo remains, European liberalism might perhaps be usurped in countries like Sweden by a European Islamic ideology, just as in Houellebecq's novel *Soumission* (2015). The liberals who defined themselves in terms of tolerance (but are not really tolerant as the mere suggestion that immigration should have some limits will be met with the most intolerant of responses) risk becoming in the most extreme outcome yes-men to a highly intolerant society based on *shari'ah* law. The secular ideology and its followers with their intemperate dislike of opposition seem thus to be headed down a rather self-destructive path.

As with certain other European countries with large Muslim populations, Sweden has become an increasingly balkanised country. The Swedes who vote for the most pro-immigration parties live in areas where there are no refugees, and thus sometimes struggle to grasp the 'invisible' problem that segregated communities create. Many live in Södermalm,

---

44 Source: https://www.youtube.com/watch?v=rcsG-u2GtZE

one of the most expensive areas of Stockholm where the cool hipsters like the idea of helping 'refugees', perhaps because they never see them. They assume that the social problems have just been whipped up by right-wing ideologues, or at least that is what they have been conditioned to think.

Swedes are increasingly living in a climate of fear and repression, but also in one of sheltered institutional ignorance. If the rapes are mentioned at all, they are committed by Swedes. It is not permitted to give the ethnicity of the rapist. This is doubly pernicious: if, say, the assailant is from North Africa or the Middle East, his identity is protected, and the ethnic Swede is seen as the criminal. Such a policy can only be insulting to its own people, and chimes with the spirit of self-loathing and cultural nihilism propagated by the liberal politicians. There are countless examples of such incidents. Two years ago, an ethnic Swedish woman was gang-raped on a ferry between Stockholm and Turku in Finland. The rapists were called Swedes, but were in fact six Eritreans and one Iraqi.[45] In a perverse turn of events, the rapist is sometimes even seen to be the victim, not the girl that has been raped. We have forgotten that signs of weakness show the opponent that one is vulnerable, and that one's system can be manipulated. Some judges in Sweden seem to be rather deluded, often sentencing Somali rapists (or 'newly arrived Swedes' to use the multiculuralist's language) to fifty hours or so in a detention centre and allowing them to stay in the country.

In neighbouring Norway, politicians and academics (Professor Unni Wikan, Social Anthropology, University of Oslo, 2001 for example) have berated Norwegian girls raped by Muslims for being intolerant, implying that had Norwegian women dressed as Muslims, these assaults would never have happened. At this point, one might recall that in countries that follow the dictates of *shari'ah* law, men can commit rape with impunity because the victim's testimony is inadmissible. If this kind of insulting thinking propagated by Norwegian academics becomes institutionalised — and

---

45 Source: http://www.thelocal.se/20150202/eight-swedes-questioned-over-ferry-gang-rape

there is a real risk of that — then one should expect the indigenous culture to continue to be undermined and marginalised, perhaps to the point of irrelevance. The social norms of the newcomers will take precedence, and perhaps parts of Western Europe will resemble the medieval governance structures of *shari'ah*. We live at a time in which Christ can be depicted in all kinds of defamatory poses, such as when the artist Andres Serrano put a crucifix in a jar of his own urine.[46] However, laughing at Islam merits the *fatwa*. Islamic accommodationism would appear to be the norm in large parts of Western Europe.

Sweden decided that the best way to deal with returning *jihadists* who have raped and pillaged in Syria is to ensure that they are well integrated into a community by giving them a job, free housing and access to benefits. In addition, they promised to cancel their debts. These killers in the name of religion should be looked after, as they will no doubt be traumatised. Denmark has also decided rehabilitation is the best response.

Islamic accommodationism is writ particularly large in cities like Malmö, in southern Sweden, close to Denmark. This city is set to become the first Muslim city in Scandinavia, and will be the site of a new mega-mosque funded by Saudi Wahabi money, the ultra-conservative branch of Sunni Islam that wishes to spread *shari'ah* law across the world. The spread of *shari'ah* law is the macro-strategic goal of the Islamist movement, funded by Saudi Arabia. This is a fundamental part of the Islamist ideology; it compels its subjects to spread the practice of *shari'ah*. From the Saudi perspective (a Muslim country which has not accepted a single refugee), the 'refugee crisis' is effectively *hijrah*, 'the moving into a place to take it for Islam'. The first *hijrah* was by Muhammed in 622 who took his followers from Mecca to Medina. *Da'wah* follows the *hijrah*. *Da'wah* refers to the process where every aspect of society is run in accordance with *shari'ah* law, and it runs in tandem with *jihad*. And, it is important to understand that *da'wah* is a part of Islamic creed. *Da'wah* propagates

---

46 The artist won US$15,000 for the work and was paid US$5,000 of tax-payers' money to do the exhibit.

extreme isolation from Western society, and encourages the creation of parallel Muslim communities run in accordance with *shariah* law which can be used to undermine their adjacent Western communities. The concern is that this is happening now in parts of Western Europe.

The Grand Mosque of Copenhagen opened in 2014. It was funded by Ahlul Bayt Foundation of the Islamic Republic of Iran. The organisation has called for the death of Israel, and is also vociferously opposed to the integration of Muslim immigrants into their host societies. Its centres in Asia and Africa have been used to radicalise local Muslim communities. The prayer room is so large it can host over 3,000 worshippers at a time. In Oxford, the new Oxford Centre for Islamic Studies is much more than any other academic department. It occupies a 3.25 acre site in the centre of Oxford, and includes a mosque with a striking dome and minaret. It took over eleven years to build, and cost more than £75 million. It was funded in part by the late King Fahd of Saudia Arabia.

It is this extreme naïvety that has characterised our universities and immigration policy for years, and particularly so in Sweden. Surely, any reasonable, half intelligent politician or university administrator could see what is really happening, as it is obvious to anybody who has not been subjected to the propaganda. It is clear for instance that the Swedish Muslim Housing Minister had an agenda when he said in October 2014 that the way to tackle ISIS recruitment was for European Governments to give money to the mosques.

Contrary to what the media with its multiculturalist agenda and the Establishment politicians wish us to believe, the problems in Sweden have little to do with 'racism'. It is about the failure of juxtaposing two cultures with utterly alien value systems in a time of turmoil and Islamist terrorism. In response, all the multiculturalist liberals seem capable of is moaning about the 'clash of civilisations rhetoric'. The Left has been conducting an experiment and has used the coercive power of the State to achieve its objectives, but things have gone very badly wrong in the Swedish social laboratory. The changes that have taken place in Swedish society are probably irreversible and will destroy any notion of the *trygghet* that Swedes seek. But worse than this is the fact that Sweden has created a repressive society where none of these important issues can be openly discussed.

If speech attacking a group is prohibited, that group has absolute power. A free society is contingent on the freedom of speech, and a tolerant society does not abandon the freedom to argue. The real problem is that we cannot talk about the problem. If one cannot tell the truth, one does not have one's freedom.

VI

SWEDISH AIR WAVES

> Only the mob and the elite can be attracted by the momentum of totalitarianism itself. The masses have to be won by propaganda.
>
> — HANNAH ARENDT

THE AFTERNOON RADIO PLAY HAS a Soviet feel to it with talk of the *Folkehemmet* ('the people's home'), a name given to the extremely generous, paternalist Swedish welfare state. The play is a twelve-part memoir with subtle undertones of communitarian associations and the conflicting imperatives of authoritarian liberalism: surveillance is the condition of trust, the State with its executive managerialism is the predominant category of political economy. The words are spoken slowly, articulated with great clarity and precision.

In Sweden, there is the sense that radio is creating an explicit 'national imaginary' (Hadlow 2004; Mrázak 2002; Bolton 1999) based on a prescribed repertoire of speech codes and cultural-political grammar. It aims to give 'stories of other worlds' (Abu-Lughod 1995: 191), carefully selected worlds where minorities are always discriminated against in some way or another. This is an ideological process concerned with social relations of power, and in the case of Sweden the State is portrayed as coming to the rescue of victims of these power relations. There is almost a fetishisation of minorities, or anybody who in some way may have been the victim of one form of social injustice or another. A sort of *caritas* FM; this characteristic maximises the role of radio as the *locus* of anti-racist linguistic hegemony.

There is no ideological balance of power on the nation's airwaves. Sweden is in fact what one might call the Gramscian end-game. Gramsci (1971) spoke of how the State would fall into the hands of the Leftists once it captured the commanding organs of culture and media. All that happened long ago in Sweden. Sweden does not have the 'talk radio' culture that America has. Nothing like it. The only outlet for conservative thinkers is the policed Internet. There is the Gramscian discourse, and there is the spiral of silence and self-censorship, previously discussed in the 'The Groupthink Trap' essay.

The Swedes are a microcosm for their quasi-totalitarian Government and its all embracing system of prescriptive thinking. If one criticises the system, one criticises the Swede. The two have become synonymous, coterminous. The individual struggles to differentiate himself from the governing system; the individual and the collective act as one. A quasi-totalitarian State such as this defies Kant's (1993: 30) moral philosophy, which states that moral beings can think for themselves and act on the basis of their independent judgements. And in a society where the historic religion is gradually becoming irrelevant, the State has usurped many of the previous functions of the Church. In Sweden at least, it is there to care for one from the cradle to the grave; it tells one what to think, when to feel guilty, how to express oneself etc., and perhaps most importantly it tells one that there are subjects that can only be discussed if one pursues a certain coded, accommodationist stance.

The radio gives voice and texture to news events, and is of course a public body with an instilled authority. McLuhan (1968: 340-45) speaks of radio as 'the cradle of the collective environment of voices'. With its acoustic authority, radio can have a monopolistic effect in certain communities, and can be indicative of linguistic intimacy, consciousness and acoustic presence. The 'intimacy' of Swedish radio is torn apart by its explicit attempt to appeal synchronically to multi-norms, the cultural and linguistic apartheid that modern Sweden has become.

When it comes to the Swedish radio, there are no normative frames for speech communities. On any single day, one can be acoustically teleported to a Somali, Sámi or Arabic speaking community in contemporary Sweden. All these communities make up apparently the acoustic national imaginary, but of course they do not. Nobody is fluent in all of these minority languages. Instead, it divides the Swedish radio sphere, the acoustic *Lebensraum* into linguistic islands, a discography of strange voices, reinforcing the ethnic separateness that has come to characterise Sweden. The inclusiveness of radio sociality has been undermined by multiculturalist objectives.

The radio crackles into life. It is 'Summer on P1', a very popular Swedish radio programme, P1 being roughly equivalent to Radio 4 in the UK. In the summer months, the programme is broadcast every day. A lady with a soft voice and dulcet tones reads out the programme highlights for the forthcoming week. In one week in the summer of 2015, there were three documentaries on P1 with these titles: 'Does God hate women?'; 'Does God hate homosexuals?'; 'What is Sweden's homosexual geography?' In the final programme, the objective is to understand why there are fewer homosexuals living in the countryside ('Is it because farmers are homophobic…?' is the subtitle). Permutations of these topics crop up time and time again. Three years later it was no different with programmes on sexual domination. There is an obsession with gay rights and feminism on Swedish radio: topics which should have marginal value at best at a time of economic crisis, war and burgeoning extremist movements.

Beyond the series on whether God is homophobic, in the summer of 2015 we were told there will be a series of discussion programmes on menstruation, transsexuality, unrestricted immigration and masturbation. What is more, we can look forward to programmes on discrimination against transsexuals with a focus on how difficult it is to live as a transsexual in Sweden. Despite being considered perhaps the most 'liberal' country in the world, ethnic Swedes are apparently transphobic.

Liberal groupthink and a sense of consensus are created on these radio programmes by choosing people that only represent radical views, quite unashamedly so. Here is a selection of guests in the month of July 2015: Hans Mosesson, who worked with the leftist theatre and musical group, Nationalteatern, Kristina Sandberg, the liberal author, Auschwitz survivor Hédi Fried and Liza Marklund, the multi-millionaire author who will make a special plea for immigration to be completely unrestricted. She would like to see the population of Sweden rise to 180 million (from 9.8 million today).

A week later, a Swedish cartoonist is on the radio, discussing her orgasms. No objective listener could say that this is anything but far left-wing propaganda mixed up with idiotic outpourings blurted out by people with a twisted worldview. The topics chosen are peripheral, trivial, often perverse, and the conversations are one-sided and lack substance.

Does the Swedish media really represent the interests of so many? State media journalists present the image through a demoralising discourse that attacks spiritual values, implying that if one is a true intellectual, one must be an atheist, ready to scorn any higher authority and of course engage with this matrix of preoccupations about minorities. The epistemological assumption is that intellectuals have apparently a monopoly on legitimate forms of knowledge. Religious belief cannot be computed in any scientific fashion, and therefore cannot act as a catalyst to the moral high ground. The Swedish media portrays those who have faith and go to Church as akin to people believing in fairies, lacking in intellectual heft. The media couples intellectual activity with the boorish, profane pursuit of atheism. Religion (unless it is Islam, it would seem) should be trivialised. Christianity might even be considered fundamentalist since it appeals to authorities that are not recognised by the anti-traditionalist media (but once again Islam is an exception). Kalb (2008: 108) speaks of the 'world's turn away from transcendent realities and towards this-worldly constructivism'. That seems to be explicitly the case in Sweden.

If one is a Church-goer, one is not a 'thinking type' and perhaps somehow 'deviant', threatening the secular consensus model that imprisons Swedes intellectually. Swedish journalists and left-wing politicians work in concert to create this image. It is almost unheard of for a Swedish journalist to criticise anything that a politician from the secularist *Miljöpartiet* says, even if the party has shown that it has been infiltrated by Islamists. They share the utopian vision of a world free of borders, and populations enlightened by the abolition of cultural and national identities. They aspire to a Kindergarten view of the world.

Listeners to Swedish public radio are spoon-fed radical feminism and mass immigration rhetoric as this appears to be the rather flimsy intellectual foundation of the Swedish political elite. The radio wishes to continually present Sweden as structurally racist. In doing so, it is almost as if they see it as their job to shield Swedes from the truth of what is happening in their country. It is noticeable that they can only introduce the information in a way that intellectualises it. The information provided on national radio programmes is packaged in often very conceptual ways, sometimes quite abstract, but seldom factual. State media journalists gloss over the facts, and quickly move on to an intellectual discussion.

The journalists know that the average Swede is kind, generous and slightly naïve, and they wish to do everything to perpetuate this naïvety, so that they can continue to promote the multiculturalist agenda by stealth. They also understand that Swedes overwhelmingly comply. Few Swedes would for instance dare criticise immigration policy on the radio, and if there is any risk of doing so, one would have little chance of being invited to participate. Programming for Swedish radio follows an unequivocal liberal-left agenda.

Sweden needs desperately an alternative to State radio; free, private channels where people can call in and speak freely about all the big topics. The silence on the most important topics has meant that alternative media has become increasingly popular. But, one wonders if this will be possible for much longer. Will the next step be for the Government to close down websites that are critical of Sweden's immigration policy? Many fear this is in fact imminent which is why so many (almost all of them) are no longer hosted on .se web addresses. They know they are being monitored by the Big Brother Society.

The content of Swedish State radio programmes and its agenda journalism shows just how ideological the media is, how bound up with the utopian vision they are. This notion of attempting to create a post-racial, post-gender universe is the fanatical iconoclasm of late modernity. Race and gender are part of who we are. Racism is always framed in terms of intolerance, but the media's approach to the subject wishes to prohibit certain speech acts and modes of thinking. It aims to tackle what it perceives as intolerance by imposing its own intolerant, totalitarian system. One cannot beat the State, and in Sweden the media is the State.

A few more turns of the chrome dialing knob, and the radio springs to life with Kurdish folk songs. For five hours every day, Swedish Public Radio (P2) broadcasts live on air in Sweden in the following languages: Finnish, Meänkieli, Sámi, Romani, Albanian, Arabic, Assyrian/Aramaic, Bosnian/Croatian/Serbian, English, Farsi, Kurdish, and Somali. The equivalent in the UK would be to turn on Radio 3 and hear for a couple of hours every day nothing but Polish and Lithuanian. The Swedish acoustic universe is partitioned in a rather essentialist manner by the media into cultural reservoirs of semiotic proportional distribution. This is the State philosophy of egalitarianism, attempting to represent the nation as a linguistic pluralist whole with its internal diversity and is tantamount to what Vidali-Spitulnik (2012: 250-67) calls in a Zambian context 'culturalisation of ethnicity'. Sweden has institutionalised anti-fascism and this has led to a curious obsession with minorities. Hearing such a diversity of languages on private radio channels is something that one could only applaud, but of course this ethnolinguistic democracy in the name of the social imperative of 'inclusion' just results in practice in Swedes turning the radio off. When multilingualism is low, such a cultural codification of diversity cannot achieve its objectives. Swedish radio reproduces unthinkingly the notion that it is a language that emblematises people, and thus hypocritically conforms to the essentialism that they are meant to be distancing themselves from.

There is a tendency to select radio plays that invite a sense of self-loathing, and nurturing of some kind of collective guilt: productions for instance about the Swedish *Rasbiologiinstitutt* (an Institute established in the 1920s and supported by all the political parties with an objective of measuring the racial make-up of the Swedes), Nazi concentration camps to remind listeners of the horrors of racism and to speculate on whether Swedes were somehow complicit. It is not unknown for Swedish radio programmes to exaggerate wildly the scope of the Swedish slave trade on Guadeloupe before it was handed over to the French at the end of the

Napoleonic wars. There is a desire to constantly judge past actions by our own repudiative values.

Radio dramas feature invariably an immigrant who is always cast as the 'victim', bullied at school, denied opportunities etc. One programme recently centred on an Iraqi refugee to Sweden called Fatima. She was encouraged to think about whether she had had any unpleasant experiences as a child that she had never overcome. She spoke of how one day her father made her have her haircut like a boy. Swedish radio was quick to describe this as an 'assault', and devoted a whole programme to what they perceived to be a human rights issue. It is a familiar theme. If the theme is not the hard-done-by 'refugee', the focus is on the Swedes themselves. The intention is often to play on the alleged Swedish complicity in the atrocities committed in the earlier part of the twentieth century during the Second World War, and to portray the ethnic Swede as somehow the arrogant, racist colonial master. The implication being always that we must make amends, even if the fabricated image is of course far from the truth.

Artists, playwrights and authors with foreign background are often interviewed on P1 and asked to talk about the 'racism' they experienced. The assumption is that Sweden must be racist, and that the immigrant must somehow feel like a victim. Plays are chosen for their anti-racist agenda, and the Swede is presented as the guilty party. The implication is that to cleanse this image, Sweden must play the humanitarian superpower, be the conscience of the world (even if it is per capita the world's third largest arms exporter).[1] It is a peculiar variety of nihilistic propaganda which leaves one struggling to come up with historical precedents. It is not possible to eliminate all inequalities among human beings. The Swedish media is failing its own people by focusing somewhat exclusively on such overly politicised themes.

In July 2015, there was a programme on P1 on child abuse. As always, it is obvious from the reporting that it is the 'ethnic Swede' that is guilty. And yet when the reports are followed up with individuals, often related

---

1   Source: Stockholm International Peace Research Institute (2014).

to the assailant, it is evident in fact that the offender is not a Swede, as he invariably does not speak Swedish. It is very disconcerting to see programmes aimed at Swedish men in this manner, especially as so many of these effete, androgynous men do not seem capable of speaking up for themselves. National radio is clearly being run by a group of radical, left-wing feminists. Man-hating is a theme in these Swedish radio plays. There is a temptation to portray men as misanthropic pre-rapists, but only if they are white ethnic Swedes. One is left wondering whether these editors really understand the purpose of journalism, or whether they are just blindly following a culturally nihilistic Government agenda. Along with the judiciary, they just seem to want to make a career out of obsessing over 'equality' and other such shallow thinking best reserved for demure housewives.

It is State feminism and anti-racism devoid of common sense.[2] Men are often portrayed as potential enemies. Women are the 'victims' and thus they are by definition right, as he or she who has achieved victim status is never in the wrong. In a fraudulent manner, Swedish politicians explain away the sudden increase in rape by claiming that men are having trouble dealing with gender equality or the 'feminist revolution'. But, femininity is also being demonised, in Sweden at least. If women do not describe themselves as 'feminists', then they are not considered real women. If men do not describe themselves as feminists, they are considered sexist. Both men and women are deviant if they do not behave within the constraints of the State ideological norm. There is no established alternative voice in Swedish media. There is no space for the non-feminist, and the anti-feminist might be guilty of hate-speech. By only giving voice to the feminist, the media wants us to believe that the non-feminist simply does not exist, and so selection of radio themes serves the same objectives as political correctness.

---

2   Even in the 2016 Swedish Government Budget Statement, the Government describes its philosophy as 'feminist': 'The proposals are informed by a feminist philosophy based on...'. Available at: http://www.government.se/articles/2015/09/the-2016-budget-in-five-minutes/

There is a very different kind of journalism in Sweden as compared to the UK. Swedes do not seem particularly interested in making headlines. If rapes in the UK had increased astronomically, newspapers would report it and it would be all over the front pages. That is because the print media in the UK at least works as a 'checks and balances' mechanism. Journalists in the UK would crave this kind of factual information because it could mean they could expose something or somebody. This element of shock exposure seems to me to be very important to journalism in the UK, but is curiously absent in Sweden. One can only assume it is because Swedish editors would not accept these articles because they have been told such sensitive topics are unacceptable. Journalists who are keen to advance their careers know that they have to tow the line. This goes against, no doubt, many of the perceptions that people have of Sweden and its media, but it is true. Like so many other aspects of Swedish society, the media's principal focus is 'control'.

The irony is that Sweden was in 1766 the first country in the world to abolish censorship and guarantee the freedom of the Press. Sweden has gone from being a freedom advocate to a subtle, pseudo-totalitarian state; this sounds like an oxymoron, but in this case it would appear not to be.[3] It is important to understand that there is no freedom of the press in Sweden; unlike in neighbouring Finland, the newspapers have been partially subsidised by the Government since 1971.[4] According to the former Swedish Minister for Culture and Sports, Lena Adelsohn-Liljeroth, newspapers that criticise immigration policy or multiculturalism will be threatened with subsidy removal.[5] For the more indoctrinated journalists, there is little risk that the subsidy will be in fact removed for many of them perceive criticism of immigration policy to be a form of 'hate-speech'. And thus, we have a situation where the Government reports the 'facts', and

---

3   Available at: https://www.britannica.com/topic/Freedom-of-the-Press-Act-of-1766
4   Available at: https://reutersinstitute.politics.ox.ac.uk/sites/default/files/Press%20Subsidies%20%26%20Local%20News%20the%20Swedish%20Case_0.pdf
5   Source: SVT debate, 27th September 2013.

the newspapers reproduce it. When one reads newspapers in Sweden, one is not reading the news, but State propaganda. In 2013, the Government made it possible for police to access IP addresses in order to identify when 'online hate-crimes' occurred, and granted the Swedish Media Council SEK 1 million for initiatives to combat online xenophobia, sexism and similar forms of intolerance.[6]

In such a context where editors of Swedish newspapers are not only accountable for all content published on the newspaper's website, but also for all the archived material put online by their predecessors, it is not surprising that voices of dissent are few and far between.[7] As with the multi-party political system, the Swedish media looks extremely democratic and diverse with its seventy-eight daily newspapers (2007 statistics), but they are subsidised to say more or less the same thing.[8] It is a 'smoke and mirrors' democracy with allusions to free speech. It says quite a lot about a country when the leading newspaper with the widest circulation (*Aftonbladet*) is controlled by the Swedish Trade Union Confederation, and when politicians debate whether private individuals should be able to own satellite dishes.[9] The news reporting on television is so biased that high-profile news presenters have resigned. The key positions in the media are filled by the Social Democratic party. It is extraordinary to think this can happen in a Western democracy which is billed as one of the most 'free and open' states in the world.

It is a similar story with Swedish radio. There was no commercial radio at all until 1993, and then it was only reluctantly allowed after many

---

6 Available at: https://freedomhouse.org/report/freedom-press/2015/sweden
7 Available at: https://freedomhouse.org/report/freedom-press/2016/sweden
8 Available at: https://www.ofcom.org.uk/__data/assets/pdf_file/0021/23952/subsidies.pdf
9 Private individuals are not allowed to own satellite dishes in some countries such as Singapore where the People's Action Party (PAP) has maintained its unbroken rule in Government since 1959. One reason contributing to the ruling party's predominance is their strong control of the Press and the news media.

years of debate.[10] Today, 35 per cent of the content is from commercial radio, but news items are produced centrally. Thus, there are no originally produced news items, and few alternatives to the feminist, multiculturalist State propaganda. When it comes to the media in Sweden, change is cosmetic (and not real). As mentioned previously, where Swedish media is concerned, there is a disturbing silence regarding the big topics. If one constantly cuts out the voice of opposition, one risks creating a very volatile and explosive situation. We are moving towards a state of psychological warfare, and in Sweden this is happening at a time when society is in great flux.

It is not really totalitarianism, not of the Soviet type with the secret police and *samizdat* publishing. There are few dissidents amongst the intelligentsia. There are of course no gulags; nobody is being put up against the wall and being shot. One language and one norm are needed for that kind of totalitarianism. Instead, it is more akin to a kind of rational totalitarianism. Whatever one chooses to call it, all ideologies have to some degree totalitarian elements or at least mechanisms for enforcing their legitimacy. The template that successive Swedish Social Democrat Governments have been trying to create is one of a social, humanistic utopia. Governments in centralised Sweden have had the power to implement policies and operationalise control mechanisms over the Swedes. Other Governments could only have dreamt of having this kind of power and control where for decades the same party could continue to implement its *Folkehemmet* policies.

It might be an understatement to say that totalitarianism has an intolerance for autonomy and freedom. Totalitarianism is a state of mind that at its extreme attempts to destroy private opinion and transcend the human condition. The current status quo in parts of the West is that the private opinion, if it does not adhere to the liberal, multiculturalist outlook, has been silenced (but not destroyed). If people think they want to say something which might not adhere to the supposed liberal consensus

---

10 Source: http://www.pressreference.com/Sw-Ur/Sweden.html

or something that is considered politically incorrect, they look around before saying it. The PC police are in your heads.

In an environment of an ideologised public consciousness, nobody wants to be caught apparently swearing allegiance to a heretical philosophy. A significant freedom is being erased. The last time we lived in this kind of context must have been in a totalitarian society. This time around, the dissidents are not marginalised intellectuals (as in the Soviet Union), but those who paradoxically enough speak up for the cultural heritage and traditions of the country, be it Sweden or Britain. They are in a sense, curiously enough, what one might call anti-dissidents as they are dissenting against the State-supported undermining of their own indigenous culture. Their opposition is against an anti-culture; it is perhaps the national Governments and the EU that are the dissidents as they are embracing a muddled ideology of multiculturalism which is misrepresented as egalitarian. Ideological struggles were pushed 'underground' in the Soviet Union, but in multiculturalist Europe, they appear on the Internet, the modern platform for political dissent where opponents to the mass liberal consciousness are monitored in microscopic detail by the State, using the latest search tools.

Totalitarianism is a form of State-sanctioned authoritarianism that historically speaking, Nazism aside, has gone hand-in-hand with Leftist thinking. A totalitarian regime is informed first and foremost by an ideology, and this ideology penetrates all aspects of social life, curtailing individual freedom and stifling creativity. Totalitarianism 'liquidates its internal enemies' (Revel, 1985: 4). The objective is for the Government to control the thoughts and actions of its citizens. Totalitarianism is now reasserting itself in new forms: surveillance is total and privacy is being decimated. The little bit of privacy left is even in some cases being monetised. Much of this extraordinarily banal content now appears as reality TV. Every human act is now fodder for social media in the endless public display of the Self. The GPS on our phones track our whereabouts, and all digital communication is passed through centralised servers and kept in storage banks (alongside one's DNA if one has committed a crime).

Some companies in America are now using facial recognition software and biometric technologies which will be able to detect and identify anybody. Indeed, such software showed that some of the 'child refugees' from Syria were in fact nearly forty years old. Whole cities in America, such as Baltimore, are being spied on by the police day and night. The police have adopted a surveillance system used in Iraq, whereby they fly Cessna aeroplanes over cities with wide-angle 200 megapixel cameras capturing an area of thirty square miles that continuously transmit real-time images to analysts on the ground. Everything is recorded, every movement, and all images can be played back and fast-forwarded. These surveillance aeroplanes were flying for over six months before people realised what was going on. No public disclosure of the programme had ever been made.[11]

Mass surveillance is emerging in a context of the polarising, totalitarian language of Leftist institutions. Such language is increasingly unchallenged, and has filtered through most of the strata of our society. As in any totalitarian regime, language in the West is manipulated and employed as a form of Orwellian doublespeak where words used as slogans have come to mean the opposite of their defined meaning. There has been rather thorough semantic recoding. The meaning of words has become sufficiently destabilised, and the truth is becoming blurred. Thus, 'tolerance' means privilege status for the ideologically protected.

'Democracy' is considered something beyond reproach, but when used as a slogan by the multiculturalist it seldom refers to the democratic process. Instead, it is more likely to refer to the 'democratic rights' of minorities which Drummond (2014: 178) describes as 'sacred' in a multicultural society. Following the failure of two previous totalitarian regimes, people have been led to believe that 'democracy' is unquestionably the best model of government in every sense. To even question the supposed infallibility of democracy as a model is semi-scandalous. And so using the word deceptively to refer to the 'rights' of the 'persecuted', one creates a statement whose falsification would be socially quite unacceptable.

---

11 Source: https://www.bloomberg.com/features/2016-baltimore-secret-surveillance/

The idea that democracy is always the best form of government irrespective of the country's political history has become a truism, even if only half the population vote, and the winner in the American version is often determined by which candidate has the most money to spend. It is as if 51 per cent of the electorate vote for one party, then that party is able to do what it likes and we should support it nonetheless in the name of 'democracy'. Individuals should have certain inalienable rights akin to the American Bill of Rights that are off-limits for an incoming government. Many countries such as Sweden and Germany where individual freedoms are being undermined by the State would benefit greatly from such legislation.

Unlike in many parliamentary elections, democracy becomes the champion in national referendums, because here voters know that their vote can actually make a difference. Switzerland is a model for democracy, not Sweden. And of course, the Brexit referendum with a 72 per cent turnout was democracy working at its very best. People went out to vote because they knew the result could actually lead to change, unlike with a General Election. Transforming the demographic and ethnic make-up of a nation and pursuing utopian, federalist fantasies without public or parliamentary debate is democracy at its worst.

The totalitarian multiculturalists, the pioneers of cultural entropy and repudiation, believe they are right by definition. This form of totalitarianism is being led by the antagonistic post-modern Left (more so than what one may call the traditional Left), and by, in particular, academics, bureaucrats and journalists, some of whom refuse to accept the inherent values of the West: the very people whose role in society is surely to promote and ensure an open and fair intellectual discussion. Herein lies a paradox: the enemies of freedom are disguised as the guardians of tolerance and openness. And the so-called victims are often 'quite proud of their intolerant traditions' (Drummond, 2014: 178).

Unlike Russia, Sweden is not an authoritarian State. There is no monopoly on political power, and its leader is by no stretch of the imagination a demagogue. Instead of a charismatic leader, Sweden has an insipid trade unionist who is inclined to feel sorry for himself. Neither is there any demagogic control of the psychology of the masses for which there is normally required some kind of appeal to a religious basis (Le Bon, 1982: 36). Huntford (1971) describes the situation in Sweden as 'benign totalitarianism'. He showed how the Swedes sacrificed personal liberty in order to have a 'benevolent' modern welfare state. Undoubtedly, this has been the case. These observations ring true in the context of the discussion about home-schooling in Sweden. Home-schooling has been effectively banned (except in very few exceptional cases). Those that want their children to be home-schooled have left the country because the fines are so onerous. With cases like this and others, it seems that Sweden does not want the individual to think for himself, especially not in an educational context. For a country that loves to talk about human rights, it is ironic that when it comes to freedom, certain fundamental rights appear to be denied to Swedes. People who like to rule over others have understood for a long time that if one can create dependence on the system that one is trying to build, the job of ruling becomes a lot easier. And the Swedes are certainly dependent on their system, many quite happily so as it is so generous.

Whilst much of what Huntford writes about in his book still stands, the current totalitarianism is of a different kind because it embraces what the State calls multiculturalism (as has been observed, it is not very *multi-*). Given that we live in an age of Islamist terrorism, one might not wish to call it 'benign'. Huntford concludes (1971: 285): 'To judge solely by its mass media, Sweden appears to be run by a tolerant dictatorship. Press, radio and TV show remarkable similarity, as if guided by some Ministry of Propaganda'. And so it is the case that totalitarianism of this kind can exist without tyranny and charismatic leaders. It is an attempt to govern 'in the name of the truth'. Sweden wishes to imprison its members in regimes of truth. In the twenty-first century, the regime operates in a context of technological and media control where 'acoustic and audiovisual media have a particular media for exercising political power' (Zakharine, 2010: 158).

No totalitarian state of the twentieth century had anything like the kind of power that modern communication technology enables where digital surveillance systems can tap into every conceivable mode of communication and collect endless amounts of mass metadata on every citizen. With such extraordinary capabilities, the Internet could soon become a force of oppressive control in a post-Orwellian world instead of a force for democratisation. It would seem the conditions for a new totalitarianism are already in fact in place. Our lives have been technologised and the five companies that monitor our every movement are all Californian companies that endorse the globalist liberal-left agenda. What is more, there is now one principal source of knowledge: Google, an omnipresent, omniscient (one might say) company embedded in the social justice warrior ideology. This alone should be cause for alarm.

Once again, in this domain, Sweden has managed to engineer an image of the ultimate free, open country, an image that is at odds with the truth. We know for instance from Edward Snowden that Sweden is a key partner to the US in mass Internet surveillance, and the Swedish FRA law (broadly in line with the proposed 'snooper charter' in the UK, and far beyond the scope of surveillance sanctioned by the European Commission) permits rather broad snooping.[12] The Swedish state keeps a record of everything said in telephone conversations, surfed on the web or written on the Internet. The entire population is tapped all the time, and no courts are involved. By law, every telephone and Internet operator in Sweden has to have a cable linked to the Government's server. Every single piece of communication is examined using 250,000 search criteria.[13] Technological and digital registration means that we have little choice but to hand over control and surveillance to potentially a small number of people who may at some point in the future and for a variety of reasons abuse the control they have over the data. Once again,

---

12 It is perhaps worth pausing for thought at this moment, and bearing in mind that the US is a country that has, with the exception of five years, been at war for its entire existence.

13 Source: https://policyreview.info/articles/analysis/do-swedes-do-internet-policy-and-regulation-sweden-snapshot

transparency is particularly poor in Sweden. The Stasi could only have dreamt of this kind of surveillance.

From the Snowden leaks, it can be ascertained that Sweden spied on Russian leaders, and shared the data with the US. Leaked documents show that Sweden is a key NSA collaborator because 80 per cent of Russia's Internet traffic passes through Sweden.[14] Once again the traditional image of Sweden as a politically neutral, pacifist country was shattered. Wikileaks from 2011 show that Sweden adopted the new controversial wiretapping law because they were under pressure from the NSA. The whole Snowden case shows how truth-telling has been problematised in contemporary 'democratic politics'. It might be perceived to be 'unpatriotic' to reveal the truth that the NSA spies systematically on its citizens all of the time, and to demonstrate that various Government and NSA officials lied under oath when talking about these revelations.

Sweden had a bilateral agreement with the NSA long before the FRA law was introduced, and Snowden reported that the NSA gave Sweden access to XKeyscore, the most comprehensive system that allows the monitoring and wire-tapping of millions of people worldwide.[15] XKeyscore is a gigantic electronic trawler that can search in real time through tapped fibre optic networks, satellite links and enormous electronic databases. So, for instance, it could give lists of people in Sweden that visit a certain anti-immigration forum. In Sweden and elsewhere, there appears to be a collective indifference to the growth of the surveillance state. People feel with a sense of holistic resignation and disempowerment that it is just completely beyond their control. In a 'securitised' world, individual liberty is crushed, and we are left feeling helpless because the threat is felt to be existential. Through the 'grammar of security', the threat is felt to be immediate and ubiquitous. In Sweden, the threat can be real. People who have been critical of immigration policy have had Swedish journalists

---

14 Available at: http://www.globalresearch.ca/swedish-intelligence-service-spying-on-russia-for-us-national-security-agency/5362967

15 Source: http://www.svt.se/ug/read-the-snowden-documents-from-the-nsa

knock on their door, threatening to 'expose them'. ISPs must be passing on data to journalists (perhaps via the Government). There can be no other explanation.

Electorally speaking, Sweden does not feel like the open democracy par excellence that people believe it to be either. At the polling booth in Sweden, the voter is invited to take a slip for the party that he wishes to vote for. If the voter wishes his voting intentions to be private, he would have to take several slips of paper to disguise who he intends to vote for. One might infer that voting is done in this manner to deter people voting for SD, the anti-mass immigration party.

Totalitarianism can come about in various different ways, but one way Sweden attempts to control its people is by the media telling them what to think. This is at least the view of the editor of the major Danish newspaper, *Berlingske*, Anne Knudsen. This kind of control is not new. Sweden has for centuries rather obsessively collected large amounts of data on its people. From 1686 onwards, laws regulating parish registers came into effect. The State collected comprehensive demographic data on population structure, mortality, fertility, health, marriage, occupation, illegitimacy, migration etc. The primary purpose of this was for the clergy who were State employees to control the Christian and moral belief of their parishioners (specifically to collect information on people's knowledge of the catechism), and to keep track of the population (Sogner, 2016: 443). Sweden boasts amongst the most comprehensive historic demographic records in the world, and is therefore of much interest to academic demographers. This obsessive control took a controversial turn during the 1930s when the State started to sterilise young women that it thought might pose a threat to society because of mental illness, feeble-mindedness or social problems. These policies lasted for forty years and were arguably an extreme attempt at 'controlling' the future behaviour of Swedish citizens. This is apparent when one looks at the census in 1970 where there was an enormous amount of information collected on almost every Swedish citizen. However, these reproduction policies which the Swedish media loves to discuss were not connected with ideological goals of the State, and thus comparisons to Nazi Germany are largely unjust. Nowadays, with ID numbers and mass electronic surveillance, control has become so effortless few would ever question it. This is a country where one cannot even order a bathtub without an ID number.

VII

Societies at Risk

> This multicultural approach, saying that we simply live side by side and live happily with each other has failed. Utterly failed.
> — Angela Merkel

Can a human society where inherited forms are under constant attack survive in the absence of tradition and conservative forces? We will discover here that our explicit attempt to create a so-called 'multicultural' society is based on perverse thinking. In the case of Sweden, we are importing outsiderhood and dependents, breaking up organic communities and replacing them with a generation of individuals whose roots rather obviously belong elsewhere. Intercultural fluidity exists and the aesthetics of modernity can be challenged, but the idea that we are all somehow 'citizens of the world' evokes a fake universality. It might give some hope to confused transnationals, but is ultimately a meaningless objective that tries to conjure up a false, Panglossian worldview where 'everything is the best in the best of all possible worlds'. The idea that we should all be these rootless, globalised citizens of a utopian, multicultural world where we have forgotten there are limits to growth has been coupled with the notion of a 'progressive' society, the *sine qua non* of modernity.

The contemporary cultural imperative in the West is to be 'progressive', but there is zero critical thinking as to what 'progress' really should mean in our overpopulated, *panem et circenses* consumerist-obsessed societies where materialism is coupled with intellectual regress. The consumer good is the *summum bonum* in the world where the transcendent in any of its permutations (cultural, religious or otherwise) is frequently ridiculed. In such a society, one sometimes finds even a contempt for learning. Kalb (2008: 4) describes 'progress' as 'in effect, movement to the Left', and at a meta-level, that is of course correct. But, meta-politics aside, one might question whether it is progress if modern, secular society erases any moral teleology, and is reduced to little more than hyper-consumerism. Is it progress if we live in a world where children grow up knowing nothing about their cultural heritage? Is it progress if Christian holidays become nothing more than consumerist orgies where any public display of Christian iconography is considered multiculturally insensitive? Well, it certainly is for those that cheer these kinds of secularist practices which chime so conspicuously with the totalitarianism of Nazism and Communism. In Nazi Germany, ideologues saw religion as an enemy of the totalitarian state. It was the same in 1980s Ceaușescu Romania where massive apartment blocks were built in front of churches in order to conceal them from view.[1] In liberal democracies, multiculturalist secularists see religion as an enemy of 'progressive liberalism'.

In the long term, this will surely unravel somehow. The liberal centre will not hold; even some liberals now recognise that the ideology that was once based on rationality is no longer rational. When one looks at developments on American campuses, few rational people could claim that they are the outcomes of a liberal consciousness. Identity liberalism has had its day, and left a deep scar on our public institutions. It is time for a post-identity liberalism to return to its rational roots. One cannot organise a society along the lines of consumerism and political correctness without it looking eventually like little more than a self-parody. These are not 'real' connections. At some point, any such society will surely implode and people will be left looking for a more transcendental dimension. Now that we live in a continent where a Catholic priest is beheaded during a Church service in a sleepy French town or where a Belgian priest is stabbed by an asylum seeker whom he is trying to help, the secularisation multiculturalist project pursued by the liberals might perhaps be reassessed.[2]

---

1   In Romania, I have seen great crowds queue to enter churches at Easter in the way that shoppers in the West queue outside department stores on Boxing Day.

2   Available at: http://www.telegraph.co.uk/news/2016/08/01/belgian-priest-stabbed-in-his-home-after-refusing-to-give-cash-t/

What some perceive as 'progress' may be nothing more than ongoing decline. Taking people away from their roots and placing them in some kind of egalitarian cultural soup might not result in 'progress', but might be a formula for disaster for the regressive liberals that spearhead these changes. It collapses the bonds which tie people together, destabilises the moral consensus and risks turning a country into a schizophrenic army of conflicting personalities. In the name of cultural relativism, Norway abolished in 2012 the State-sponsored Church of Norway ending a 1,000 year tradition. The nation no longer has an official religion.[3] This radical change was framed in terms of 'progress' and 'freedom', but it has nothing to do with either. Those who practice other religions are free to practice in Norway. Norway wants to escape from religion, but it has just sleepwalked into another religion of rational, consumerist scientism. The new religion is based on political correctness, feminism and egalitarianism. Practicing an ancient religion might even be considered by some to be politically incorrect, unless it is Islam of course. When it comes to the treatment of Islam in the West, it seems that cultural relativism even trumps equal rights for women.

One wonders how far we might go with this rather extreme cultural relativism and equality demagoguery. At Palaiseau, 17th December 2008, President Nicolas Sarkozy said that the challenge of the twenty-first century was interracial marriage (*métissage* 'miscegenation').[4] Ten years later, President Macron spoke in very similar terms in Brussels. If white ethnic French did not submit to it, Sarkozy promised that the State would take measures to force it upon them. This is still the thinking of some of our leaders today who nurture a strange fantasy of a multiculturalist utopia, apparently in the name of equality and diversity, the *a priori* apodictic cultural truths. Certain politicians speak of these notions as if they have

---

3   Source: http://www.loc.gov/law/foreign-news/article/norway-change-in-churchstate-relations/

4   Available at: https://www.youtube.com/watch?v=qwPPRYl0xQE. An extraordinary speech which he must have regretted after the change in the political climate in France eight years later when he lost the the Republican candidacy to Fillon.

become entirely incontestable. But, following the rapid increase in the popularity of the alternative Right, their claims are being dismantled bit by bit, sometimes (as in the case of Sarkozy) by the same people that promoted such thinking. They have perhaps paused to remember the lessons of Soviet Communism — manufactured utopias are self-destructive and end in failure.

Some of our leaders demonstrate a hatred for the West and the whole superstructure that has put them in the privileged position that they occupy. If we wish to preserve our culture, these people would need to be voted out of office, for otherwise the guardians of our civilisation risk disappearing. Echoing Sarkozy, Frans Timmermans, a Dutch diplomat and Vice-President of the European Commission, made recently a disquieting speech saying that 'Europe must face diversity or face war'.[5] He urged all members of the EU parliament to increase efforts to '*erase* single, monocultural nation-states'. It is no wonder that Iceland and the Faroes lost interest in joining (or rejoining) the EU. One does not want to give up a culture established over centuries, just so it can be replaced with an incoherent muddle. One does not want to be 'erased' for having a sense of national identity, and one certainly does not want to be told to do so by an overpaid, unelected good-for-nothing bureaucrat. Very soon, such speeches, which are online and available for the world to see, will backfire and destroy the careers of these individuals. The sentiment is changing very fast, and they risk looking like vacuous demagogues of diversity who are promoting ideas which are self-destructive, and ultimately serve an abstract concept and nothing more.

Peter Sutherland, the late UN special representative for migration, non-executive Chairman of Goldman Sachs and Bilderberg Group member said in 2012 that the EU should 'do its best to undermine the homogeneity of its member states'.[6] In a separate discussion, he said that sovereignty must end. Three years later, this globalist with diplomatic

---

5 Available at: https://www.youtube.com/watch?v=q94syUDDhxA
6 Source: http://www.bbc.co.uk/news/uk-politics-18519395

immunity appealed for unlimited immigration into Europe from Africa. With Heads of State, European Commissioners and billionaires such as George Soros talking like this, it is not surprising that there is conspiratorial talk of a globalist destabilisation programme whereby globalists step in to run great trading blocs once the complete chaos that they have engineered ensues. One might think of this as the economic version of the migration crisis. It is certainly the case that destabilisation programmes have been discussed before. We know from General Wesley Clark that the US had planned a mass destabilisation programme after 9/11 with the plan to invade seven countries in the Middle East.[7]

If there is no conspiracy, then multiculturalist liberals have seriously misunderstood the multicultural project. The people coming to Western Europe from the Middle East and North Africa are considerably less liberal than the people here already. The result will not be the liberal, atheistic paradise they crave. They are peddling a new consciousness, but it is a false one. It might be an illiberal theocratic society based on *shari'ah* law juxtaposed to a Western, secular society. Islam as it is spelled out in the Qur'an (and not necessarily as it is practiced by the millions of moderate Muslims) is illiberalism as a religion and is based on a contrary civilisation.

It represents a different way of being human, for it is total and absolute; it is absolutism as enforced uniformity and these pressures can lead to demagoguery, as we have seen with Gaddafi, Hussein, Assad etc. The West has drifted into secularism to such an extent that it could not even begin to understand the metaphysical objectivism which is so absolute in Islam. Muslims must surrender to the slavery of God — a concept that is complete anathema for people living in the West, even Christians. If one cuts off the matrix of relations embodied in history which define who we are but which are external to us, then one cuts off an individual's vitality, and leaves him 'etherised upon a table'.[8] If one were to run around a town in Nietzschean fashion in the West shouting

---

7   Source: https://www.youtube.com/watch?v=9RC1Mepk_Sw
8   Source: T.S. Eliot, The Love Song of J. Alfred Prufrock.

'God is dead', people would just ignore you, shrug their shoulders and think you were mad. They might even laugh. This is the extent to which we have lost our theological foundation. If one did this in parts of the Middle East, one would have insulted the prophet, and might face the death penalty under *shari'ah* law. This is the extent of the culture clash we are busy orchestrating.

One must remember that a community is more than just wages and consumer goods. How can one have a *Gemeinschaft* ('community') if people have nothing *gemein* ('in common')? To have a big welfare state such as Sweden, one needs a proportionate sense of commonality, not a pre-existing national commonality based on some kind of Herderian romantic *Volksgeist*, but one based more simply on an agreement on and sharing of the procedures, precepts and institutions that make up the country. A nation's culture is its proverbial glue binding together these institutions and its citizens. It implies a sense of shared process. One would have thought this was rather obvious, and yet reductive liberalism wants to undo this collective identity, erase our common habits and loyalties, remove our badges of membership, dismantle our meanings and beliefs, which have been inherited from generation to generation. The modern liberal instruction is that we must question orthodoxy (in all its guises) — the default position of mankind. The Christian West must constantly question its roots and belief systems, but Islam forbids investigation into the origins of the Qur'an. Just imagine the hullabaloo that would have ensued had *The Life of Brian* been about Muhammed, and not Christ. John Cleese would have been hanging from a mature English Oak tree.

Multiculturalism and the political correctness that guides it amounts to an oxymoronically sounding 'dictatorship of virtue' (Bernstein, 1995). It emerged from the laudable impulses of the American civil rights movement, but has become quasi-dictatorial in nature as it attempts to demonise any opposition and seeks complete and absolute ideological control over people in the West. Bernstein shows how multiculturalism is a code-word for an expanded concept of moral and cultural relativism, and that this relativism has become the orthodoxy of our age. It acts as a form of totalitarian thinking because nobody wants to appear to be against it, and 'hiding behind the innocuous, unobjectionable and entirely praiseworthy goal of eliminating prejudice from the human heart lies a certain ideology, a control of language' (1995: 36). Bernstein called multiculturalism 'nobility perverted' (1995: 11): it appears as something noble, but its effect is alienating and self-condemning unless one is a minority. Courage and 'nobility' will be required to transgress this dictatorship of virtue. Bernstein's description could be no more fitting than in a place like Sweden where virtue as meant here is put on a pedestal.

Despite all the rhetoric, the objective of eliminating all prejudice by creating multi-ethnic societies might seem praiseworthy, but it is in fact, one suspects, a rather shallow ideal. It is largely unrealistic and might even be the stuff of fairy-tales. It is not valid in any way as a policy for a Government that sees itself as something more than *Blue Peter*, something more than naïve, blind liberalism which many Swedish politicians seem to stand for.

A society with a tightly shared culture and inviolable principles at its core, where there prevails a clear collective sense of 'who we are', and a love for one's fellow men, will be replaced by a muddled, confused or worse, conflicting imbroglio because a pluralism of diverse values leads to a loss of social solidarity. There might not even be any shared sense of what the nasty prejudice that certain politicians wish to eliminate actually amounts to. A so-called multicultural society — and by that is meant a formerly rather homogeneous society along ethnic grounds that has through a system of open borders allowed millions representing very different cultural and moral values to settle in its land (and not a society that has had historically diverse ethnic groups) — is one that is prone to conflict if the incomers represent a culture or religion which teach a different interpretation of tolerance to that that exists already in the country. With this admittedly rather narrow definition, one has of course Sweden in mind, where tradition as a source of insight is inclined to be denigrated.

The contemporary cultural grammar does not permit a distinction to be drawn between culture and race. And thus one risks being accused erroneously of preferring a world with one dominant, single race, which is certainly not the case. The deduction is flawed, but convenient, because of the Nazism precedent. And thus, it opens the door to the new cultural grammar lexicon — the universe of -*ist* suffixing adjectives to be employed at every conceivable occasion.

Multiculturalism, as it has been practiced, is in essence an anti-European, anti-White ideology with political correctness, the legacy of Blairism, as its doctrine. A doctrine which when combined with the economic management of the EU has left parts of the European continent hamstrung and paralysed in both material and non-material terms. In Sweden, this multiculturalist ideology manifests itself in what one might call the 'politics of folly', putting fabricated emotion before reason; folly because it represents the pursuit of policies which are ostensibly against Sweden's own national interest.

Multiculturalism might be perceived to be the result of relativism, or racism, post-modernism, multiculturalism and deconstructionism can be seen as the intellectual descendants of relativism; but it goes one stage further than that. Multiculturalism is a politicised form of relativism, since the incoming culture is given preferential treatment, often explicitly so as we saw with hate-speech legislation. In practice, it is thus not about treating cultures equally. Cultures in any case have a determinate content; they represent worldviews and function to exclude other cultures. If one tries to destroy the common culture, one runs the risk of being left with an anarchising society as the foundational matrix of values is washed away. The 'progressive' impulse in the Western mode of consciousness threatens the foundations of culture and erodes the basis of belief because it is an agenda based on constant change. In this sense, conservatism is anti-ideological because in contrast to liberalism, it is based on a system of fixed, guiding principles.

Unlike cultural relativism, multiculturalism excludes the worldview of Western civilisation because it is perceived to be elitist and sexist, as it is thought to be exclusively the product of white heterosexual males — those enemies of anti-individualistic liberal fascism where each person is expected to agree with the judgements of the group. There is no place for the autonomous thinking individual in this rather vulgar, secular worldview. If one has a certain name, speaks with a certain accent, dresses in a certain way, then one will be assigned irrevocably to an out-of-favour group and discriminated against. The individual will be burdened with a politicised collective guilt which is a conduit for the liberal principles of egalitarianism and anti-discrimination, pursued so obsessively and unthinkingly. Europe is paralysed by the memory of Nazism, but no German of my generation or my parents' generation can possibly internalise this neurotic guilt. A 'strong' nation cannot constantly ruminate on old evils.

Images of multiculturalism are being pressed on the Swede everywhere he goes in an attempt to dictate the impression that this is the norm. Billboards and advertisements for furniture and any number of things for the home are always multi-ethnic, showing typically black men with Swedish girls (interestingly, it is always the Swedish girl with the Muslim or the black man and not vice versa); the interracial relationship is the expected norm, just as Sarkozy insisted. A monochromatic advert might be 'racist'.

A recent Volvo car advert features mainly ethnic minorities in what might be called a quintessential Swedish landscape. It is a conspicuous attempt to change the way we think, a clear attempt to superimpose a multicultural trope on what for centuries has been a rather monocultural human landscape. This kind of racial profiling in favour of ethnic minorities is to be found right across Western Europe, in every magazine, on every billboard. There is a fear of presenting anything as monoracial, as this will fall foul of the diversity prerogative. Compliance with the regime is not only essential, it is monitored. UKIP was accused of being 'racist' by a BBC journalist for not including more photographs of ethnic minorities in their election campaign literature. That does not constitute racism. This kind of smearing left-wing bigotry that UKIP and other anti-immigration parties faced should be silenced in the same way that the Left has silenced any dissenting voices. As with the Swedish media, the BBC is always investigating some case or other on the grounds of alleged racism. The concept of 'diversity' as applied is arguably racist because it means in practice 'anti-white'. If a place is considered 'diverse', it means simply there are very few white people around. 'Multiculturalism' and 'diversity' can be understood as code words for suppression and discrimination against white people.

These are concepts that are only found in countries which are majority white (Western Europe, US, Canada, Australia etc.), so it is not surprising that some colourful political commentators label this as 'white genocide'. It is the ultimate paradox: it is self-imposed auto-ethnic repudiation or self-hating neurosis by white people, and one is not permitted to speak out against it. One wonders whether this has ever happened before, and so overtly. On the 23rd of November 2015, Green Party MP Stefanie von Berg spoke in the Bundestag of how it would be a good thing when ethnic Germans are a minority in their own cities.[9] In Frankfurt, they already are. She spoke with joy about the *superkulturelle Gesellschaft* ('the super-diverse society'). Here we have an elected parliamentarian calling for the marginalisation of her own people. This is a perverse attempt at being anti-ethnocentric in the name of a culturally nihilistic political correctness.

Such a total commitment to the diversity ideology, the plurality ontology that West Germans felt they should accept in order to come to terms with their fascist past is surely indicative of Gehlen's (1969) 'hypermorality'. By destroying the past, they think they can control the future. It is the 'end process of rationalisation' (Bell, 1976: 4). It is a means of coming to terms with a psychological trauma which cannot in any way afflict this young generation of Green multiculturalists. At least, not directly. Indirectly, they are perhaps wreaking revenge on their grandparents' generation, but that is an extremely twisted thought process. One might ask why one would create a system of potential chaos which you and your children have to live in just to vent some vicarious, misplaced anger. This does not seem to be a very likely explanation. If the sense of post-war guilt was so

---

9   Source: https://www.youtube.com/watch?v=9pk2UMqqyfY

tangible, then why wait sixty years to do anything about it? Surely, there is a better explanation than simply *Vergangenheitsbewältigung* ('coming to terms with the past')?

But hypermorality does appear to account partially for what is happening. If one looks at who votes for the Green Party in Germany, and its equivalent in Sweden, it is people living in the wealthiest parts of Hamburg and Stockholm. In Sweden, they get the trendy, hipster Södermalm vote. In Hamburg where the Green Party scored 11 per cent in the 2011 State Election, it seems it is more the old money set. The most 'privileged' social group comprising the largest percentage of ethnic Swedes and Germans seem to vote for the party that is most committed to undermining precisely this group. One might call it hypermorality, a heightened modern consciousness vis-à-vis liberal guilt or just cultural and epistemological nihilism. Understanding this nihilistic impulse is of course problematic in times of extreme modernity, but it is perhaps in part 'a result of socialisation to a culturally specific language code that not only makes critical discourse possible but also provides the ideological justification, that is notions about progress, moral integrity etc.' (Bowers, 1985: 469). The language of 'progress' has created a new conceptual orthodoxy, and because it is 'new', it must be modernising, and thus good. Our social intelligence is reluctant to question this teleological view of society because to do so might make us romantic reactionaries *qua* 'unprogressive' members of the community. The only criterion for 'progress' seems to be 'progress' itself: social tradition is a mere constraint on a more rationally ordered future. But it is the experiential ground that has reality — the entangled comings and goings of everyday life, be it in the mega-city or the four-road Lapland village — not intangible exhortations.

For some of the deluded social progressives, nihilism where a Dostoyevskian figure makes destruction the only creative art is preferable to racism. Indeed, for the ideologised hypermoralists, there appears to be no bigger evil than racism. Islam scholar Lamya Kaddor said on German television that 'being German no longer means having blonde hair and blue eyes, but being a Muslim migrant and wearing a *hijab*'. The audience responded with a big applause.[10] It was as if the people in the audience were just totally ideologised in the way that starving North Koreans applaud missile launches.

---

10 Source: https://www.youtube.com/watch?v=Qb9QAUsUA98

VIII

Don't Just Point the Finger at Russia

> I cannot forecast to you the action of Russia. It is a riddle wrapped in mystery inside an enigma; but perhaps there is a key.
> — Winston Churchill

The Soviet era, rusty trolley-buses claw at the bloated cables suspended above the boulevards: an electric, rasping hum. The sky is dove-grey, full of snow perhaps. I walk for hours down streets that creep into obscurity. Laden-down *babushkas* with silk scarves tied firmly under chin inch in their senectitude up the snowy, tree-lined pathway to the huddle of expecting golden cupolas. A gaunt, urban landscape on a bleak afternoon. Bulbous onion-domes top the Corinthian columns and Baroque stucco architraves light up the drowsy city towards the end of daylight. Inside, it is dark, but gilt-edged. Puffs of incensed air linger reverently amongst the faded murals whose shades merge in a *sfumato*. Even if I am not Orthodox, these Russian Orthodox churches and cathedrals are the most holy, sacred places I know. There is a reverence to be found here which I have never witnessed in the West. Unlike the vulgar mega-churches, Russian Orthodox churches respect solitude. They appeal to the inner-self, the private inner sanctuary of peace, and the nature of that appeal seems rather Russian to me. I find them magical, and am constantly drawn back to them. Vespers at such a place could surely convert any sceptical soul. The appeal is not a religious one *per se*; it is the metaphysical sensitivity, the mystery and irreducibility of the human spirit that these churches inhere.

Enigmatic, multi-genuflecting ladies with the look of salvation in their faces and cowled in head-scarves, light candles and form orderly queues to kiss ancient icons that portray a multitude of saints. They move like chess pieces between relics lit by lamps and candles, kissing the glass and then quickly rubbing away the mark. I am drawn into the blessed silence of the icon. The gaze of memory looks down upon me. Kissing and communicating with multiple images of Christ permits an intimate immediacy with the Saviour not readily obtainable in non-Orthodox worship. Their azure-coloured eyes never meet mine. I feel invisible amongst the funereal expressions. Soft, fervent whispers echo around the vaulted, frescoed naves. Russian, a language of soft sibilants and palatal fricatives, is made for whispering and chanting homophonic Slavonic chants. I stand, letting myself float in the harmonic consonance of the language. I want the sounds to be impressed on my brain.

Vigil lamps hang from brass chains. Mystical and heavenly, the First Antiphon is chanted from somewhere high above me in a cappella harmony; fragments of a mystical vision, a bridge to the beyond. The purity of the human voice, the most perfect instrument of praise, with no musical accompaniment to trivialise things. No guitars or gospel here; just continuity, authenticity and tradition. Unmodernised, its appeal is as transcendental as the faith it is show-casing. Rooted in past traditions and with the immediate symbolism of the relics, it transcends time and the world. Immutable and indifferent to temporal necessities. The Liturgy remains virtually unchanged, still enshrouded in the mystery of the Church Slavonic language whose zigzagging sentences and repetitive poetics are just beyond the reach of the standing Congregation. From the beginning, Russians had always heard the Gospel preached in the vernacular.

Surely weary, they have been standing for over an hour now. I stand with the upright poise of the spiritual man, lost in borrowed thoughts, indulged in the inner lyrical grace of the words being issued forth. Bearded men in heavy cassocks emerge from hidden doorways behind the gilded iconostasis, swinging chinking censers. Then they disappear dragging their shadows behind them, only to reappear moments later from another concealed door, grasping a heavy, ancient tome with marbled fore-edges. The booming *basso profondo* of the priest's voice resonates from the ambon, saturating the church with an oppressive spirit. Shoulder-to-shoulder in the packed nave. A silent, congested train of people in the narthex. It is New Year's Day, and the day is beginning to bloom.

The great lure of the Russian Orthodox Church is its continuity, its steadfastness. Religion aside, it has a philosophical magnetism. The evangelical, happy-clappy churches which Russia is rightly trying to render illegal seem pathetic in comparison with their teary sermons and people waving in the air as if they were attending a rock concert. These churches do not belong perhaps in Russia. They may have mass appeal, but some might say they make a mockery of religion. A service at the Russian Orthodox Church is timeless, sacred and authentic. It is sincere, deep and as the superlative of church services conveys a much more meaningful, transcendental *Mitsein*.

The Orthodox Church appears to have remained somehow immune to liberalist thinking. It has preserved its sanctity by never bowing to the demands of that fatuous evangelism which is creeping into churches right across Western Europe, and indeed much of the world, turning Church services into some kind of self-parody, a sort of pathetic, childish skit with guitars, mindless emotionalism and grizzling adults. It is not exactly *vox populi*, but if religion is more private, it is more likely to achieve a sacred appeal through detachment, not via giant screens and bad acting. These evangelical services replete with their emotional paroxysms make religious practice look like some kind of desperate self-help group. And if the contrast to these churches is the explanation for the reversal of what looked like the Russian Orthodox Church's impish fate some years ago, then Russia seems more appealing than ever before. It is comforting to know that spiritual solemnity can still have an appeal somewhere in the world. In this vein, a Russian Orthodox thinker might offer, 'Why the constant need to *engage* with the contemporary world and its modernist, universal liberalist discourse?'

Amidst all the trash and self-imposed cultural decay in the West, Russia represents class, constancy and cultural preservation. Unlike the West, Russia has not joined in the race to the bottom in terms of standards and decency. The icon of femininity, a Russian woman would not dream of covering herself in tattoos and dressing like a failed gangster with baggy jeans hanging beneath her *derrière*. Russia understands old-fashioned values, the importance of preserving its own culture, but also the threat of radical Islam. In terms of conceptual orthodoxies, Russia is the inverse of the West in all these respects, and for this reason is chided for being a thorn in the liberalist hegemonic side.

Despite living in an age of Islamist terrorism, in the Putin era Russia has been consistently demonised by the West, with all the Western criticism bearing down on its leader. It is difficult to find any alternative view in the West. Russian officials, including Putin, have said repeatedly that the migration crisis is the result of the US-European destruction of Iraq, Libya and attempts to topple Assad in Syria. That is undeniably the case. A consequentialist could only take a dim view of any US-led invasion in the Middle East or North Africa. What is more, cables published by Wikileaks show that the US planned on destabilising Syria as early as 2006.[1] Every time this Western alliance seeks regime change in an Arab country, it ends in disaster (one would say 'unprecedented disaster', but sadly there are now a whole list of precedents).

An alternative view, such as Putin's take on the Middle East, might be somehow politically incorrect, and an affront to liberal groupthink because of the conservatism which Putinism is perceived to characterise. Scholars such as Clowes (2011) love to describe Putin's Eurasian Economic Union as 'fascist' and 'imperialist', but have no problem with the expansionist European Union which left behind any notion of economic union years ago. Putin's Russia is determined to maintain her sovereignty and identity in the face of globalisation, and for that she should be applauded. Not everybody wants to live in a world of globalised clones who live in 'identity-free' areas without borders where there is no alternative to

---

[1] Source: https://wikileaks.org/plusd/cables/06DAMASCUS5399_a.html

homogenised chains that sell the same junk food and where everybody is tuned into the same trashy TV that could barely entertain a half-intelligent ten year old. Russia has its faults, most certainly, but Putin wants a Russia based first and foremost on tradition, a traditional morality and Christianity, whereas the globalists seek the truth of a nihilistic creed. An identity is formed from roots and connections, not from consumer goods, but the globalists seem to wish to do away with identity.

There prevails currently a liberal imperative to be anti-Russian. And yet, the revolutionary events in Ukraine in 2014 were seldom described for what they were: an illegal coup of an elected leader, President Yanukovich. Overzealous with its imperialist ambitions, the EU supported regime change in Ukraine, and as such unreasonably provoked Russia. It continues to do so to this day, having given Ukraine (not a member of the EU) 1bln Euros of financial assistance in 2018. The EU always defends its stance by invoking the discourse of sovereignty, but hypocritically represents itself a body that wishes to do away with national sovereignty.

The US was also quick in its support. It likes to remind us of its noble intentions of spreading liberal democracy, but it is never about that. The objective, be it Egypt (2011), Guatemala (1954), Iran (1953), Chile (1973) or Ukraine (2014) is always to put in place a pro-American Government, and the US does not hesitate in facilitating 'regime change' of democratically elected leaders in order to achieve this. Ukraine is also rich in natural gas, and the US wasted no time in getting their hands on it. The EU's moves were fully supported by Joe Biden, the US Vice-President who liked to go to Ukraine to lecture on corruption. At the same time, his son was elected to the Board of Burisma Holdings, the largest independent natural gas company in Ukraine.

With the Bucharest Declaration in 2008, the West had broken the promises agreed between Gorbachev and Reagan, with its intention of expanding NATO membership to both Ukraine and Georgia. Russia made it perfectly clear after the announcement that this would be wholly unacceptable to them, and indeed after the Declaration there was war with Georgia in that very year. Subsequently, NATO placed its nuclear warheads and US$800 million missile shield in Romania aimed at Russia, all in the name of a spurious Iranian threat.

NATO expansion was the deep cause for the crisis. Ukraine is of absolutely key strategic interest to Russia, and great powers are always sensitive about their security. One just has to look at the American response in the Cuban Missile Crisis (1962) when Russians placed nuclear weapons in Cuba, but only after Americans had deployed nuclear weapons to Italy and Turkey in 1961 and aimed them at Russia. The US assumes that the world believes it to have benign intentions, but that is not the Russian and Chinese opinion. And so, under Putin and in the face of such provocations, Russia had of course to respond. If China were to hypothetically form a military alliance with Canada and Mexico and then place its weapons on the American border, one can be rather sure that the US would not respond by saying that these countries had a right to form a military alliance with anybody they wanted, as the US said about Ukraine. Despite this, the conventional wisdom in the West remains that Putin is responsible for the crisis in Ukraine. One might not want to condone the accession of Crimea, but the West had created an extremely dangerous situation: they provoked the key strategic interest of a country (Crimea is the only ice-free naval port for the Russians) with thousands of nuclear weapons, and followed it up by imposing economic sanctions. It is an act of folly for the US to put a nuclear power such as Russia into a corner over Ukraine, a country that is no strategic interest to the Americans. The provocations by the West since 2008 have been deliberate, unnecessary and continue to this day.[2]

The Stalinist-styled Hotel Ukraine commands the perfect position in

---

2   Readers might want to remind themselves of the contents of Victoria Nuland's (US Assistant Secretary of State for European and Eurasian Affairs at the State Department) intercepted phone call where the extent of American plotting in the run-up to the overthrow of Yanukovich is detailed, and where she shouts 'Fuck the EU'. https://www.youtube.com/watch?v=2QxZ8t3V_bk

Kiev,— overlooking the central Maidan Nezalezhnosti and the broader skyline: a curious juxtaposition of the dehumanising Lego of Kruschchyovka, obelisks, Byzantine glory, stucco candy-floss and magnificent Baroque churches. The hotel, State owned, is pure Soviet nostalgia: the Rosa Klebb-like *offiziante* that man each landing with poker-like faces, the bugged bedrooms and tapped telephones of former days, the enormous reception and dining rooms built to serve Soviet delegations that just weeks later would tragically become morgues for the protesters.

In the final days of 2013, barricades blocked the entrance to the square, groups of men gathered around fires and sung Ukrainian songs throughout the night. Ukrainian nationalists climbed up onto the stage and addressed the crowds in increasingly fiery rhetoric that boomed out across the city centre. Just weeks later, charred pavements would be ripped up for ammunition, and the unease would escalate into a full-blown revolution.

I saw with my own eyes those demonstrators on Maydan Square, many of whom were anarchist thugs. All the media in the UK painted a picture of a suppressed people fighting a vicious regime. They did not tell you that the EU was supporting militias of neo-Nazis, or that the accession of Crimea was entirely peaceful. In Kiev, policemen had fireworks thrown in their face night after night just because they were trying to protect the elected parliament. EU officials had been meddling more than the Russians, and yet it was never presented that way.

Ukraine must be free to decide its future (or futures in the event of a split), but it is undeniable that culturally, linguistically and in every other way, Ukraine is much closer to Russia than anywhere else. Russia has been provoked for years by the West as NATO has pushed further and further East until it came right up to the Russian border. The problems facing the world in the first instance are the work of the West (and in particular the US as global aggressor), not Russia. The demonisation of Russia and the response to the conflict in Russia is another chapter in the bigger ideological clash between liberalist multiculturalism and its cultural nihilism on the one hand, and the preservation of cultural-national identity structures in the face of a globalist threat on the other.

* * *

The 'progressive liberalism' of the West is beginning to appear autumnal; many in the West have lost their faith and convictions, and the Brussels politicians swaddled in this ideology are busy trying to deny the remnants of our culture. Western traditionalism has been in pell-mell retreat for decades, and until recently there was almost no opposition to the prevailing ideology. Liberalism in conjunction with mass digital communication is everywhere, so omnipresent that people have forgotten it is a system of beliefs. Believing that we must 'delegitimise the Eurocentric heritage of Western nations, which is thought to transmit a reactionary consciousness' (Drummond, 2014: 174) does not have to be the norm. Putin's Russia is fighting for a multi-polar world where there can at least be some alternative to secular liberalism and the modernising form of secular consciousness which some believe to be inherently unstable (Eliot, 1939; Berdyaev, 1933; Scruton, 2014). This consciousness is nihilistic in its emphasis on individuals selecting their own values.

Putin's Russia is preserving its self-consciousness and culture, and for that at least it should be respected and its leader should be listened to. After years of totalitarianism, post-Soviet Russia has again found its soul even whilst the European soul is being dismantled. Europe might want to learn from Russia, a country whose Christian identity was systematically undermined under Communism. By insisting on a one-world liberal secularist ideology, we will only create more terror and warfare. The crisis of globalisation is that the alternatives are constantly disrespected. It has to be that way because the essence of globalisation is that there is only one ideology. But, thankfully we have not got to the point where that is acceptable to everyone.

In Putin's Russia, there is of course a very close link between the Government and the Orthodox Church, and this should be rightly viewed with some suspicion. There has been a focus on Orthodoxy as opposed to 'Christian churches', implying that the Orthodox Church is somehow beyond-Christian. A Wikileaks report describes the Orthodox Church as a 'Government agency'.³ All the criticism of the implied corruption and Patriarchal politics is no doubt justified, but the fact remains that under Putin, the Church has been revived at a physical and psychological level in a way few imagined. The State and the Church share a sacralised vision of Russian exceptionalism, and according to Forbes (May 21st, 2015) around 25,000 Russian Orthodox Churches have been built since the early 1990s, many with money from the oligarchs.

It is also clever politics: Russia is able to use the Orthodox card in discussions with countries such as Serbia, Macedonia and Greece, and it acts as a bond with former Soviet states that have become Westward-looking, such as Georgia. It acts as a useful bond at a time when Russia is trying to reassert itself. The clue is in the Patriarch's full title 'Patriarch Kirill of Moscow and all the Rus'. It also enables Putin to tap into the social trust that the Russians had invested previously in the Orthodox Church.

There is of course an anti-globalist connection between Putin and Trump. Beyond Trump and those who surface in his wake, most political leaders in the West are, however, still little more than globalists who prioritise faith in global networks of interdependence over sovereignty and who live under a protective cupola. They see the world as one big, inevitable economic and cultural convergence play. London, that bogey-blackening lost Moloch and global-citizen bubble, is one of the centres of this convergence play, increasingly filled with homogenised globalists funded by multinational corporations with their own distinctive worldview and creed—liberal Christianity without Christ. For many of these political leaders in the West, their primary concern is to secure a seat at the big globalist table and hob-nob with other globalists like Jean-Claude Juncker at the G8, G20, G40 and the EU. Some of them seem to care little about the nations they are meant to be representing. It is the apolitical monarchy with its stable, transcendent legitimacy that cares. It is the monarchy (best epitomised by Her Majesty the Queen of England, and not certain

---

3   Available at: https://wikileaks.org/gifiles/attach/133/133780_Foundations%20-%20-1.doc

European Royals who have lost their dignity and try to be 'normal' celebrities with their tattoos, Pizza and pornographic film appearances) that maintains and symbolises order in society, preventing nationalistic excess.

Even the all-signed-up Christians in the West today are far less pious than they were just a hundred years ago. The old systems of belief, like religion and morality, exist only at the edge of our consciousness. Christianity was an overarching system that shaped culture in the West for two thousand years. Now, there is just nothingness, an absolute inner emptiness—the secular void that liberals celebrate, a shallow world with its prevalence of base interests, desacralised by science, with no higher purpose than to enjoy consumption and the modern idiocracy of the entertainment world that plays to a dysgenic universe.[4] But without an overarching system, society has no organic structure, meaning or unambiguous identity. Liberals, and particularly those at the heart of the EU project, want our nations just to become 'economic zones' stripped of identity. If this happens, one might assume we will be left with just decadence, rampant materialism and the cultural decay that comes with this. What is more, unaccountable transnational governance risks superseding centuries of national parliamentary accountability in countries beyond Britain that have denied their citizens a say in the European political union project.

Liberals are in fact losing their enamoured secular freedom to an increasingly Muslim fundamentalist Europe. The secular *jouissance* might not be maintained *ad infinitum* in the manner that liberals aspire to. This truth is being hidden; those with dissenting views are being intimidated

---

4   It seems that Heidegger shared my concerns when he described the plight of many modern Germans as follows: 'Hourly and daily they are chained to radio and television. Week after week the movies carry them off into uncommon, but often merely common realms of the imagination, and give the illusion of the world that is no world. Picture magazines are everywhere available. All that with which modern technologies of communication stimulate, assail, and drive man—all that is already much closer to man today than his fields around his farmstead, closer than the sky over the earth, closer than night over day, closer than the conventions and customs of the village, thus the tradition of his nature world' (*Notes on the Return and Kapital*: 49).

by a partisan cultural grammar. We have entered the era of falsity and inverted reality. Our nations are threatened by Islamism and the EU which is enforcing mass immigration on Western Europe. The future will be the history of another people, coming with cultural values that have never been a part of our past. Our notions of 'belonging' or more precisely perhaps, *Zusammengehörigkeit* (with its undertones of 'belonging' and 'togetherness') will be strained because the sense of continuity will be irreparably broken. Unless man feels as if he 'belongs' somewhere, he is overcome by individual insignificance. The foundation of the communities that we have belonged to will not be the same. Those who speak out against it will be ridiculed for living in the past and clinging to outdated concepts and social structures which are *a priori* negative because they are culturally framed.

As Schmitt said, liberal states extend rights of membership to those who do not truly belong to the political nation, but being a member of a nation must come with duties as well as rights. Instead of creating functional, pluralistic societies, liberal states such as these will be overwhelmed by external enemies who are more politically united (Schmitt, 2007: 69-79). Liberalism is undermining the political basis of our societies, trying to do away with markers of identity that can ground political decisions.

It is clear that Europe needs rethinking meta-politically, i.e. at the level of the collective consciousness. As a matter of urgency, national identities must be strengthened with a focus on Judeo-Christian values. Sovereignty, independence, national and cultural integrity should be red-lines for every European country, but instead they have just become marks in the sand washed away by the surf of the European bureaucratic machine. Not everybody wants to see their country thronging with people who either choose not to integrate or who are unable to do so. Muslims tend to identify themselves firstly as Muslim, and not British, Swedish, French etc. This is fundamental, and unlikely to change.

Western leaders have become appeasers, not defenders of freedom. But we must not forget that freedom is supremely valuable. Freedom is what makes an individual 'complete'. We cannot let the political system close our minds or cloud our thinking. Following two Islamist massacres in one year, France became a police state in a 'state of emergency' for months on end which 'monitored several thousand people'.[5] Such large-scale terrorist attacks are likely to lead to significantly more authoritarianism in the capital cities of Western Europe. Security is becoming increasingly prominent in everyday vocabulary as the role of the State is more and more explicitly that of 'ensuring security'. In parts of Western Europe, the price for allowing large-scale immigration from countries that have supported terrorism may well be to live in perpetual, authoritarian police states.

Since November 2016, French police have conducted more than 2,500 raids. Laws were passed to allow France to censor the Internet and to arrest people in their homes without a warrant, to search people's devices and copy any data they wish. Living in such an authoritarian regime, freedom and authority dance with one another in an intimate, awkward fashion. Arguably, the only real freedom left is the freedom to consume and spend one's days lost in the circus of consumerism. France cannot possibly function as its parliamentarians wish: immigrants to France have to, quite correctly, enter into a contract with the OFII (the French Immigration Service). The contract states that the newcomer must respect French values: *liberté, égalité, fraternité* and *laïcité* (secularism). And here lies the problem: how can one ask a Muslim from West Africa that prays to Allah five times a day to respect secularism? France is simply creating a subversive pastiche of contiguous dissonance with compartmentalised ethnic groups wallowing in different hierarchies of belonging. The future of Europe might be authoritarian police states and not free liberal democracies, as we assume.

It is right to stand up for one's nation. It is wrong to be called a racist for wishing to defend one's nation and its values. This is persecution. We share a loyalty to our nation, and this political loyalty need in no way be an aggressive one. Nobody can claim to have a loyalty to the EU, a bureaucratic body that disenfranchises the citizens of nation-states. Liberals insist

---

5   Bernard Cazeneuve, the French Interior Minister, speaking in March 2016.

on associating nationalism with aggression and war. This view is absurdly crude. It is a fallacy to constantly equate nation-states with belligerence. One cannot reduce nationalism to a politics of aggressive self-assertion. Nationalism can take many forms: left, right and ambivalent. The Norwegians and Faroese are amongst the most nationalistic people in Europe, but who has ever been threatened by them?

Instead of standing up for one's nation, there is a constant attempt to stimulate a specious Western guilt. To defend oneself and speak up for one's Judeo-Christian values might be deemed nationalistic, and thus anachronistic behaviour. This would represent 'old thinking', conservative, and therefore something negative because it cannot map out its objectives in terms of 'progress' or rather 'change'. This guilt and malaise is becoming commoditised and has begun to sound like a kind of anti-Occidentalist secular confession.

We must not let the film of political correctness — the contemporary nexus of intellectual life — muddle our minds. The more open discussion and debate is suppressed by the 'tolerance mob', the sooner counter-extremism will arise to tackle Islamic extremism (as we saw in the Slovak elections of 2016). Many on the Left do not hesitate to oppose the Christian Right in America. If they are against extremism in all forms, then they must surely rather more conspicuously oppose militant Islam which is a far more immediate threat to our societies than any Christian church. One might ask how the Left can be supportive of gay rights, and yet apparently find excuses for radical Islam whose ISIS members threw gays off roofs into bloodthirsty crowds in Iraq and Syria. If they survived the fall, they were then stoned to death. One cannot promote secularism, but condone in the name of cultural relativism radical Islam at the same time.

The correct response is one that is rooted in a kind of level-headed common sense that addresses the day-to-day reality of the dystopia that open-borders liberalism is creating. Multiculturalists who are indifferent to their country and culture, and who so frequently double up as Islamic apologists, may be naïvely acting as *jihadist* facilitators. Certainly, there appears to be an alliance between the two. This is not scaremongering.

This is reality. We are living in a time of creeping *shari'ah* and stealth *jihad*, and juxtaposing ideologies such as secularism and radical Islam that have immediately conflicting objectives can only end badly.

We have worried too much about offending the Other. It is time to move beyond Teddy Bear politics. The liberal multicultural consensus must be to some extent a fabrication. Otherwise, right-wing, anti-immigration parties would not be on the rise throughout the West. A true leader will only emerge in a time of crisis, and that time is rapidly approaching. One can see why one might object to him, but Russia has found a strong leader after years of kleptocracy, corruption and systematic collapse under Yeltsin. Putin will defend Russia's cultural heritage, and will attempt to ensure that it is not undermined by the forces of globalist consumerism: a difficult task.

Just as with their thinking, many people in the West have internalised their preoccupations, turned in from society, dragged down by a defeatist sense they cannot do anything about it. For the more individualist amongst them, representative democracy is becoming a questionable concept. The average person in the West today wants to live his own life with enough income that he can be surrounded by the requisite material goods; but he lacks any higher purpose or any engagement with the enormous changes in society which are happening around him. In his daily hermetic life he 'makes money', sleeps and indulges in the idiocracy that has been forced on him through watching television, some of which plays to the lowest cultural denominator and over-clichés our existence. One might think of reality TV as the ultimate symbol of this cultural excrescence. Spend half an hour watching that nonsense, and one might conclude that this is being unleashed on people to lower their IQ (it is sometimes publicly recognised that this is the objective of artificial intelligence), so that some sinister globalist project can proceed unchallenged. And so, the effects of mass media and *la toute-puissance* of its popular culture which both seem to wish to celebrate mediocrity should really be reconsidered.

Other symbols of cultural excrescence emerge through any number of things, but perhaps most conspicuously through the mendacity of graffiti, urinals and soiled beds sold at Sotheby's, Christie's and Bonhams posing as 'modern art'. When one sees such 'exhibits', it would seem to suggest the process of dissolution is well underway. Such exhibits are not *objets d'art*, but are simply there to shock, as is the case with much contemporary architecture. Forgive me the authoritarian subjectivism. There is a mass dumbing down in the arts and the media in the West. The void is not just spiritual, but cultural. A secular, liberal modernity impedes self-understanding, and liberal thought has a near monopoly on Western education.

It is perhaps not surprising that our societies have become so consumerist when political thinking in the West now is more or less concerned with one thing: economics. Political parties are dancing to the same tune as their masters — big business. Profits come before cultural heritage, national identity and environmental preservation. Political leaders in both Germany and Sweden have surrendered to mass Muslim immigration because they think it will create jobs, even if it takes on average eight years before a refugee gets a job in Sweden.[6] But, if it really is just about jobs, one might ask why Sweden is letting in hundreds of thousands of uneducated workers from the developing world when it had a youth unemployment of 19 per cent just a year ago in July 2017.[7] Swedes are so ideologised into thinking mass immigration from the Middle East is a good thing, they cannot see the tremendous harm they are doing to their own society, even in pure economic terms.

Mass immigration is apparently good for the building industry because the need for new housing stimulates economic activity and increases GDP. But, not everybody wants the UK to be covered with endless, grim suburbs of crowded tenements where strangers, in clogged streets, have no bond to the place. Not everybody wants to live in ugly utilitarian cities of square shapes. And all so we can say that our GDP, an indicator which tells us nothing about the actual condition of a society, is increasing. Community

---

6   Source: Stockholm's County Administrative Board, *Länsstyrelsen*, 2011.

7   Source: http://ec.europa.eu/eurostat/statistics-explained/index.php/
    Unemployment_statistics

values and national cohesion are being flushed away in the non-stop race of frantic economic activity, the rush to add every new face to the supermarket culture. This might create a 'booming economy' in the short-term, but in the long-term such policies might lead to societal breakdown. Even if these initiatives led to tremendous economic growth, so what? By pathologically pursuing this pseudo-religion of economic growth and diversity at all costs, our countries, which were once breathing motherlands teaming with life, will be nothing more than cancerous, sterile 'anywhere-in-the-world' housing estates and identikit, soulless shopping centres full of outsiders trapped in their own cultural bubbles. Places are becoming homogeneous, and perhaps ultimately interchangeable — a horrendous thought. The visible has replaced the invisible of indigenous cultures, and the cultural explorer is left to eke out the diminishing *locus* of 'otherness'.

We have to start confronting these unpopular truths, to realise that what matters is preservation and conservation (not growth). Conservatism (meant here in the British sense, and not in the sense of American religious conservatism) must concern itself again with 'conserving'. As a political philosophy, it has lost its way, strayed too far from its roots and original meaning. Some Conservatives nowadays are so liberalised, they have discarded many of these responsibilities. They are not 'conserving' anything, and might even consider it anathema to attempt to do so. As I have argued previously, conservatism must rekindle the conservation ethos, and start conserving our social and ecological inheritance. We cannot continue to absolutise the liturgy of economic growth as so many Conservatives do. Growth can be cancerous, and this is indeed one of its dictionary meanings.

There must be principles of higher order by which we can organise our society. These are nowhere to be found amongst the *données* of liberalism. There must be inner change to overcome the prevailing state of doubt, and sense of indeterminacy. To converge every single issue and interest on the economic plane and to perceive work as the perennial 'sacred cow' is demonic. Evola (2002: 74) wrote about the hegemony of work and the need to regain inner freedom. He said: 'action, not work is what is performed by the leader. [...] In the present economic civilisation, even action is increasingly attributed to the action of "work". The Evolian critique of society and the need to restore a hierarchy or sovereignty of values applies more today than ever before. Inner freedom and strength is required to stand against the inexorable current, the wave of changes crashing on our shores. Cultural values must take priority over the economy. Reflecting this Evolian spirit, Putin is not afraid to defend the sovereignty of values when he speaks of Russians being the embodiment of the highest moral values. By this he inspires the Russian psyche to look beyond the personal yardsticks of success in the West which are defined so frequently by an inward-looking, individualistic materialism.

Putin likes to remind Russians of their deeper sense of patriotism, sense of sacrifice, honour and generosity of spirit. He criticises what he rightly perceives to be Western 'quasi-values'. He wishes to protect Russians from the Western cultural hegemony which has become rather aggressive. As he has said publicly: 'Without a sense of tradition and the values that come with it, society begins to decay'.[8] His language is Evolian in this regard. He evokes Berdyaev's conservatism, defined in his own words as the kind of 'conservatism that does not get in the way of moving forward and upward, but does prevent from sliding backwards and downwards'.[9]

In times of cultural insecurity, we might learn from a much-needed *rapprochement* with this Russian spirit. We might begin by not prefacing every attempt at being strong by saying 'I am sorry'. Young people would benefit from a splash of Spartan stoicism and an ingratiating smile, not pity and ontological malevolence. Linguistic norms are such that we are left apologising for any view that does not reflect the pervasive liberal ideology by saying: 'I am not a racist, but...'; 'I am not Islamophobic, but...'. We have been taught to police prejudice in our minds. Yet, as a nation or an 'economic zone', if the globalist liberals have their way, we will only go backwards with such feeble, policed thinking and spiritual defeat.

---

8 Available at: https://www.youtube.com/watch?v=HSX2ALtIejw
9 Available at: https://www.youtube.com/watch?v=Vhhdh6vwFW0

We must transcend this impartiality of administered public opinion and break free from the rhetoric. To put an end to this policed thinking would require changes to hate-speech jurisdiction, a reformed and re-balanced 'old media', an abandonment of the 'diversity religion' in the public sector and totally new principles of education.

Fortunately, to some other leaders, this is obvious. If one is looking for common sense, one needs to go further east. Here, the former Communist countries were spared the decadent liberalism that has had such a negative impact on the West. Despite religion having been effectively closed down in Russia during the Soviet period, today these countries celebrate largely Christian values, and are anxious to preserve their cultural identity in the face of what they perceive to be a threat. The Patriarch Kirill of Moscow (2011: 7-10) has written of how we must be free to critique liberalism, and not just from a theological standpoint. If one cannot even critique liberalism, then one is clearly living in an ideological ghetto.

Fico, the former Prime Minister of Slovakia, said in January 2015: 'We [Slovakia] will not tolerate mass Muslim immigration and building of mosques'.[10] But short of building a wall, it is difficult to see how they will stop this, as the Slovaks are members of the EU and the Schengen Area. Prime Minister Fico spoke out against multiculturalism, calling it a 'failed project'. He stated that his country is first and foremost Catholic, then it is Lutheran; and thus he cannot accept 300,000 Muslims 'who want to build mosques all over the place'.[11] He was not prepared to subject his country to the kind of dramatic and irreversible cultural shift that Brussels bureaucrats are anxious to bring about. Central Europe, Eastern Europe and Russia have not been subjected to incessant political correctness. Ironically for ex-Soviet countries perhaps, they enjoy the privilege that we once had of being able to speak their minds without having to worry

---

10   Available at: http://www.euractiv.com/section/justice-home-affairs/news/refugee-crisis-reveals-fundamental-splits-in-european-political-parties/

11   Available at: https://www.washingtonpost.com/news/worldviews/wp/2016/06/21/the-next-e-u-president-says-islam-has-no-place-in-his-country/?utm_term=.f3668f5309f1

about cultural grammar. In the West, we have compromised this terribly important freedom.

Another example of somebody who is prepared to speak up for his country (and not discard a national identity established over the course of centuries in the name of globalism) is Prime Minister Orbán of Hungary. In his State of the Nation address in 2015, he rejected multiculturalism, saying: 'Europe is facing questions which can no longer be answered within the framework of liberal multiculturalism'.[12] He is one of the very few politicians (whose country is in the EU) to push the boundaries of political correctness from within the system. Orbán continues: 'Europe has built a wall of taboos and dogmas around itself'. Bravely, he says: 'We decided to face the barrage of unfair attacks and accusations, and also let go of the dogma of political correctness'. It would be unthinkable for a leader of a Western European nation to say this, but it could not be more accurate. The conservative Hungarian leader has chosen the route of common sense, and has thus stayed faithful to the wishes of his electorate. There are many reasons to criticise Orbán, but he has at least grasped the problem of liberalist modernity: its totalitarian temper. He continues: 'Liberal politics only ever recognises two kinds of opinion: its own and the wrong one. [...] As far as I see it, Hungarian people are by nature politically incorrect — in other words, they have not yet lost their common sense'.[13]

Putin and other leaders beyond Europe seem to see the world for what it is. He can see that militant Islam is trying to split our societies. Putin made it clear in his address to the Duma in February, 2013 that minorities who want to live in Russia should speak Russian and respect Russian laws, and if they want to practice *shari'ah* law, they should leave.[14] He went onto say that Russia must learn from the 'suicides' of America, England, Holland and France. If we are to defeat militant Islam, the UK will need a

---

12 Available at: http://www.dteurope.com/politics/hungary/hungarian-pm-evaluates-2014.html

13 Available at: http://www.kormany.hu/en/the-prime-minister/the-prime-minister-s-speeches/the-next-years-will-be-about-hardworking-people

14 Available at: https://www.youtube.com/watch?v=5hnq5gEzZ8Q

Putin and not a Chamberlain. Suicide is the right word because the West has actively chosen this path of cultural repudiation.

The West could learn much from these leaders. Russia has found its King, the true voice of conservatism, and broken free from its ideological vacuum. We must now fight for our respective nations, take back the powers from the European bureaucrats and globalists, and preserve our cultural heritage. We must send unambiguous messages like this to people who want to dismantle our societies. To do this, we will need our King, somebody who can show how a cultural and political life can have a higher value, a meaning that transcends the pure satisfaction of private desires. Transcending is knowing, placing thought in a meta-, trans-, *über-* sphere, as Heidegger would have said.

Putin is the boss (the *vozhd*) and passionately defends the values of his nation, and for this he is loved in Russia. He will not subscribe to the self-imposed cultural stagnation of the West, but wishes instead to promote a patriotic consciousness reconciling ethnic and civic identity into a singular, pro-Russian allegiance. His opinions are welcome in a country where conservative thinking is inherently popular and linked to respect for established religions. He understands that political correctness and the instrumentalisation of 'liberal' identity politics is a reductionist discourse with execrable consequences.

The EU bureaucrats and leaders of the West look spineless and pathetic in comparison, wrapped up in their politically correct doublespeak. If they were to put aside the political correctness, as Trump, Farage and others have done, the Brussels politicians might find they become slightly more popular amongst the electorate that they claim to represent. The liberal media in the West responds to politicians that speak the truth and tell the electorate how things really are by labelling them 'populist'. And, then they employ the familiar technique of reprimanding an opponent with the normal barrage of -isms etc. to disenfranchise him and close down the debate. And we are left in a pool of lies and ideologised doublespeak, distorting and obfuscating the beclouded reality.

In a speech in September 2013 at the Valdai Club, President Putin commented that 'Euro-Atlantic states have taken the path of denying or rejecting their own roots, including their Christian roots which form the basis of Western civilisation'.[15] The implication is that we all, that is every society, need a *sobornost* ('a spiritual community that engenders social harmony'). Every Briton, Swede and American listening to President Putin must know, in those scarce, private, ideology-free moments, that he is absolutely correct. Here is a man, one of the very few statesmen, that understands what is happening in the West. He goes on to say:

> In these countries, the moral basis and any traditional identity are being denied — national, religious, cultural and even gender identities are being denied or relativised. [...] And these countries try to force this model onto other countries, globally. [...] Without the moral values that are rooted in Christianity and other world religions, without rules and moral values which have formed and developed over millennia, people will inevitably lose their human dignity.

What Putin is doing is dialectical. He refuses to allow Russia's past to cloud its future. He will not allow Russians to adopt the nihilistic, defeatist tact that we have seen in Sweden. In this respect at least, Putin is the face of what conservatism should be today. Blair — surely the most hated and repugnant man in Britain — and his fellow Soros-funded EU cronies are the face of meta-political malaise.

In his infamous 2009 address to the UN General Assembly, Colonel Gaddafi makes some extraordinarily judicious comments. He tells the European nations that they should pay 7 trillion dollars for the colonisation of Africa, or they might face mass immigration.[16] Ironically, this effectively happened when in 2016 the EU paid Turkey 6 billion euros as a bribe to stop President Erdoğan letting Syrian refugees into Europe. In return for turning the refugee tap, Turkey was promised EU accession talks and very large amounts of cash. This happened at a time when Turkey is clearly sliding into

---

15 Available at: https://www.youtube.com/watch?v=P2dgmKElZA8

16 Available at: https://www.youtube.com/watch?v=YuMTzyxAuzs

dictatorship, with the State assuming control of the media and the freedom of speech being suppressed. A few months later, there was a coup attempt. Turkey, a country that houses some of the US' nuclear weapons, is now, like France, under a state of emergency rule. Erdoğan is currently using these powers to arrest anybody that opposes his dictatorial ambitions.

The mass immigration that Gaddafi spoke of is what Greenhill (2010) neatly called 'weapons of mass immigration', and Greenhill shows in her book how liberal democracies are very vulnerable to such unconventional forms of coercion because they have codified commitments to human rights through instruments such as the 1948 Human Rights Declaration, the 1951 Convention and the 1967 Protocol. These conventions place certain legal obligations on states to meet the responsibilities they impose. There are many such case studies of political leaders attempting to bring about destabilisation through mass immigration: Cuba in the 1970s when Castro threatened to use immigration as a weapon; Milošević in Serbia in 1999 during the Kosovo conflict.

Significant cross-border movements create severe ethical difficulties for liberal democracies. In such situations, liberalism is a weakness and prevents countries from making a swift, appropriate response. Human Rights Conventions become a hindrance, a national burden. Aware of this conflict, the likes of Gaddafi, Milošević, Castro and Assad have exploited it to the full. With an unfeasible EU open-borders policy, this liberalism will be surely abused to such an extent that the open-borders policy will have to be reversed in the face of civil unrest and a breakdown of the nation-state. This is what is beginning to happen.

In subsequent speeches and interviews, Gaddafi threatened to 'turn Europe black', just as Raspail (1973: 50) predicted would happen in his prescient novel *The Camp of the Saints*:

> There's no Third World. No, not anymore. That's only a phrase you coined to keep us in our place. There's one world, only one, and it's going to be flooded with life, submerged. This country of mine is a roaring river. A river of sperm. Now, all of a sudden, it's shifting course, my friend, and heading west...

It is difficult to believe that this book was written in 1973, and not 2015. Both Gaddafi and Raspail knew very well what the future would hold.

As Viktor Orbán recognises, liberalism has resulted in an intellectual hegemony which is strangling the West, depriving it of meaningful dialogue and any fruitful exchange of ideas. He inveighs against liberalism for presuming to speak for the whole of humanity. Freedom of speech is one thing, but one would surely not want to dispense with freedom of opinion as well. This late liberalist modernity appeals to an unthinking person, internationally mobile with an iPhone but with little grip on political reality or emotional investment anywhere. It is no doubt politically incorrect to call parts of the population 'unthinking', even if one will find the same dichotomy in the Bible (Psalms, 92: 6-8; Jude 1:10; Peter 2:12). In reality, it is unquestionable that the world can be divided up into those people who are constantly preoccupied with the problems of the world, and think critically and philosophically about a whole swamp of issues, and those who simply seldom stop to consider the world they live in, who they are or where they come from. Perhaps because they are too busy just surviving, trying to get through in their lives.

What is needed is realism, not a kind of Pavlovian political correctness conditioning that prevents any discussion. Instead of realism and debate, we have repression and mass immigration policies that have internalised the problems that used to be external to our societies, and have led to us producing difficult-to-find, home-grown Islamist terrorists. As we see with the Labour leader in the UK, Jeremy Corbyn — that very pomegranate of learning — the Left is more determined than ever before to pursue a new, multicultural demography rather than national security which seems to stand for nothing. This comes at a time when social media and other aspects of our lives are becoming increasingly 'securitised'. As observed previously, we are living in the age of 'security', and the world is not very 'secure'.

And nor can it be, because privatised, internalised thought about authoritarian fear and oppression is likely to encourage, by definition, lone-wolf attacks of the Breivik style. The quiet, shy man who kills the British Member of Parliament or who guns down children in a German McDonald's is potentially everywhere. Heinous private thoughts have perhaps just not yet become public actions. I do not worry about the piety of radical Muslims. I care about the obfuscation in the West; the media that is deceiving freedom-loving people. I am against the totalitarian nature that liberalism has come to represent and its post-democratic direction. The first priority has to be to beat the liberals in the information field. Liberals overwhelmingly dominate the information space. In the name of preserving the tried-and-tested model of European nation-states, there needs to be a diversification of the ideological discourse. True conservative thinking has more or less disappeared. It has been silenced.

It is an uneasy feeling when the parent culture dissipates, when the church bells fall silent on parts of England's ancient land (such as West Yorkshire) where place-names tell the story of our Viking heritage. The soft chime of the bells is being increasingly replaced by the loudspeakers that resonate the *adhan* called out by the *muezzin*, the call to prayer and the repeated praise for Allah and Muhammed. The call can be heard twice a day across the cities of Bradford, Blackburn, Manchester, Oldham, Bolton and Coventry where churches have been converted to mosques (such as Didsbury Mosque, Manchester; Jamia Mosque, Oldham).

The documentary *Undercover Mosque* (2007) proved that British *imams* right across the country have been calling for Muslims not to accept the rule of the *kaffir*; *imam* Abu Usamah praised the killer of a British soldier serving in Afghanistan, stating: 'The hero of Islam is the one who separated his head from his shoulders' and his advice on meeting a homosexual was to 'throw [the homosexual] off the mountain'. Then, you have *imam* Abdullah el-Faisal: 'You have to bomb the Indian businesses, and as for the Jews you kill them physically'. *Imam* Al Jibali said: 'By the age of ten, it becomes an obligation on us to force her to wear *hijab*, and if she doesn't wear *hijab*, we hit her'. Some *imams* in Britain and elsewhere in Europe are spewing out hatred and vengeance, calling for the persecution of Christians in Pakistan. No charges were made, and no doubt their pronouncements have been taken out of context.

London, the capital city whose mayor is a Pakistani Muslim, is no longer an English city in any way. When Zac Goldsmith debated alongside Sadiq Khan in the London mayoral election of 2016, many British Conservatives must have surely wondered how it was possible for Zac to lose by the margin he did. The answer is simple: the London voter base is no longer made up of people representing the values that he stands for. London has become a pluralistic, hybrid *à la* Toronto where the ethnic minority population has gone from three per cent to over fifty per cent in fifty years. In years to come, the rich language of Churchill will err towards some kind of multicultural pidgin as new multi-ethnolects emerge in London, creating new and more fundamental barriers. Not only will any sense of common hope be forgotten, but also communication could even be impaired ultimately as recent sociolinguistic research shows.[17]

In these post-modern places, the imperative is not to be wedded to any one culture unless it is a non-Western one; monoculturalism might be perceived as racist or imperialist, but ethnocentricity if one is a Muslim is unobjectionable. White Canadians are now the ethnic minority in the biggest city of their own country. In Frankfurt, ethnic Germans are also now a minority. These changes are irreversible. Publicly, one can *only* celebrate this diversity, even if it is one big mangled diaspora of confused allegiances and hyphenated identities, an aggregate of unconnected individuals, living with mythical shared, secularised values. But for societies to work, its members must have some kind of historical commonality and collective inner experiences. Even if the language is shared, if the understanding of the concepts that the words designate is slightly different, then they will not have the same experience of events.

There is nothing wrong with urban diversity *per se*, but one needs a core in order to celebrate 'difference', and celebrating 'difference' is the

---

[17] Source: Prof. Jenny Cheshire lecture, General Linguistics seminar, University of Oxford, 2015.

ordre du jour. If diversity becomes the state-sanctioned discourse, as it has in Canada under Trudeau, the indigenous group is just disenfranchised because of the blank-slate ideology. One wonders whether there are any frontiers or limits to this celebration of diversity. Is one meant to jump and cheer in the name of anti-racism if we elect a Muslim Prime Minister, or if our greatest cathedrals become mosques? Diversity in the true sense of the word (and not in the sense of ideologised privilege bestowed upon minorities, which has become the meaning of the word in the public sector) is of course what makes the world utterly fascinating. Discovering just a tiny fraction of the cultural and natural riches of this planet is the best education one could ask for, and has given me personally more pleasure than anything else. But if every country and city were genuinely diverse in the perverse sense in which the word is used, the world would be significantly less interesting, as culturally it would be the same everywhere because every community would be multi-ethnic along the same lines. And thus the advocates of diversity would end up celebrating homogeneity or *undiversity* (on a global macro scale at least) and not the diversity they craved to make them feel better and less guilty about themselves.

People who identify as 'white British' are now a minority in London, their capital, and in some parts of London a tiny minority (2011 Census). They are also a minority in England's second biggest city, Birmingham, as well as Luton, Leicester and Slough (2011 Census). The Muslim population of England and Wales has doubled in the last ten years. In parts of London such as Tower Hamlets, there are more Bangladeshis alone than there are white Britons (2011 Census). Arguably, none of this matters. But what does matter are the establishment of entirely 'separate' communities with religious (and not political) accountability and with a system of values which are alien and sometimes conflicting with the rest of Britain. It is not about immigration *per se*, and absolutely never about race. It is a question of ideology and cultural norms. It would be easier to integrate English-speaking, Christian Africans from Commonwealth countries such as Uganda than Muslim Afghans or Syrians that wish to live in societies run in accordance with *shari'ah*. At the risk of repetition, this is absolutely not a *race* issue. It is the Left that insist on trying to make it that, so that they can close down debate and claim the moral high ground by labelling the mass migration sceptic 'racist'.

Research from Oxford University shows that Britons will become within this century minorities in their own country, changing its culture forever, and descending us into an unknown fosse.[18] Mass immigration and open borders have been imposed on a people without ever asking them. The Government cannot so much as put a figure on the number of newcomers, and does not even appear to care, content to rip up the English countryside in the name of economic growth and housing starts. Currently, the Government believes there may be up to half a million migrants unaccounted for in the UK, but nobody is really sure what the number is. We are living in the age of super-mobility and mass population shifts, and governments cannot possibly keep up with the new paradigm.

These days will leave an indelible mark on our future, leaving our children and grandchildren to grow up in rootless societies built around secular cathedrals that serve little direction and that might not stand for much more. If the attempts by the Left and the EU technocrats to erase national identity succeed, there might arise a risk to social solidarity, and this might lead ultimately to societal breakdown. History shows that social cohesion is possible and is best achieved through nations which have a democratic legitimacy and a shared set of cultural beliefs and anchors of belonging. As has been noted, thanks to cultural nihilism, the current intellectual *Zeitgeist*, an incoming 'strong' culture could trespass across this Hamletian 'muddled pile of identities [...] this congregation of vapours' and create a stronghold out of a self-imposed vacuum. At the moment, it looks like that will be Islam, a rigid theocratic monotheism, and this time there will not be much left of Christendom for it to overrun.

When considering these issues, it is important to recognise that there

---

18 Source: See Projections of the Ethnic Minority Populations in the United Kingdom 2006-2056 (2010: 31-4, Conclusion), University of Oxford: 'If overall net immigration continues as projected by the ONS, and if the ethnic distributions assumed here are even approximately correct, then the ethnic composition of the United Kingdom would be irreversibly transformed within the current century'.

is a difference between immigration and colonialism. Colonialists bring their culture with them and live under their own laws, whereas immigrants may be willing to learn the ways of their new home, to integrate and perhaps assimilate. Sweden and other parts of Europe look increasingly like countries that are being colonised by groups which are *in moribus et artibus* alien, but also alien in terms of *Weltanschauung*. From a European perspective, the twenty-first century is beginning to look like the inverse of the nineteenth century. And yet it would be unthinkable to ponder colonialism models that differed from the white, settlement colonialist model, which is inherently racist, to speculate whether the empowerment of minorities might be tantamount to a transition in control.

It is in this manner that the West has nurtured an overdeveloped capacity for self-criticism, a fetishised historical guilt, and a passion for self-laceration, and in so doing has become a 'penitent State' (Bruckner, 2010). The culture of remorse has become a disabling, debilitating form of narcissism that makes it almost impossible to criticise non-Western crimes or actions. A lingering sense of culpability that is explicit in the outpourings of the liberal elite, the anti-traditional 'aristocracy of the *parvenu*' (Evola, 2002: 289). It has committed itself to systematic cultural narcissism, wallowing in the barbed words that it aims at itself. The former Archbishop of Canterbury, Rowan Williams, implied in a speech given in 2008 that we could not expect Muslim communities to live under British Law, and responded to a question by agreeing that 'the application of *shari'ah* in certain circumstances would achieve cohesion because it would show that we are treating peoples' religions seriously'.[19] This relativist remark suggests that the former Archbishop of Canterbury endorses the *affaiblissement* of the civic and legal identity of British society.

This is the naïvety of callow youth and will lead ultimately to completely segregated communities answerable to utterly opposing legal systems: one based on a system of divine commands with no distinction

---

19 Source: http://rowanwilliams.archbishopofcanterbury.org/articles.php/1135/sharia-law-what-did-the-archbishop-actually-say

between morality and law, and the other a common law system built up by the courts. These kind of concessions would be extremely dangerous and irreversible. The implication of *shari'ah* is that the secular, Western law lacks authority because the opposing system is divine, and thus supersedes everything else. Islam dictates that the authority of God is always sovereign. Anything that does not respect the 'divine' system of judgement is potentially blasphemous. We know from the *Undercover Mosque* documentary that this is what is being taught in some British mosques.

In such a context, Europeans might become ultimately *dhimmis* (indigenous non-Muslims that surrender to Muslim domination) in their own countries, pariahs in what were once their own societies. Having surrendered to the armies of *jihad*, the *dhimmi* loses his territorial rights and his sovereignty. Our commitment to a liberal ideology states that we must accept multiculturalism and afflicted by our imperial past, we must reject our cultural and national pride. It is argued that once the 'multiculturalism project' is complete, there will no longer be any need to go to war. But the Arab states of the Middle East, Russia, Japan and China are quite ostensibly not pursuing the same multiculturalist policies. The countries with the largest armies in the world such as China, Russia, North Korea and Pakistan are united instead behind a national identity and nationalist ambitions. At the same time as we are being educated in the benefits of globalisation and multiculturalism, it seems that it is essential to remain ignorant about the history of Islamic imperialism; that way we can be 'infidels' in our countries and live up to the dictionary meaning of Islam and 'submit'.

We are living in a time where the violent Islamist ideologist meets the European milksop, who has become an easy target. In the face of totalitarian Islam, this is not a time for spineless accommodators, new-age wimps or rose-tinted spectacles. This is a time for Promethean thinkers and open, intellectual debate first and foremost. It is time for realism, common sense and honesty. Leftist thinking has become disconnected from reality; political correctness has failed and morphed into something much more sinister. Sweden needs to respond to protect its democracy.

In the face of ritual assassination, we cannot continue just to talk in terms of dialogue and respect. Militant Islam is an ideology, and it must be defeated and rendered defunct by any means possible. It is antithetical to the freedom we should cherish, the freedom that our grandparents and ancestors fought for.

If one criticises the Christian Crusades, that does not make one anti-Christian. One might note that the Left has cleverly coined the term Islamophobic, allowing any critic of Islam to have this label affixed to him. This is what Bruckner (2010: 48) calls the 'semantic buckler', and is employed by the politically correct brigade, the apostles of identity liberalism. The notion of Islamophobia denies the reality of worldwide *jihad*. To comment negatively on the Islamist offensive would be Islamophobic. The rhetorical crime of speaking common sense trumps the actual terrorist crime where innocent civilians are killed.

There is no recognised equivalent adjective for other religions. Criticism of Christianity does not make that person 'fear' this religion, just as criticism of Islam should be allowed to be made without being reprehended. It also means that Leftists can couple homophobia with Islamophobia; these substantives, which are endowed with such rhetorical force, are used alongside each other by liberals who criticise right-wing thinking. The implication is that adherence to a traditional sexual morality or Christian ethics is indicative of some kind of disorder. The term Islamophobia is nothing but a propagandistic term used to defend Islam in a context of paranoia. The Left likes to conveniently package these things together, and the vocabulary allows them to, even if there is absolutely no reason why somebody who 'fears' Islam should 'fear' homosexuals. However, one could see why a homosexual might fear Islam. A survey (April, 2016) where over one thousand Muslims were polled shows that fifty-two per cent of Muslims in the UK want homosexuality to be banned.[20]

---

20 Source: https://www.theguardian.com/uk-news/2016/apr/11/british-muslims-strong-sense-of-belonging-poll-homosexuality-sharia-law

IX

The Globalists in Brussels

Europe is France and Germany: the rest is just trimmings.
— Charles de Gaulle

There was panic in the skyscrapers, blanched faces at Brussels; frowns of disapproval at the universities. The long faces at the BBC on the night of the 23rd of June 2016 said it all. This was never meant to happen. In the morning that followed, the furious Brussels Politburo stood on the podium with faces like smacked bottoms, giving monosyllabic answers to journalists' questions. They dished out veiled threats and spoke of 'consequences' and a 'painful process'. Subsequently, Jean-Claude Juncker spoke like a dictator, telling the British to get on with Brexit and invoke Article 50, reminding that anybody in Europe who shows dissent towards his project should expect to feel the 'consequences'. Anybody that stands up to this arrogant globalist project, such as the Hungarian Prime Minister, is called a 'dictator' by the President of the European Commission. Juncker is clearly determined to punish the British people for their decision to dent his empire. Juncker admitted that he has a little black book called 'Little Maurice' in which he lists the people that have betrayed him. The British people and Nigel Farage in particular clearly make for a significant entry in the book.

The media, the intellectuals, the IMF, the NGOs: they were all committed to the globalist project, and all used threatening language, speaking about the dire consequences of leaving the EU before the event: economic collapse and even war apparently. But the fight back against them and their mantra of political correctness had begun. First Putin, then

Brexit, Trump and subsequently a series of election wins for anti-globalist parties in Europe. Putin and Trump do not play by the globalist rules, and are therefore deemed to be a threat. Anybody that does not sign up unthinkingly to the European federalist project is a threat. Even after the Trump victory, Juncker and his stubborn brigade of Brussels oligarchs still do not apparently understand that his globalist vision is not the wish of the people.

Following Brexit and Trump's victory, the rules of the game must change, but the Western media is still reluctant to let one hear the alternatives. When was the last time anybody in the West actually listened to a speech by Putin? One doubts anybody who voted for Trump or Brexit, i.e. the majority of Britons, would disagree with much of what Putin has to say. His speeches are perhaps the most important since Churchill's, but there is a media blackout on them in the West. The media would not want the electorate to be exposed to an alternative, anti-globalist message. When one listens to his words, it is worth asking the question: why does the Western media never let us hear this?

The Brexit referendum must become a Berlin Wall moment, for Britain has shown that we can be liberated from Europe. We now have an opportunity to change the world and introduce a new national politics. The Brexit result is an excellent opportunity for Britain to look outwards, and not inwards. It is a chance for people to put freedom and sovereignty over GDP statistics and globalist sensibilities. Britain has shown that it can regain its place as a powerful, sovereign nation, and that it is stronger than the globalist, bureaucratic sand-castle in Brussels, which lacks both in a sense of common *demos* and mutual *telos*. The globalist groupthink dictated that any criticism of its project amounted to cultural atavism. With this kind of discourse, there is an insidious attempt here at invoking a falsified moral panic. The imperative is always that one must align oneself with the moral, cultural relativist community, and that this community has hegemony over morality issues.

The anti-globalist vote has just laughed at that absurdly simplistic, unilateral vision. The road-map to a one-world Government is now in tatters. Putin said he would smash the New World Order (NWO) in 2016. Through Russia's actions in Syria, he has shown that Russia can challenge any such order. He always said that 'ordinary people' would reject the ambitions of the globalists, and the Brexit vote has thankfully shown that he is right once again. The people voted against a single currency, a single banking system, a single army and most importantly a single political entity. The world now needs the age of anti-globalism, and there is every reason to believe its arrival is imminent, if it has not arrived already.

Things can now change. Charmless, painfully mediocre Clinton offered nothing new, just walking in the shadows of her husband. Americans have perhaps grown tired of the Establishment globalists running the White House. Hillary Clinton was just another personification of the globalist elite lie: she pledged the same old, tired identity politics, and was a politically correct open-border pioneer who thought she had a right to be elected just because she was a woman. She would have put her country on a war footing with Russia. But it is all fine as long as we have gay marriage, which in a typically unprincipled manner she decided was a good thing only once polls showed people were on average in support of it. What was unthinkable prior to the Brexit Referendum and the Trump victory is now very much on the table. It is clear that globalisation benefited a tiny elite and countries such as China and India, but not the average man on the street in the West. This failure of globalisation and unconventional monetary policies explains in part the Brexit and Trump victories.

As we have heard, political leaders in the West are no longer defending their country's interests, but instead are ceding power to something untested, a globalist, bureaucratic machine in Brussels that has led to widespread economic misery on the Continent, where in some countries such as Portugal, over 20 per cent of the population live below the poverty line. Others such as Greece have become failed states, little more than pathetic EU protectorates. Since it joined the euro, Greece's economy has shrunk by one third, and Italy's economy has not grown at all. This machine extinguishes not only democracy and political legitimacy at every turn, but it does not even create economic growth.

The leaders of European nations are willingly compromising their sovereignty and our democracy—that thing which is held dear by so many, or who at least have been told so many times we should defend it that they do so unthinkingly. Even for the sceptics, the argument is that we are too far down the road, and so in the words of Margaret Thatcher: 'we agree for the sake of agreeing, and being Little Sir Echo we say 'me too' '.[1] Surely, one cannot stay in something just because it is difficult to get out. One does not stay in a house that is burning down, just because it is difficult to get out.

From its very inception, it has in fact been the plan amongst the armies of Mephistophelean EU bureaucrats to get to the point where nation-states feel sufficiently uncomfortable about going into reverse that they introduce political union through the back door. And, indeed, with the Brexit debate it is clear that this has in fact worked as a policy. The majority of those who voted to stay in understood that the EU was corrupt and unworkable, but that we had gone so far that a reversal would be somehow more detrimental. Only once we voted to leave, did people realise how far we had gone down the federalist path (and potentially how difficult it might be to extricate ourselves from it).

The EU technocrats realise that a crisis represents an opportunity. That is why Hollande, the most unpopular President in French history, and Merkel allowed the 'refugee' crisis to happen. When the problem looks overwhelming, they can respond by saying that challenges such as climate change and mass immigration cannot be dealt with at a national level. Apparently, only an army of EU bureaucrats can tackle such issues. In other European countries, the general public seems to fall for this reasoning. The result is that national governments look weak, and the impression created is one where the 'big issues' can only be solved by a small oligarchic group who have their hands on the levers of power. This is undoubtedly the plan. The EU is now absolutely open about the fact that it intends to create an EU superstate. However, there is now at least reasonable hope that this may backfire spectacularly, and people will see this deception for

---

1   Source: https://www.youtube.com/watch?v=U2f8nYMCO2I

what it is. We have not yet entirely lost the grip on sovereignty, and the obvious flaws of the Schengen agreement were there for all to see after the Paris attacks of November 2015, and again in Berlin a year later. Now, that agreement is in tatters and effectively finished due to Merkel's pig-headedness, arrogance and her unilateral invitation to all Syrian refugees to come to Europe in the absence of any European agreement. After a string of terrorist attacks in the summer of 2016, she could only manage to insult her own people further by saying *Wir schaffen es*.[2] *Wir schaffen* what exactly? To turn Germany into the exact vision that ISIS portrayed in their policy document, *Libya: The Strategic Gateway for the Islamic State* (page 10), where militants were told to converge on Europe disguised as refugees. If she refuses to back down on her deeply unpopular policies, then we may see the incipient sociopolitical revolution move from the periphery to the centre of Europe. With recent challenges from the CSU on the issue of immigration, Merkel is left barely clinging onto power.

There is a strong parallel here between the phalanx of liberal groupthink found in academia (commented upon in the essay 'The Groupthink Trap') and the thinking of elected leaders of EU nation-states. There are many that sense there are very serious mistakes with the EU project, but they dare not speak out. The EU body has become so big and powerful that nation-states feel there is more to be lost from not being in it, even if there are many aspects which alarm them.[3] Those European states outside of it such as Norway, Switzerland and Iceland feel no doubt very differently about the matter, and must be breathing a sigh of relief that they did not concede to the bureaucratic monster.

---

2   Available at: https://www.youtube.com/watch?v=85UjD5sWnlQ

3   It is wrong to assume that big economies are necessarily successful ones. Of the ten countries in the world with over 100 million people, only the US and Japan are prosperous, and both of those are indebted and in decline. In a context of free trade and globalisation, it is better to be a small, flexible economy. Evidence for this comes from Iceland which was bankrupt in 2008, but just a few years later was one of the fastest growing economies of Europe when other larger European economies were still stagnant.

The defining characteristic of tyranny is the diversion of power from the people to an *unelected* elite, and thus it is reasonable to assume that the EU is a tyranny in the making. A tyranny is successful if the awareness of other possibilities has been removed. The EU Commissioners want more power, and intend to get it by replacing the nation-state model with a more virulent ideological substitute. Europe's politicians are complicit in this: for example, the former Swedish Prime Minister, Fredrik Reinfeldt, pushed through constitutional changes in 2009 to make it harder to leave the European Union (*En reformerad grundlag*, Prop. 2009/10: 80: p193). Many Swedish politicians claimed that they were given minimal time to discuss the proposed changes.

The European Union is profoundly undemocratic and is anxious to remove all national electoral accountability and subsume it under an unaccountable European Commission. After ignoring the 'No' result in both the French and Dutch 2005 referendums on the Lisbon Treaty, we were told that we needed the Lisbon Treaty to 'enhance democracy' in the European Union. It sounds like a bad joke. The Irish cancelled their referendum on the Treaty establishing a Constitution for Europe as they had assumed the Dutch and French results would put an end to the Lisbon Treaty, but also perhaps because the result of the Irish referendum on the Nice Treaty, where the Irish people voted 'No', was simply ignored. Wolfgang Schäuble, the German Interior Minister at the time, famously said: 'A few million Irish cannot decide on behalf of 495 million Europeans.'[4] Martin Schulz, the former President of the European Parliament, said, 'Those who supported the No vote have opened the door to fascism' (the much used tactic discussed in previous essays). It is quite right the EU needs to 'enhance democracy', but with every new treaty, it seems to be moving further and further away from any concept of representative democracy. The same Martin Schulz responded to Brexit by saying: 'The British have violated the rules. It is not the EU philosophy that the crowd can decide

---

4 Source: http://www.nytimes.com/2008/06/15/world/europe/15iht-union.4.137228 83.html

its fate' (27th June, 2016).⁵ This really tells us everything we need to know about the EU.

The horrendous fudge of the Lisbon Treaty which amends the Maastricht Treaty and the Treaty of Rome, both of which form the constitutional basis of the European Union, takes democratic authority away from the people. The Irish voted 'No' in 2008 which should have killed the treaty, but instead they held another referendum, because the European Commission does not accept national opposition to its totalitarian plans. The same thing happened with the Treaty of Nice in 2001 and 2002. Unbelievably, both French and Dutch voters voted in 2005 against the Treaty establishing a Constitution for Europe. Along with the French, the Dutch, as founding members of the European Economic Community, voted with a 61.5 per cent majority against the European Constitution. The French National Assembly ratified the treaty, and thus it is clear that this representative democracy does not in fact represent anybody at all. If democracy stood for anything, this should have stopped the process of forming a European Constitution. Instead, member states were bullied and legislation riddled with subterfuge clauses was introduced through the back door. This will always be the way the European Union does business, because it is totally impractical to expect twenty-eight nation-states to agree on everything.

The EU uses a familiar tyrannical methodology to deal with opposition. If an electorate votes against a treaty, then the result will either be ignored, or they will keep holding elections until they say 'Yes'. It was the same with Denmark and the Maastricht Treaty. With Brexit, the former British Prime Minister, David Cameron, claimed that he had reached an agreement on the reforms that he petitioned for. The agreed concessions were absolutely insignificant, but were sold to the British public as if it would be a whole new EU, the product of a fundamental renegotiation. All of the benefits of membership could have been accrued through free and bilateral independent trading with European countries. Free trade does not require a supra-governmental bureaucratic crucible. That only

---

5   Source: https://twitter.com/mediaserviceseu/status/748137210516504576

slows the process down, and sometimes makes it impossible.[6] Fortunately, the British public saw through the lies.

Only fanatic liberals want some kind of world governance run by concealed fiscal and technocratic groups. The EU wants to standardise and homogenise our thinking with one set of policies and values instilled in a mass psychology: liberal capitalism, multiculturalism, one foreign policy to overthrow dictatorial regimes and replace them with 'liberal democracies'; i.e. the message to the developing world is 'come here and work to support our indebted service economy, and we will bomb to smithereens the regimes we do not like'. What is more, we will do it in the name of democracy. This is apparently what a progressive, open society based on globalised enslavement should look like. The brutality of the West is dressed up in the soft, comforting quilt of equality, tolerance and diversity.

With every European treaty, more and more powers are taken away from national Governments and given to unelected European Commissioners. With the Lisbon Treaty which came into force on 1st December 2009, national parliaments are no longer able to amend European legislation, member states' veto has been removed in the Council of Ministers and the EU has expanded into many new policy areas (common fisheries policy, competition rules, customs union) where it has 'exclusive competence' excluding any action by member states.

---

6   The UK would have struck a free trade deal with the US years ago (as the US has already done with Singapore and South Korea) had it not been part of the European Union, whose mass, complexity and multiple interests means every negotiation process is endless. Negotiations on the Transatlantic Trade and Investment Partnership (TTIP, the proposed trade agreement between the EU and the US) have been going on for three years already (and now look to be completely dead-in-the-water) whereas the US-South Korea Free Trade Agreement was completed in thirteen months. It took the European Union four years to agree on the Chocolate Bill and issue a new directive. In October 2016, the Canadian Trade Minister, Chrystia Freeland, announced that the EU was 'not capable' of an international trade deal. 'Not capable' because twenty-eight countries cannot agree on anything except to pay the EU institutions' useless officials' inflated salaries for meddling with national sovereignty and for creating thousands of new, unneeded laws.

The shift in power and the manner in which it is enforced is scandalous, and has no place in any permutation of a free democracy. The European Parliament, which is of course not a parliament at all as there is no government and no opposition, is the first parliament in history not to have the power to propose or repeal legislation. The Parliament represents nothing more than a gesture to convince national electorates that the European Parliament is the ultimate democracy, when in fact it is little more than a fraudulent gesture. The European Parliament, so distant from its citizens, is effectively a talking shop; its power is symbolic. With very low turnout for European Parliament elections, it lacks any kind of democratic legitimacy. Legislation comes from the unelected Commissioners, the Politburo, and their 230,000 staff. It is only on the basis of a Commission proposal that EU Council Ministers are allowed to deliberate at all. So it is not necessarily the case that British representatives at the Council can stop laws that go against our own interests.

Powers have been transferred to unaccountable and anti-democratic bodies such as the ECB, who claim that such a transfer was necessary in the name of crisis management — a crisis which they (in conjunction with Germany's export mercantilism that led to the balance of payments crisis) themselves engineered. These bodies decided they will have complete legal immunity for themselves (as set out in Protocol on Privileges and Immunities of the European Communities). European Monetary Union was a fudge from beginning to end. Everybody in the financial markets knew that. The debt ratios of Belgium, Italy, Spain, Ireland, the Netherlands and Austria all failed the Maastricht criteria in 1998. Belgium's debt-to-GDP ratio was 124 per cent at the time of entry, but it had to be below 60 per cent. The agreed criteria written into the Treaty on the Functioning of the European Union were simply ignored. It was also obvious that the political desire on behalf of a few leaders (and not the overall population, which was largely against it) was such that it would be forced through even if that meant serving up lies, misinformation and never-ending compromises.

Financial convergence aside, a conspiracy theorist would surely suggest that the EU has allowed mass immigration to destroy the coherence of nation-states and undermine national sovereign Governments, so that they can impose their non-virtuous EU governmental oligarchy. Following the Greek financial crisis, the response by the French President Hollande was to say on the 20th of July 2015 at the height of the migration crisis that the problem was that 'we needed more Europe, and not less of it'.[7] He went on to say that it is time to create a Government of Eurozone countries. Tragically, member states signed off on this hand-over of power to unelected oligarchs when they signed the Amsterdam Treaty and the Treaty of Lisbon (which was not even signed by the British Prime Minister). Just as Jacques Delors predicted in 1998, the irremovable European Commissioners might be making up to 80 per cent of the laws that affect member states.[8] According to the House of Commons Library, 59 per cent of laws affecting the UK in certain sectors over the last five years have been made in Brussels.[9] These overpaid, grey bureaucrats wish to control the global masses, even their thinking. And most people do not even know who they are. As Margaret Thatcher said: 'What is the point of being elected to this Parliament, just to give all the powers away?' (30th October, 1990).[10]

The European Commission, the executive branch of the EU staffed largely by rootless transnationals, wants to strip out the last vestiges of national sovereignty and make national elections irrelevant. The unelected EU President has been explicit about this, and it represents frankly the ingredients of a revolution. The former Vice-President of the European Commission, Viviane Reding, said in her speech at the University of Passau (8th November, 2012):

---

7   Available at: http://www.bbc.co.uk/news/world-europe-34468694

8   A former German President once put it as high as 84 per cent: http://www.telegraph.co.uk/news/worldnews/europe/8067510/Up-to-half-of-British-laws-come-from-Europe-House-of-Commons-Library-claims.html

9   Source: http://www.telegraph.co.uk/news/worldnews/europe/8067510/Up-to-half-of-British-laws-come-from-Europe-House-of-Commons-Library-claims.html

10 Source: https://www.youtube.com/watch?v=U2f8nYMCO2I

At Maastricht people wanted to have us believe that we could irreversibly establish a monetary union and a new world currency without creating a United States of Europe at the same time. That was a mistake, and now that mistake needs to be corrected if we want to continue to live in a stable, economically prosperous Europe; I believe a United States of Europe is the right vision to surmount the current crisis, but above all to overcome the failings of the Maastricht Treaty. Ultimately, as a European Christian Democrat, I cannot allow my vision of the future to be dictated by British Eurosceptics.

What we are witnessing now is a silent crisis of democracy at the heart of Europe, an emergence of a bureaucratic oligarchy on the pretext of being the only medicine for financial turmoil. Europe is now a continent of EU-sponsored *coup d'état*, led by the world's expert on tax evasion, Jean-Claude Juncker. One might ask what kind of democracy chooses its President in secret meetings, as the EU did. What is more, the first President of the European Union, Herman Van Rompuy, who liked to tell us the nation-state is dead, appeared to be completely unknown to everybody outside Belgium. It is ironic that we should have to hear this message from somebody who comes from a country that is so torn along nationalist lines: it has two parliaments and two Governments.

In time, many people might look back at this Europe and ask how this federalisation was ever allowed to happen. The answer is: just as with mass immigration, the vast majority of people were never asked, and when they were their opposition was overruled. Now that euroscepticism has shown its true colours with the Brexit result, we must campaign to ensure that every member state lets its people decide the future of this dictatorial project. According to the European Commission's own research, only 23 per cent of the EU population believed in May, 2013 that 'things are going in the right direction' when it comes to the EU.[11] And, no wonder. Sometimes the EU is even explicit about creating a European Government by stealth. The final report of the Future of Europe Group (September, 2012)

---

11 Page 59 of the Eurobarometer 2013 report: http://ec.europa.eu/public_opinion/archives/eb/eb79/eb79_publ_en.pdf

includes a proposal for 'a directly elected Commission President who personally appoints the members of his European Government'.[12] The people of Europe were told this was necessary as it was the only way to hold the peace in Europe, because nationalism always leads to war. But it has nothing to do with peace and belligerent nation-states. In my opinion, it is much more likely that the emergence of a totalitarian superstate — the multiculturalist juggernaut — will lead to war.

The number of nation-states have multiplied since 1945. There are new nations and new concepts of nationalism all over the world following the decolonisation period in the 1950s and 1960s and the dissolution of the Soviet Union in 1991. The non-violent Velvet Revolution led to the emergence of two new nations at the heart of Europe: the Czech Republic and Slovakia. There are now fifty-four independent member states of the African Union, but at the end of the Second World War only Ethiopia, Egypt and South Africa were independent.

So why do people assume that in the absence of the EU, we would all be at war? It is first and foremost propaganda used to justify the new, multicultural EU federalist empire. It is a pretext for creating a superstate whose Commissioners are answerable to nobody, whose accounts have never been signed off on and whose enormous power encompasses twenty-eight countries. We should not be relinquishing sovereignty to unelected European Commissioners at a time of crisis. We cannot take the passports away from British passport-holding ISIS jihadists, of which there may be over 1,000, because of the European Convention on Human Rights which litigates for the protection of stateless persons. This is no time for nations to be ceding such powers.

In 2011, elected Prime Ministers in Italy (Berlusconi) and Greece (Papandreou) were removed by bullying European technocrats and replaced by former Goldman Sachs employees after the ECB deliberately suspended its support for the Italian bond market by buying the bare minimum of bonds. During the Euro Crisis, the European Council of the

---

12   Source: http://www.cer.org.uk/sites/default/files/westerwelle_report_sept12.pdf

Heads of the Eurozone governments emerged as the key decision-making body. Unregulated by law and aloof from democratic constituencies, it managed the crisis by authoritative decision-making. In 2016, Goldman Sachs employed Barroso, the President of the European Commission who supervised the removal of national, elected leaders. This is how far the 'liberal' authoritarianism has gone. Greece was told by the EU President when it should have an election. The implication was that in order to calm the markets, conventional politics must be suspended. With these kind of actions, it is clear that the policies of the European Union will lead to its own collapse.

The EU oversaw a financial crisis so extreme that national economies can only be kept afloat by an ECB that buys up all their debt. The EU has used the financial and migration crises as an excuse for full fiscal and political union amongst member states. It is apparently only those that created the crisis that can get us out of the crisis. Putin is watching this and like the rest of the sane world can barely believe what he is seeing. In the heart of Europe, there is a system of thought which is sufficiently destructive, it will completely undermine the nation-states and lead to a United States of Europe run by a few grey technocrats. Attempts to undermine, ridicule and transcend national borders and identities end up in centralised totalitarianism, as in the Soviet Union. The former Eastern Bloc countries joined the EU to regain their sense of sovereignty, but have now discovered that they just passed their sovereignty from the Soviet Union to the European Union.

X

In Denial

From husks and rags and waste and excrement
He forms the pavement-feet and the lift-faces;
He steers the sick words into parliament
To rule a dust-bin world with deep-sleep phrases.

When healthy words or people chance to dine
Together in this rarely actual scene,
There is a love-taste in the bread and wine,
Nor is it asked: "Do you mean what you mean?"

But to their table-converse boldly comes
The same great-devil with his brush and tray,
To conjure plump loaves from the scattered crumbs,
And feed his false five thousands day by day.

— Robert Graves

The view from Château Hill is serene. The palm-tree lined Promenade des Anglais encircles the pale sand and the rhythmically grating surf of the Côte d'Azure. Pebbles hastily in retreat mark the shank of the evening. The shadowed mountains undulate in the evening crimson and crayola sky. With its imperious façades and pink roof, Hotel Negresco — home to red-haired grande dames — sashays as the epitome of French faded elegance, of *temps passé* when the truly wonderful Sir Roger Moore with his luxuriant dulcet tones would be seen playing Lord Brett Sinclair of *The Persuaders* beneath the Baccarat chandelier. With all its eccentricity, froth and from above the mink bed-spreads, the spangling Bay of Angels sweeps effortlessly past. French poodles feeling confident and in the pink sniff the fragrant breeze.

It is Bastille Day, commemorating the beginning of the French Revolution, and the *Maralpins*' celebrations will continue long into the night. After the military parades in Paris, great crowds of people have gathered on the Prom to watch the renowned fireworks display. The sky lights up and young children gasp, tightening their tiny grip on their parents' hands. Then, the horror begins. A lorry mounts the pavement of the Promenade des Anglais and accelerates into a crowd of terrified knee-height children. The Tunisian *jihadist* careens down the promenade in a frenzy, swaying and swerving to crush as many people as possible. He smiles and laughs aloud as the blood of his young victims first spatters and then floods the wind-screen. Bodies are smashed onto the bumper, dragged under the lorry and then crushed under the weight of the vehicle. Young women soaked in blood lie helpless on the pavement, screaming, trying to resuscitate their dead babies lying next to them. The nineteen-tonne lorry drives for just over a mile along the promenade smashing into the dispersing crowds, the killer shooting at those desperately trying to flee before the home-grown mass murderer is shot by the police.

A man in a lorry killed eighty-six innocent people and injured 434 others, all of whom had gathered to celebrate the French national holiday. Mohammed Lahouaiej-Bouhlel is one of a reservoir of do-it-yourself *jihadists* living in France. In the wake of the attack, Hotel Negresco's main hall was used to triage the hundreds of wounded. Porters donning blue frock coats, red knee breeches and top hats and looking as if they belonged to another era were seen ferrying mangled bloody bodies of children into the Royal Lounge, commissioned by Czar Nicholas II. This is the new norm in France.

Shortly after, the French police destroyed all the CCTV footage of the attacks. Twenty-four hours of footage was destroyed from memory cards. As with every Islamist terrorist attack in Europe, the media reproduced the factual information, and then quickly moved on to puerile stories about celebrities' weight loss. Within a few days, all was forgotten and the evidence had been erased. Life goes on. After all, there was no *jihad* here. The films of Islamists savaging Westerners are broadcast all over the internet by ISIS, but any footage of Islamist atrocities that ends up in the hands of the police in the West is erased. There was no *jihad* either in France in December 2014 when a driver in Dijon did the same thing, mowing down dozens of pedestrians shouting Islamic slogans. We were told once again it was the work of a mentally unbalanced man whose motivations were vague and 'hardly coherent'. His intentions could not have been more coherent if he had tried to make them so. Just two months earlier, a spokesman (Al-Adnani, 22nd September 2014) for ISIS announced that Westerners should be attacked using any means possible: 'Smash his head with a rock, or slaughter him with a knife, or run him over with your car, or throw him down from a high place, or choke him, or poison him'.[1]

As mentioned previously, another part of our new cultural grammar is obfuscation — covering things up — preventing people from knowing the truth. The fact that obfuscation exists implies that political leaders realise that the impact of telling the truth about what is happening could be just too incendiary. Obfuscation of aspects of the Muslim migration issue has created a dangerous cocktail of lies and cover-ups in Sweden. In August 2015, an Eritrean man who was about to be deported entered an IKEA store in Sweden on a Saturday afternoon and partially beheaded a fifty-five year old Swedish woman who was shopping with her son. Her twenty-eight year old son was also killed. This brutal atrocity was completely covered up by the Swedish media who described it as a 'knife attack', which in 2015/16 has become something of a ritualised term.

The Government is feeding Swedes a diet of lies, trying to conceal the reality of the fiasco of its immigration policy. Somebody at the crime scene took a photo with a Smartphone. It is clear that a customer's head was (partially) removed using a knife. The advent of social media means it is not possible to cover-up these terror acts, and expect to get away with it. After the double murder, IKEA closed the shop and put up a notice saying that the store was closed because of a 'technical error'. As we have seen

---

[1] Source: http://www.independent.co.uk/news/world/middle-east/isis-urges-more-attacks-on-western-disbelievers-9749512.html

previously, it is reasonable to assume that in a pseudo-totalitarian country like Sweden, the media and politicians collude on a regular basis to ensure the multiculturalist project is not tarnished in any way. We know that this happens at a corporate level with the Wallenberg family, which owns a third of the Swedish stock market and collaborates closely with the Government. So much for equality.

This kind of thing is not happening just in Sweden: the Enemedia (to use Pamela Geller's term) across Europe (but not in the UK where there is to be found fortunately a much more aggressive kind of journalism) gloss over the facts. If one listens to the accounts the nuns gave who witnessed the beheading of the French Catholic priest in July 2016, they speak of how the ISIS attackers filmed the beheading while laughing and how the hostages were forced to speak Arabic at the altar on which the Sacrifice of the Mass is offered.[2] The symbolism of the barbaric event is beyond taboo, with a Catholic Priest being 'sacrificed' at the altar in his own church by two thugs who claimed to be acting in the name of religion. Forcing the Congregation to chant the synecdochic *Allahu Akbar* is a metaphor for the attackers' desired Islamification of France. The French media were quick to suppress the details, saying that the Priest had his 'throat cut' and making no mention of the forced invocations. The news item was quickly replaced with a piece of celebrity gossip about somebody or other potentially being pregnant.

Back in Britain, the BBC went a step further in accommodating radical Islam by providing a platform for hate-*imams* such as Choudary. Such media complicity might suggest that liberal modernity is beginning to subside into nihilism. A resurgent Islam is being juxtaposed with a self-deprecating ideology of failure. If an ideology turns in on itself like this, it surely means that its life is coming to an end. Liberal society will end when the Islamist attacks in Europe are so sustained that the electorate has no choice but to vote for parties that offer radical solutions, or

---

2   Source: https://www.theguardian.com/world/2016/jul/26/men-hostages-french-church-police-normandy-saint-etienne-du-rouvray

when immigrants from the Middle East become the majority group in European countries. That moment is rapidly approaching, and the first option is being chosen by many voters.

With the exception of SD, it seems all the political parties in Sweden are reluctant to question this culture of obfuscation. The twenty-two year old Swedish girl working in a Swedish refugee centre who was stabbed to death by a fifteen year old asylum seeker in January 2016 was headline news in the UK, but was barely mentioned in the Swedish newspapers.[3] It was just another 'knife attack'. The Swedish media covers up the crimes of asylum seekers and illegal immigrants. It was *The Daily Mail* that showed his photograph in the UK newspapers. In Sweden, he was anonymous.

Unable to tell the truth about the mass rapes in Stockholm which were covered up in Sweden (but reported by the BBC) following the migration crisis of 2015/16, journalists such as Ivar Apri are forced to express their views in publications such as *The Spectator* (February, 2016) in the UK.[4] The series of grenade attacks in Swedish suburbs in 2018 was covered in full by *The New York Times*, but ignored by the Swedish media. Such events should have been a sword of Damocles for the Swedish Government, but instead they were just whitewashed. It is more than regrettable when newspapers in apparently one of the most 'open' and 'liberal' countries in the world refuse to publish the truth, even when it is written by well-respected journalists. A spate of rapes and attacks by asylum seekers on Swedish women in the hitherto sleepy town of Östersund was fully reported on in the British Press, but absolutely no mention was made in the Swedish Press.[5]

The Swedish media will do anything to divert the hearer or reader from the truth of the crime epidemic that broke out in Sweden following the

---

3   Source: http://www.telegraph.co.uk/news/worldnews/europe/sweden/12121070/Migrant-fatally-stabs-female-refugee-centre-worker-in-Sweden-say-police.html

4   Source: http://www.bbc.co.uk/newsbeat/article/36713031/more-than-40-sex-assaults-reported-at-two-swedish-festivals

5   Source: http://www.telegraph.co.uk/news/worldnews/europe/sweden/12188274/Police-warn-women-not-to-go-out-alone-in-Swedish-town-after-spate-of-sex-attacks.html

mass migration of 2015. The media was busy in the winter of 2015 trying to convince Swedes that the real news story was Russia, and the fact that Sweden apparently faced an immediate military threat. The same tactic was used the following summer to cover up the news story of large groups of Swedish girls being assaulted at music festivals around the country one weekend after the other. The radio (P1) even managed to find a senior Army officer to tell listeners that Russia would attack Sweden within five years. In May of 2018, Sweden distributed leaflets to every Swedish household telling them how to respond to an invasion (from Russia). Swedes use Russia as a scapegoat as it is too sensitive to talk about Islam. It has been a common tactic to cast Russia as the enemy when it is obvious that the West will need her to defeat militant Islam.

Instead of imposing sanctions on Russia, a country that strongly defends traditional Christian values, it is surely time to impose sanctions on Saudi Arabia, which for forty years has financed Islamic extremism all over the world. It is estimated that Saudi Arabia, a country where running a blog promoting the freedom of speech could get you 1,000 lashes, might have spent US$100 billion on promoting Islamic extremism over the last forty years.[6] Cableleaks prove that the West has known about this for a considerable amount of time. Reports from the European Parliament and the United States Senate Committee both verify this, and even the German Vice-Chancellor has (finally) spoken out against it publicly.[7]

As has been noted, Sweden has a continuous, unambiguous national identity and a strong system of national values. But the Government wishes to present Sweden as a 'rootless' country, when its roots are in fact much less mixed and intertwined than many other European nation-states. It is precisely this cultural sharedness that underpins strong communities.

The former Leader of the Opposition, Mona Sahlin — the master (or mistress) of self-abusive discourse — said that Muslim immigrants to

---

6   Source: World Affairs Journal (May/June 2015).

7   European Parliament Directorate General for External Policies: 'The Involvement of Salafism/Wahabism in the support of arms to rebel groups around the world' (2013).

Sweden had a culture, a history and identity whereas Swedes had nothing but a Midsummer's Party (in a speech to the Turkish youth organisation Euroturk, March, 2002). Previously in 2000, the same woman said that if there are two equally qualified candidates for a job, then it should go to the one called Mohammed.[8] She also claimed that it is for Swedes to integrate into the new Sweden, not vice versa, i.e. Swedes should become Muslims.[9] Subsequently, it was rumoured that she converted to Islam. The very same woman was appointed two years ago as the first ever official co-ordinator against violent extremism. The anti-racist propaganda streamed through the State media has tragically embedded itself in the psyche of the Swede. It is attempting to negate the natural collective consciousness of Swedish society. If a culture cannot assert itself, if it is not authoritative in any way, then it will indeed wane and be replaced with something else. It is deeply troubling that one cannot question so-called multiculturalism in Sweden without being denigrated.

Europe is living in the age of *jihad*, and yet jihadist sympathisers were appointed to the Government in Sweden, and in the case of Jeremy Corbyn hold the post of Leader of the Opposition in the UK. Jeremy Corbyn has described Hamas as 'friends', and has shared a platform with the British representative of an Iranian-backed militia which killed British troops.[10] This is how far things are going awry. Only now in the light of revelations of anti-semitism in his party are prospective Labour voters beginning to reassess their opinions of him. In 2016, Sweden's Housing Minister, *Miljöpartiet*'s Mehmet Kaplan had to resign once it was proved that he had links to extremist groups. In the summer of 2014, he compared *jihadists* who travel from Sweden to Syria to the Swedish volunteers who travelled to Finland to fight in the Winter War in 1939-40.[11] And yet all one will

---

8   In an interview with the Swedish newspaper *Göteborgs-Posten*, October 22, 2000.

9   Source: *Ungt val* (eng. Young Election/Choice) section of the Swedish newspaper *Aftonbladet*, March 15th 2002.

10 Source: *The Telegraph*, 18th July 2015.

11 Source: http://www.thelocal.se/20141014/former-swedish-mp-calls-minister-an-islamist

read about in the Swedish Press is how Kaplan was on the receiving end of racist abuse, and thus his position as 'victim' is assured. Subsequently it was shown that Islamism had infiltrated the party far more deeply than suspected. Anxious to pursue a pro-Muslim agenda, Sweden became the first EU country to recognise a Palestinian state — a gesture which has left the Swedish police investigating whether the State of Israel is planning an assassination attempt on the Swedish Foreign Minister, for many in the Middle East believe Sweden is funding Hamas (via the NGO Islamic Relief Worldwide to whom the Swedish state paid SEK 24 million in 2013).[12]

There must be a sense of 'fellow-feeling' in societies, as Carl Schmitt (2007), who was keen to promote realism (and not utopianism and the fetish of diversity), would have said. Without such, Sweden will have lost its meaning and sense of purpose. It risks becoming a multicultural entity without direction and self-worth because radicals will have abnegated the heritage, traditions and history shared amongst Swedes for over a thousand years. But Schmitt would have argued that this liberal utopianism that many Swedes stand for cannot succeed. It will be very successful in making society 'diverse' (as understood in the ideological sense), but will be completely incapable of managing the conflicts that come with it and will of course never replace capitalism. We need to be able to communicate such meta-political messages about authoritarian liberalism, before it becomes a case of there being something 'rotten in the state of Sweden'.

One might wonder why one would pursue the politics of folly when it is obvious that it is not working. This is undoubtedly the hardest question to answer. Is it simply serving a small liberal elite in Government and their perverse nihilistic ideology? The liberal elite might respond by saying that accepting refugees without posing questions is just part of what it means to be Swedish. When I asked Fredrik Reinfeldt (the former Prime Minister of Sweden) at the Oxford Union why he wanted so many 'refugees' to come to Sweden, he just shrugged his shoulders and

---

12 Source: http://www.ngo-monitor.org/reports/swedish_funding_for_hamas_terror_via_islamic_relief_worldwide_the_burden_of_proof_is_on_europe/

said nonchalantly, 'Where do you want them to go?' 'Well, surely, it is in everybody's interest if they go to the Muslim Gulf States', I responded. But, no, there is always the sense that Sweden must do its humanitarian duty irrespective of the prospect of the country ending up as some kind of *macédoine* of cultural conflict.

A hard-liner might argue the aim is to destroy the traditional Western culture and weaken its civilisation in accordance with the Gramscian cultural Marxist ideologies; to divide and weaken the northern European-derived populations, break down their ethnic consciousness and national cohesion, so that they never again will have the opportunity to organise an ethnically conscious and collectivist movement like the German National Socialism of the 1930s.

Moral relativism, the belief that there are no higher values or moral judgements, and thus that all values are merely the expression of personal values, risks, as we have seen, clashing with fundamentalist radical Islam; and then the seeds of cultural destruction are sown. One society refrains from passing moral judgement on all beliefs and cultural practices beyond its own, and the other will impose death penalties on the practice of beliefs that run counter to its own. One society believes there is no one privileged standpoint and indeed goes as far as legislating against such (assertions of religious superiority might be a criminal offence in Canada and parts of Europe); the other thinks there can be only one standpoint.

Moral relativism can be defended on its own merits or at least accounted for by the declining importance of religion, but for it to practically bring about tolerance it stands to reason that everyone has to subscribe to it. If one has two neighbouring cultures that insist on moral objectivism, one might have the ingredients for cultural conflict. If one culture based on moral relativism is juxtaposed to one based on moral objectivism or absolutism, then a scenario of likely cultural wane on behalf of the relativists is likely to emerge. All that will happen is that an intolerant ideology such as radical Islam based on absolutes will be allowed to spread. An act of benevolence will be perceived as an easy opportunity, and the empty churches might be turned into mosques. Society in the West needs to be remoralised because the prevalence of moral relativism (and the collapse of moral objectivism) means in practice that we are not able to defend ourselves politically. With anti-Enlightenment relativism, the moral discourse implodes because the individual's truth must be the only truth. But morality has surely always been relational.

The problem of a nation not being able to defend itself politically is acute in Sweden and Germany. It might be asserted that the reason why Sweden and Germany are so open to mass Muslim immigration lies in the devastation of the Second World War. Europeans are living with the burden of guilt of Nazism and Communism, and in response to the former have been conditioned to be passive. Swedes might feel guilty about their neutrality during the war, for trading with the Nazis, about their economy profiting so significantly from the Marshall Plan in the immediate post-war era. It is the guilt of the Protestant variety for a nation that is discarding its Lutheranism. The fascist stigma has become too potent, closing down debate. It is often just recycled as a meaningless label. This is nothing but a misplaced *Vergangenheitsbewältigung* ('coming to terms with the past'): unlike the German, there are very few grounds for the Swede to live with a guilt complex. What is more, there are a whole list of nations trying to come to terms with their recent past (Russia, Colombia, Argentina, Cambodia) but it seems that only Germany has created a word for it. These countries have not implemented counter-intuitive policies that explicitly attempt to reverse historic events.

The guilt complex, if there should be one, has anyway nothing to do with Islam. The explanation for such an extremist immigration policy cannot be a post-colonial guilt complex. Sweden was never a colonial nation of any scale. Nor is it reasonable to state that Sweden's involvement in two world wars can be the explanation. Sweden was neutral. Many may wish to evoke the Swedish Nazi Party, but it was of little relevance, never accounting for more than one per cent of the electorate (Widfeldt, 2015: 74). It had diminished further by the outbreak of the war. The media likes to fuss over such things, but the fact is they were always statistically irrelevant.

It is presumably a delayed, and irrational response to the Swedish post-war mass hysteria—a response to the policies of racial purity and sterilisation that continued in Sweden until 1976, and which are the subject of many revisionist, journalistic publications. For this reason and others perhaps, Sweden, acting as the world's conscience, has embarked on a dangerous national project.

It is probably also a question of winning votes, as Labour's experiment with multiculturalism in the 2000s was. It is fair to assume that this has a role to play. The Swedish Social Democratic Party, which has been in Government for three quarters of the last century, needs to bolster its weakened supporter base. Until recently, Swedes would apologise for not voting Social Democrat. The party slogan was *gör din plikt, kräv din rätt* ('do your duty, demand your rights') which meant do your duty and vote Social Democrat, and make sure we see to all of your needs when we are in power. Still today, there is a sense that the election of a non Social Democrat Government (coalition or otherwise) is something of a *coup d'état*. This is a country where Tage Erlander was Prime Minister for an astonishing twenty-three years. Today, we would call that a dictatorship (even if it was not one).

As far as Sweden is concerned, it is difficult to see if there is any grand conspiracy at work, but one might not want to rule it out. Sweden apparently set off on this multiculturalist path because of a feeling of collective historical guilt regarding the Nazi supporters in inter-war Sweden. It is as if some kind of colonialist debt must be paid which was never owed. Thirty years later, it was decided for whatever reason that one way Sweden could address this problem and show the world that it meant well was to accept refugees from war zones. Thirty years down the road again, there was surely an at least private recognition amongst some of the political elite that the policy had got out of control, and that things were going badly wrong.

It started off as a form of national benevolence, but few saw the magnitude of the humanitarian crises coming, nor did militant Islam enter the equation. But, they had gone far down the road and worked so hard to get people to accept their policies by effectively outlawing any discussion of them that they could not turn round and admit that the experiment had been one enormous failure. Instead, they saw the rise of the SD party, whom they had excluded from debate and labelled fascists and racists, and proceeded on that basis to convince the electorate that they would have to continue with the policy no matter how disastrous it was.

And 'excluded' they were. Up until recently, they were completely ostracised from the public debate. Now, polling on 20 per cent, that is more difficult for Sweden to accomplish without appearing democratically flawed. Swedish journalists are open about the fact that the media should not 'reflect' what is going on in society, but that journalists should 'evaluate what they should promote' (Booth, 2015: 336).[13] The Swedish State and its journalists like to treat its electorate like children, shielding them from any 'deviant' opinions, spoon-feeding them with the multiculturalist discourse.

The Norwegian Government has calculated that the costs of supporting a refugee in Norway for a year are roughly ten times what they would be to support one in the same manner in Iraq.[14] Spending the same money, Norway and Sweden could help ten times as many refugees if they stayed where they are (and granted, this would currently be unworkable in Syria with the current situation in 2017). It is not then always about 'helping' people, but perhaps getting some kind of personal gratification for thinking one is helping people (just as we saw with many of those who work for NGOs). This is liberalism after all. Furthermore, these Governments would of course save billions on policing, schooling etc. In 2016, having watched its neighbour Sweden almost collapse, Norway offered asylum seekers £1,000 to leave the country.[15]

Having used obfuscation and criticism of the State as harmful ideological tools, Sweden went one step further by telling Swedes that race is nothing more than a social construct. But if race does not exist, how

---

13 According to Stefan Jonsson, formerly of *Dagens Nyheter* and now a Professor of Ethnic Studies.

14 As reported by the Norwegian Minister of Finance, Siv Jensen, at a speech given at the Fremskrittspartiet annual meeting (2015).

15 Source: http://www.telegraph.co.uk/news/2016/04/26/norway-to-pay-asylum-seekers-extra-money-to-leave/

can racism, the perpetual obsession of the liberal politicians, exist? If race does not exist, why do they talk of mixed-race children? The response from the spokesman for the *Afrosvenskarnas Riksförbund* (National Afro-Swedish Association), Kitimbwa Sabuni, was: 'The Government is lost in a fantasy' (31st July, 2014). Sweden's liberals are indeed lost in their own self-delusion. This is clearly a flawed attempt at controlling language and limiting the freedom of thought. These kinds of policies have Orwellian undertones, as the ultimate objective is clearly to render the very conception of race impossible.

Sweden has gone from being a country that had a eugenics programme to ensure that the State would not have to give financial support to the 'unfit' to a country that has actively promoted immigration from the least developed countries in the world. This represents a 180 degree swing from the radical right to the radical left, and presumably the latter is a response to the former. This is how politico-ideological cycles tend to work. Multiculturalism might be perceived as a reversal of an historic event. The Nazis promoted racial superiority where Arabs were at the bottom of the ladder. Sweden's current policy is the diametrical opposite of this, and thus one might call it anti-Nazist.

And, yet, Sweden has so many advantages over other countries that she need not muddle herself with such ideological self-laceration: a diversified economy, a very highly educated workforce and most importantly of all a low population. Sweden's blessing is its relatively low population. It should be something that is preserved at any cost, for most of the world's problems would be irrelevant had it not been for the silent population explosion that has taken place in the world these last fifty years. For him who comes from an overpopulated land, the benefits are absolutely obvious.

The average birth rate in the EU is 1.38 children per family, but the population of countries like Sweden and the UK is increasing rapidly. The reason for this is solely immigration. Sweden's Leftist politicians seem completely blind to the advantages that space to move gives people, and are anxious instead to fill up the country with people who share nothing in common with them. They might benefit from living for a while in an overpopulated country such as the UK; then, they would be in no doubt as to all the tremendous advantages that are bestowed upon a country with a low population density. They would see how overcrowding threatens to tatter the shires of England.

XI

OVER THE BROW OF THE HILL

A day without laughter is a day wasted.
— CHARLIE CHAPLIN

AN ELECTION WIN FOR TRUMP, the Brexit referendum result and the Italian General Election in 2018 tell us amongst other things that there is a willingness to put aside our political correctness and confront the real issues before the chaos of a *Jacquerie* ensues. Many have resolutely decided they will no longer sit in silence and bite their proverbial tongues. They do not want to wake up a few years down the road just to discover that they have become part of a different *Mitsein* riddled with angst and meaninglessness, where their social norms, customs and traditions have been washed away in the name of secularist multiculturalism.

The ideologies behind mass migration and community-denying globalism are now proving to be self-defeating. Until they are defeated, Britain risks becoming some kind of desperate prophetical microcosm for an overpopulated world where mobility is completely impossible, where London is bursting at the seams with new, inhuman skyscrapers that foster a secular, consumerist spirit that reduces productive decisions to simulacra of consumer choices and where tempers match the exigencies of overcrowding. Our overspilling island might metaphorically resemble one of those large rubber dinghies in the Mediterranean with African refugees clinging to the side. Surely, we do not just want to be left with a disappearing countryside, forlorn-looking cottages, a crippling nostalgia, and an attempt to reconfigure an identity overseas.

A small island cannot continue to take in quarter of a million people each year *ad infinitum*. But because politicians refuse to discuss the issue, let alone tackle it, we should indeed expect the system to collapse long before might even be anticipated. Analogous to this, the EU open-borders policy now looks like a bad joke. EU Commissioners ignore the outright failure of their own policies and as a result now risk causing total collapse of the EU project. One is left wondering if many of these Commissioners are complicit in the globalist project that has been referred to in some of these essays. It is not unreasonable to assume that is the case, especially as some of them are funded (indirectly) by one of the key architects of the crisis: George Soros.

In these changing times, when people have awoken to the true motivations behind globalism and EU federalism, there are now thankfully more and more islands of sensible level-headedness, with a clear vision unpolluted by globalist ideology about how the plurality of humanity should unfold. It is these few, rightly flustered by the things-being-not-altogether mood, that realise we cannot continue to turn the other cheek, that we have to confront the illiberal mob, trudge right through their groupthink and laugh at their debate-silencing tactics.

They understand that we are now at a point where more than ever before, we need 'nobility' (in the Nietzschean sense of the word), and not a demoralising legacy. We need a community of people who possess themselves entirely, are philosophically autonomous, unruffled by the weak, herd morality and the hegemony of ideologies which try to undermine sovereign nations and people. These men will greet danger and threats with splendid sangfroid, with *veritas et fortitudo*. They will not allow the principles of sovereignty to be demonised because they will have recognised the mental prison that the globalists are trying to herd us into. Globalism can only function if sovereignty, borders, notions of separate cultures and group beliefs are erased. There is an ulterior motive to their rhetoric. It might be that the unelected elite wish to rule over us without the slightest hindrance.

This community of people must be strong enough to undemonise notions such as 'tradition' and conservatism by making people realise that tradition, customs, morality and social norms are not just our past, but are our present and future. Globalism should be undermined through decentralisation and localism. This group of people will not look up to or be persuaded by any faux-utopian vision or false self-opinion because they can still experience and revel in their authentic instincts. They are not incarcerated in the mental and linguistic prison invoked in earlier essays. Instead, they look at life from within, not from above, not from the lofty unreality of inflated grandiloquence. They do not suffer from the Nietzschean 'slave vanity' (*Eitelkeit*) — the propensity to accede in one's self-estimations to the opinion of others. These forces of 'slave vanity' bring about a recognition of the liberal Holy Grail — the doctrine of universal equality — but do not translate into equality at the ontological level.

No brow of the hill is without danger. As one approaches the hill, one might feel confident about one's prospects. But then comes the moment when one has not quite reached the top. One cannot yet see down the other side of the hill. It is not a blind spot, but something could potentially come shooting the other way, shatter one's optimism and change everything forever. That is the point we are at with this migration *mêlée*, and that is why this final, incoherent, slightly stream-of-consciousness bundle of thoughts has the title 'Over the Brow of the Hill'. Like the brow of a hill, it represents a moment of potentially very false ontological security.

In looking over the brow of the hill, one of the many problems conservatives are going to have to tackle is language and the cultural grammar that has been described herein. It should be apparent to everybody that the Left in conjunction with the globalists have a monopoly on the political shibboleths of the day: universalism, human rights, equality and diversity, and all the other tired old platitudes that are trotted out time and again in the institutionalised meta-drivel. As platitudinous as they are, these terms are not innocuous, but are used by the globalists as an ideological agenda to beguile the masses. In this book, I have attempted to provide a critical analysis of the speech code that liberalism weds itself to: groupthink sceptics must now work together to expose the real intentions of this speech code.

One can call the likes of Le Pen, Farage and Trump 'racist', but any un-ideologised, intelligent person can see that their message has very little to do with 'race', and everything to do with anti-globalism and anti-Establishment. The 'race' word is almost always nothing more than a red-herring to deflect from the real issue, which is globalism. Judging by how frequently liberal globalists recycle these catch-words such as 'diversity' and 'tolerance', one might assume that they believe through their constant repetition alone that they can actually change reality, that they have entirely penetrated the liberal psyche.

Liberal globalism with its psycho-cultural agenda should really concern everybody except for the completely rootless *ensemble* of Swiss-boarding-school-educated, nose-jobbed brats. Its agenda is the global mobility of capital goods, people and information at lightning speed. Any impediment to this, such as borders, national jurisdiction, notions of belonging, but also freedom of speech, must be removed as they will create obstacles to the globalist multinationals. All these things problematise control for a global elite who hypocritically preach cultural relativism, and at the same time overthrow any regime that they oppose in the name of liberal democracy. It is always about control and power.

The constant recourse to these 'diversity' and 'tolerance' shibboleths just renders their meaning more and more vacuous. And so conservatives need to establish their own shibboleths and encapsulate them into skilful panegyric: tradition, heritage, rule of law, conservation (in the broadest sense), freedom and independence perhaps. Without such a referential frame, social conservatism will continue to flounder. It has lost direction, listing like a ship heeling to one side. Conservatism has forgotten its basic principles, and it is high time for a renaissance. It needs to rediscover its language, the terms that frame its philosophy.

In short, we need a new cultural grammar to underpin the multi-polar, anti-globalist philosophy. We don't need speech codes or double-speak, but we need a a set of rigid principles. A cultural grammar that can show rational, sensible people that 'tradition' and conservatism in the apolitical sense is not xenophobia as the liberal globalists want us to believe.

It has nothing to do with that. This cultural grammar must show that it represents an idealism of its own (and not just an antipathy towards liberalism), one that is not based on arbitrary whims but enduring realities. As such, it would be a *real* cultural grammar that described concepts pertaining to real, tangible things and not intangible ideas of global governance. This cultural grammar would rise up against the censorship, and self-censorship that is enveloping us and that allows the multiculturalist project to go ahead unheeded. We must dispel the tapestry of lies that suggest this is incontrovertible 'progress'.

Currently, our freedom and freedom of speech appears to be conditional on these liberal shibboleths. That is to say freedom of speech only exists in the sense that it conforms to the heavily politicised notions of 'diversity' and 'tolerance'. If we must have hate-speech legislation, then it should protect the ethnic majority, not criminalise them and legislate only in favour of the minority. If the German MP Stefanie von Berg addresses the German *Bundestag* and tells her peers that Germans *must* be a minority in their own cities, then that might be considered hate-speech. If we need the legislation, then that would surely be a more rational basis to litigate upon.

The problem with conservatives appears to be that they take their inspiration from the past, from traditional social structures and institutions whereas the Left seeks to reject all moral authorities that transcend human purposes. Any objection to this is a manifestation of bigotry. The conservative agenda is perceived to be 'unprogressive' because it is not socially meliorist and does not favour 'progress' over 'tradition' (Pabst, 2010: 66). Meliorism is a noble effort no doubt, but meliorists tend to overlook the fact that man is in Gehlen's language a *Sonderentwurf* ('a special project'); his heterogeneous life-world is more complex and less malleable than the meliorists presuppose.

There is a necessity for Europe to present itself as 'modern', but it cannot do this by appealing to its authentic antiquity. The telos has to be apparently secular, and thus post-Christian. But we cannot continue the European legacy without the 'archaic' idiom. 'Progress' would appear to be the *sine qua non* of any forward-looking society, and any philosophy that is part of that society. But of course one can progress without abnegating all one's customs, traditions, sense of morality etc. There are few politicians who would not stand under the moralising banner and embrace 'progress'; there are perhaps even fewer that would not advocate 'social justice'. But the 'justice' or the 'progress' that has been discussed always refers to the group (not the individual), and it is a universal abstract progress. The Left might not hesitate to put down or hold back an individual, but provided the group can pass by unfettered, then that is progress. Their objection to selective Grammar Schools in England is an obvious example of this. The demonisation of clever people can never be progress.

The Left has a vision — a flawed and unrealistic one — but it has a vision, whereas traditional conservatism has a legacy. Or at least, that is how the Left wishes to present it. It is perhaps this 'legacy' criticism that enables Leftist thinking to assume an *a priori* correctness. But far from being a positive anthropology, Leftist liberalism, as we have seen, is uniformly negative. It wants to undermine Western values in the name of economic competition, 'diversity' and 'tolerance' which, as we have seen, are code words for concepts which are potentially rather sinister. There is nothing positive in supporting an ideology which does little more than attempt to negate every inherited value and institution in the book. This has to be one of the platforms from which Leftist thinking can be attacked and undermined. It is not an ideology of 'progress' at all, but one of annihilation, a case of *schafft sich ab* ('doing away with itself'; Sarrazin, 2010). It is an admission of defeat at a time of Islamist extremism, and it is defeat without even the hint of a struggle. It is a case of *kein Kampf*, with rather a lot of topspin being put on the word *kein*.

But if the 'voice of dissent is the voice of the hero' (Scruton, 2015: 59), then perhaps the time for new conservatism, and the return to the local, has come, since it is surely time to dissent against the cultural repudiation that Leftist thinking has imposed on us. Future migration crises might shatter our societies. Certain globalist political leaders have refused to listen to their respective electorates, perhaps because their overall agenda reaches beyond them. We must liberate ourselves from the truth-denying rhetoric that feeds off false conflicts, and prevents us from drawing conclusions based on common sense. The point that has been made throughout this book is that there is really *nothing* to be gained from embracing cultural nihilism. In order to look forward to a less tragic telos of modernity, we must understand this.

The Brexit result has given us anti-globalists great hope, the *deus ex machina* that some of us have been waiting for. It has shown that we can beat the globalists, the multinationals, the overpaid antediluvian bureaucrats with their plump pensions who think they can rule over us without a mandate from their Brussels offices. Moreover, it has shown us that Brexit might mark the beginning of the twilight of liberalist modernity, and return us to a more familiar world of ethnopluralism (every nation has a right to sovereignty). Liberalist pluralism is just at the moment beginning to look rather fragile. There is now a feeling that common sense must at some point prevail. After all, why would any half-proud nation want to *schafft sich ab* in the manner that Sweden is doing?

Once we have emerged from the travails of liberalist modernity, from the globalist tyranny that uses multiculturalism to subvert sovereign nation-states, we must only hope that the façade of human sovereignty and the sanctity of the land is not inexorably blemished, and that we can again look over the horizon and find the fields still green. We must hope that more remains than just the banality of the global consumerist frenzy. We must ensure that our ancient farm lands, which have been harvested for generations by families and friends, remain what they are, and are not blotched with cul-de-sacs of tiny, terraced houses with many-hued faces, faiths and fancies staring blankly from the *fenestra*. Britain and Western Europe will have to emerge from the tangled hinterland of the gigantic tattoo parlour that it has become, and face the coarser realities.

We have forgotten one important, fundamental lesson on this peculiar relativist track that liberals have tried to lead us down: people perceive life differently because they are different. The objectives of one-world globalism and its universalist view of humanity are based on fundamental flaws about human nature. World citizenship with one proletarian state will never work for this reason. And now it is time to deliver ourselves of a searching point or two along these lines, before we find ourselves truly in the soup: politics needs to be based on reality again, and not fantasy. Politicians must rediscover their mettle and state the obvious as Trump and Farage (with different degrees of aptitude) have done time and time again: multiculturalism has been a hideous failure, political correctness leads to self-censorship, cultural repudiation is nihilistic and serves no meaningful purpose, the EU oligarchic project that has convulsed Europe has for many nations simply not worked. We need alternatives and these are independence, sovereignty and self-determination. Politicians aside, what we all as individuals must do is 'speak out'. We must smash the groupthink and speak up for what we believe is right. That is the greatest imperative. We must challenge any infringements put on the freedom of expression.

Thankfully, not everybody agreed with the former NATO supreme commander, General Wesley Clark, when he said in 1999: 'There is no place in modern Europe for ethnically pure states. That's a nineteenth century idea and we are trying to transition it into the twenty-first century, and we are going to do it with multi-ethnic states.'[1] The implied sense of purpose and agency here is worrisome, particularly as this comes from the man who was responsible for the illegal 'humanitarian' NATO bombing of Yugoslavia in 1999. It was the largest attack ever undertaken by the alliance, and was against a nation that posed no threat to a NATO member state. One might even infer from Clark's comments that an attempt to preserve a mono-ethnic nation *should* be met with a NATO onslaught of uranium bombs and cluster munitions. We cannot allow our nations and communities to be melted down by the multi-ethnic discourse like this, and spread like dripping butter on the ideologically perverse toast. And thus when Theresa May says: 'if you are a citizen of the world, you are a

---

1 Source: http://en.metapedia.org/wiki/NATO

citizen of nowhere', it looks like, in the UK at least, we are edging back to the politics of common sense.[2]

Looking over the brow of the hill, there are many things which can be done to counter-attack the kind of globalist liberalism with its rhetoric that has been commented on in these essays. It is firstly imperative that the peoples of other European countries have the opportunity to determine their future in Europe. If a democratic right to a referendum is refused, then that tells us all we need to know about the EU. If member states are permitted referendums from their elected Governments, then we will see the whole project dismantle over the coming years. That is to say, the EU is a false democracy whose Commissioners are pursuing the policies of multiculturalism (to the point of destabilisation) without any mandate to do so. Beyond encouraging democratic referendums in respective European nation-states, other measures that could be taken in the UK might include: repeal the European Convention on Human Rights and rewrite hate-speech legislation to protect the ethnic majority (and not the minority), or else just scrap it. Hate-crimes are absurd, anomalous and Orwellian. We must not waste our time trying to police synthetic anger. But, do not permit me to dwell on some sort of sanctimonious wish-list compiled at leisure over the fragments of small-talk.

Instead, let us now turn our attention to languorous Sweden where the situation is more alarming because of the deception of the State-sponsored media that likes to indulge in the agonies of perjury. The unthinkable needs to be done: the Swedish welfare state should be reformed. It is true that Sweden has an ageing population, but the solution to this cannot be to import large numbers of people from the poorest countries in the world. The Swedish welfare system is comprehensively abused. Nearly a quarter of a million people were on long-term sick leave in 2015 (for a labour force of just 5.0 million [2014]; in 2002, 298,000 people were on sick leave for a labour force of 4.6 million) and being well paid by the

---

2 Source: https://www.theguardian.com/politics/2016/oct/09/theresa-may-rejection-of-enlightenment-values

State to do nothing.[3] As many of these people as possible need to get back to work, and an Australian-style points immigration system should be introduced to make up for the shortfall in skilled labour. Egalitarianism in Sweden is such that the infrastructure in place is not there to reward people who want to work harder and get on in life. They will be simply punished through higher taxes, and all those benefiting from the system will reap the awards. This system really must be reformed and made far less generous, and then the apparent ageing population problem will soon go away because younger people will be forced back to work, and with much lower taxes they will be motivated to work harder.

As has been mentioned elsewhere, it is absolutely vital that Sweden establishes an alternative media where the facts can be heard, and not just the Swedish Government multiculturalist ideology that attempts to unscrupulously banish opposing views. Only then will Swedes understand the ultimate paradox: liberalist modernity is not liberal at all. It is quasi-totalitarian.

These private media channels must lift the lid on the collusion between politics and media, so then the obfuscation can be seen for what it is. Swedes must be freed from the blinding, patronising ideology, so that they can regain their critical awareness and see all the problems that face Sweden not just from the perspective of the mollycoddling Government and not from a perspective that is just immediately deemed to be racist. However, we should not expect the State media to reform because it is obviously in the interest of the ruling Government to have that media as its mouthpiece, as a powerful voice of party propaganda. The media is there to fulfil a political function, to smother the population in its malignant, multiculturalist rhetoric. This rhetoric is so terrifyingly powerful that it is only an outsider who listens to it with such a pained grimace. The ideologised Swedes are apparently blind to its politicised message. The purpose of this book has been to try and address that regrettable status quo.

---

3   Source: http://www.ekonomifakta.se/Fakta/Arbetsmarknad/Fortidspensionerade-och-sjukskrivna/Sjukskrivna/

It is only once a plausible alternative to the State-sponsored media has been established that the truth about what is happening in Sweden can be known, and the ensnaring totalitarian mentality can be tackled. The lies must end. Then, and only then, can Sweden become the open, free democracy that people think it is and that the erroneous league tables tells us it is. Of course, there are some small private radio channels that tell the truth, but they lack funding and most people have never heard of them. Swedes would be frightened of being labelled a racist for listening to an alternative, un-State sponsored view of what is really going on in this country. In Sweden, people serve the State. They do not ask questions. It might even be frowned upon to ask questions because that would break the bond of conformity. In a country where servitude is expected, individual rights can be suppressed. Swedes have almost no rights for instance when up against the authorities in the Swedish courts. But, Sweden has come to such a point that it is absolutely essential to ask questions. Unquestioning conformity at a time of crisis is insidious.

Sweden must of course deal with the problem that it has created, that of segregated Muslim communities of outsiders. This is not the place for a discussion of how to go about this, and I do not have the mental complacency to dictate to a country how to run its affairs. One is concerned here with ideologies, and not dry political manifestos. But permit me a few unsubtle observations. One objective measure of integration is surely the ability to speak the language of the host country. If after three years of help and tuition, a 'refugee' still has no fluency in the language, then this is probably because a conscious decision has been made not to integrate into Swedish life. Swedish is not a particularly difficult language to learn. Where possible, the future 'refuge' options of these people should be reconsidered, as it is obviously in nobody's interest to create diaspora of unintegrated exiles.

Sweden should ban *shariah* law, for equality, which is after all the national creed, is blasphemous according to *shariah*—equality for men and women, homosexuals and heterosexuals. So, surely, *shariah* must be legislated against. It would be contradictory to talk endlessly about equality, but oppose this. What is blasphemy to them is the *raison d'être* for many Swedes. The country should send a strong message saying that incomers must adapt to the Swedish way of life, accept the basis upon which Swedish law is founded, and not vice versa. Those that drink, those that are gay, those that are Christian, those that are having extra-marital affairs — I have just described Stockholm — all of them are punished under *shari'ah* law and some of them would have to be stoned to death. Not a single European country bans *shari'ah* law.

As an all signed-up feminist country, other measures that should be taken are a ban on the *burqa*, *niqab* and *chador*, as indeed Denmark has recently done. It is clear that this kind of Islamic dress has no place in the most feminist country in the world. That is the stuff of cartoons. These are basic, reasonable measures that have a very simple message: if you come here, you respect our customs, public culture and way of life. You have to play by the rules.

As a good UN member, Sweden should really determine whether those that have sought 'refuge' still actually require it. Repatriation is the preferred UN outcome, but that seems to have been forgotten in Sweden. In cases where peace and stability has returned to the country, then the refugees that have not yet gained Swedish citizenship (i.e. recent arrivals) should, where possible, be asked to leave. Voluntary repatriation should be sought in the first instance, but then the cases for the repatriation of recent Afghan and Pakistani 'refugees' for instance might be taken up. These few measures alone would send an unambiguous message to any plotting migrants that things have changed, the door has closed and that Sweden, that 'end-of-history paradise' as *The New York Times* called it (December, 2015) has not completely lost its sanity.[4]

Arguably, more important than all these measures is the need for the Swedish Government, media and social institutions to foster again a positive belief in Sweden and its heritage. It should be a statement of

---

4   Source: https://www.nytimes.com/2015/12/27/opinion/sunday/cracks-in-the-liberal-order.html

affirmation, and not hostility to others. The ongoing migration crisis cannot be tackled until this process of affirmation takes place. As has been noted, the crisis of identity in Sweden is unnecessary and entirely self-inflicted, and so the re-establishment of positive beliefs will require a degree of ideological unwinding. In so doing, the Swedish heritage, public culture and social norms must be first defended against all internal and external threats. If they are not, then the prerequisite of social attachment is jeopardised and Swedish society risks becoming undone with adjacent communities living in accordance with very different value systems, as is the case in parts of the war-torn Middle East.

Europe cannot go on the way it is. Any European that goes to the US is shocked by seeing unapologetically right-wing presenters on television. It is perhaps only then that they realise such a thing would be totally impossible in Europe, and that we have drifted so far into a whirlpool of Leftist thinking that relies on naïve, secularist visions of the world. The European media no longer reflects on the whole the views of the advocates of the sociopolitical revolution that is unfolding. The biased media coverage in certain European countries will have to change, and there are signs now that this is beginning to happen (but not yet in Sweden). The phlegmatic layers of society, the intelligent people with some common sense, are beginning to stir.

If all European countries were to implement some of the measures suggested above, then this would deliver a *coup de grâce* to the globalist project of border-free multiculturalism, which seeks to entirely undermine our socio-cultural legitimacy. And, as we have seen, with its toxic cultural grammar, it seeks to do this by devious means. Measures such as these would help our countries to remain free, but also for us as individuals to remain free. I believe this can be done and I believe there is now some hope. These and similar measures might maintain a shaky *pax Europaea* and enable us to fret a little less over the atlas of the future.

BIBLIOGRAPHY

Abu-Lughod, Lila. 1995. 'The Objects of Soap Opera: Egyptian Television and the Cultural Politics of Modernity', in *Worlds Apart*, edited by D. Miller. London. Routledge: 190–210.

Adamson, Göran. 2015. *The Trojan Horse: A Leftist Critique of Multiculturalism in the West*. Malmö: Arx Förlag.

Arnstberg, Karl-Olov and Sandelin, Gunnar. 2013. *Invandring och mörkläggning*. Stockholm, Debattförlaget.

Assange, Julien. 2015. *The Wikileaks Files: The World According to US Empire*. New York: Verso Books.

Austin, John Langshaw. 1962. *How to Do Things With Words: The William James Lectures Delivered at Harvard University in 1955*, edited by J. O. Urmson. Oxford: Clarendon.

Bakhtin, Mikhail. 1984. *Problems of Dostoevsky's Poetics*, edited and translated by Caryl Emersen. Minneapolis: University of Minnesota Press.

Baudrillard, Jean. 1993. *Symbolic Exchange and Death*, translated by Iain Hamilton. London: Sage.

Bauman, Richard and Charles L. Briggs. 2003. *Voices of Modernity: Language Ideologies and the Politics of Inequality*. Cambridge: Cambridge University Press.

Baumgartner, Frank and Jones, Bryan. D. 1993. *Agendas and Instability in American Politics*. Chicago: University of Chicago Press.

Bawer, Bruce. 2007. *While Europe Slept: How Radical Islam is Destroying the West from Within*. New York: Anchor.

Bell, Daniel. 1976. *The Cultural Contradictions of Capitalism*. New York: Basic Books.

Berdyaev, Nikolai. 1933. *The End of Our Time, Together with an Essay on the General Line of Soviet Philosophy*. London: Sheed & Ward.

Bergson, Henri. 1899 (1975). *Le rire: essai sur la signification du comique*. Paris: Presses universitaires de France.

Berman, Paul. 2011. *The Flight of the Intellectuals*. New York: Melville House.

Bernstein, Richard. 1995. *The Dictatorship of Virtue: How the Battle over Multiculturalism Is Reshaping Our Schools, Our Country, and Our Lives*. New York: Vintage.

Bessire, Lucas and Fisher, Daniel. 2012. *Radio Fields: Anthropology and Wireless Sound in the 21st Century*. New York and London: New York University Press.

Bloom, Allan. 1987. *The Closing of the American Mind: How Higher Education Has Failed Democracy and Impoverished the Souls of Today's Students*. New York: Simon and Schuster.

Boghossian, Paul. 2007. *Fear of Knowledge: Relativism and Constructivism in Academia*. Oxford: Clarendon Press.
Bolton, Lissant. 1999. 'Radio and the Redefinition of Kastom in Vanuatu'. *Contemporary Pacific*, 11 (2): 335–60.
Booth, Michael. 2015. *The Almost Nearly Perfect People: Behind the Myth of the Scandinavian Utopia*. London: Vintage Books.
Bowers, C. A. 1985. 'Culture against Itself: Nihilism as an Element in Recent Educational Thought'. *American Journal of Education*, Vol. 93, No. 4: 465–90.
Browne, Anthony. 2006. *The Retreat of Reason: Political Correctness and the Corruption of Public Debate in Modern Britain*. 2nd Revised Edition. London: Civitas, Institute for the Study of Civil Society.
Bruckner, Pascal. 2010. *The Tyranny of Guilt: An Essay on Western Masochism*. Princeton, NJ: Princeton University Press.
———. 2007. 'Enlightenment, Fundamentalism or Racism of the Anti-Racists?' http://www.signandsight.com/features/1146.html: German version 'Fundamentalismus der Aufklärung oder Rassismus der Antirassisten?'
Burke, Edmund. 1790. *Reflections on the Revolution in France*. London: James Dodsley.
Burnham, James. 1964. *Suicide of the West: An Essay on the Meaning and Destiny of Liberalism*. London: Jonathan Cape.
Churchill, Winston. 1899. *The River War*. London: Longmans.
Clover, Charles. 2016. *Black Wind, White Snow: The Rise of Russia's New Nationalism*. New Haven: Yale University Press.
Clowes, Edith W. 2011. *Russia on the Edge: Imagined Geographies and Post-Soviet Identity*. Ithaca: Cornell University Press.
De Benoist, Alain. 2011. *Beyond Human Rights: Defending Freedoms*. London: Arktos Media.
De Benoist, Alain and Champetier, Charles. 1999. 'Manifeste: la Nouvelle Droite de l'an 2000'. *Eléments*, No. 94, February 1999: 11–23.
Drummond, Nicholas W. 2014. 'Immigration and the Therapeutic Managerial Government'. *Telos* 166 (Spring 2014): 174–80.
D'Souza, Dinesh. 1998. *Illiberal Education: The Politics of Race and Sex on Campus*. New York: Free Press.
Dugin, Alexander. 2012. *The Fourth Political Theory*. London: Arktos Media.
Eco, Umberto. 2007. *Turning Back the Clock: Hot Wars and Media Populism*. Translated by Alastair McEwen. San Diego, California: Harcourt.
———. 1970. 'Codes and Ideology'. In *Linguaggi nella società e nella tecnica*. Milan: Ed Communità: 545–57.
Eliot, T. S. 1939. *The Idea of a Christian Society*. New York: Harcourt, Brace and Company.
———. 1933. *After Strange Gods: A Primer of Modern Heresy*. The Page-Barbour Lectures at the University of Virginia. London: Faber & Faber.
Evola, Julius. 2003. *Ride the Tiger: A Survival Manual for the Aristocrats of the Soul*. Rochester, Vermont: Inner Traditions.

———. 2002. *Men Among the Ruins*. Rochester, Vermont: Inner Traditions International.
———. 1995. *Revolt Against the Modern World*. Rochester, Vermont: Inner Traditions International.
Finkielkraut, Alain. 2015. *La seule exactitude*. Paris: Stock.
———. 2013. *L'identité malheureuse*. Paris: Stock.
Foucault, Michel. 1983a. 'Discourse and Truth: The Problematisation of Parrhesia'. Six lectures given by Michel Foucault at the University of California at Berkeley, Oct-Nov, 1983.
———. 1983b. 'The Subject and Power'. In *Michel Foucault: Beyond Structuralism and Hermeneutics*, edited by H. Dreyfus and P. Rainbow. Chicago: University of Chicago Press: 208-26.
Fromm, Erich. 2004. *The Fear of Freedom*. London and New York: Routledge.
Garnett, Mark. 2004. *The Snake that Swallowed its Tail: Some Contradictions in Modern Liberalism*. Exeter: Imprint Academic.
Gehlen, Arnold. 2004. *Moral und Hypermoral. Eine pluralistische Ethik*. 6th edition. Frankfurt am Main: Vittorio Klostermann.
———. 1967. 'Die Sekulärisierung des Fortschritts'. In Arnold Gehlen's *Gesamtausgabe, Einblicke*, 1978, edited by Karl Siegbert Rehberg. Frankfurt am Main: Vittorio Klostermann.
———. 1940. 'Der Mensch. Seine Natur und seine Stellung in der Welt'. Translated as 'Man, his nature and place in the world'. In Arnold Gehlen's *Gesamtausgabe*, Vol. 3, edited by Karl Siegbert Rehberg. Frankfurt am Main: Vittorio Klostermann.
Gellner, Ernest. 1987. *Relativism and the Social Sciences*. Cambridge: Cambridge University Press.
Goldberg, Johan. 2009. *Liberal Fascism: The Secret History of the American Left, From Mussolini to the Politics of Change*. New York: Crown Forum.
Gottfried, Paul. 2002. *Multiculturalism and the Politics of Guilt: Towards a Secular Theocracy*. Columbia: Missouri: University of Missouri Press.
Gramsci, Antonio. 1971. *Prison Notebooks of Antonio Gramsci*. London: Lawrence & Wishart.
Greenhill, Kelly. 2009. *Weapons of Mass Immigration: Forced Displacement, Coercion and Foreign Policy*. Ithaca: Cornell University Press.
Hadlow, Martin. 2004. 'The Mosquito Network: American Military Radio in the Solomon Islands during World War II'. *Journal of Radio and Audio Media*, 11 (1): 73-86.
Heidegger, Martin. 1990. *Being and Time*. Translated by Joan Stambaugh. New York: Wiley, John & Sons.
Herodotus. 1996. *The Histories*, translated by Aubrey de Sélincourt and edited by John Marincola. London: Penguin.
Horowitz, David. 2006. *An Unholy Alliance: Radical Islam and the American Left*. Washington, DC: Regnery Publishing.
Hosken, Andrew. 2015. *Empire of Fear: Inside the Islamic State*. London: Oneworld.
Houellebecq, Michel. 2015. *Soumission*. Paris: Flammarion.

Howell, Signe. 1982. *Chewong Myths and Legends*. Singapore: Malaysian Branch of the Royal Asiatic Society.
Hunter, James Davison. 1991. *Culture Wars: The Struggle to Define America*. New York: Harper Collins.
Huntford, Roland. 1971. *The New Totalitarians*. London: Allen Lane.
Janis, Irving L. 1972. *Victims of Groupthink*. New York: Houghton Mifflin.
Kalb, James. 2008. *Tyranny of Liberalism: Understanding and Overcoming Administered Freedom, Inquisitorial Tolerance and Equality by Command*. 2nd edition. New York: Intercollegiate Studies Institute.
Kant, Immanuel. 1993. *Grounding for the Metaphysics of Morals*, translated by James W. Ellington. 3rd edition. Indianapolis: Hackett Publishing Co.
Kimball, Roger. 1990. *Tenured Radicals: How Politics Has Corrupted Our Higher Education*. Chicago: Ivan R. Dee.
Kirkpatrick, Bill. 2013. 'Voices Made for Print'. In *Radio's New Wave: Global Sound in the Digital Era*, edited by Jason Loviglio and Michele Hilmes. New York: Routledge.
Laidlaw, James. 2013. *The Subject of Virtue: An Anthropology of Ethics and Freedom*. Cambridge: Cambridge University Press.
Le Bon, Gustave. 1982. *The Crowd: A Study of the Popular Mind*. Atlanta, Georgia: Cherokee Publishing.
Leiken, Robert. 2011. *Europe's Angry Muslims: The Revolt of The Second Generation*. Oxford: OUP.
Lewis, Wyndham. 1977. *The Code of a Herdsman*. Glasgow: Wyndham Lewis Society.
Linkola, Pentti. 2009. *Can Life Prevail?* London: Arktos.
Löwith, Karl. 1995. *Martin Heidegger and European Nihilism*. New York: Columbia University Press.
McLuhan, Marshall. 1968. *War and Peace in the Global Village*. New York: Ginko Press.
Milbank, John and Pabst, Adrian. 2016. *The Politics of Virtue: Post-Liberalism and the Human Future*. London: Rowan & Littlefield.
Mrázak, Rudolf. 2002. *Engineers of Happy Land: Technology and Nationalism in a Colony*. Princeton: Princeton University Press.
Nawaz, Maajid. 2012. *Radical: My Journey Out of Islamist Extremism*. Guildford, Connecticut: Lyons Press.
Nietzsche, Friedrich. 2003. *Beyond Good and Evil: Prelude to a Philosophy of the Future*. Translated by R. J. Hollingdale with an Introduction by Michael Tanner. London: Penguin Books.
O'Dell, Tom. 1997. *Culture Unbound: Americanisation and Everyday Life in Sweden*. Lund: Nordic Academic Press.
Orwell, George. 1944. 'What is facism?' *Tribune*.
Pabst, Adrian. 2010. 'The Crisis of Capitalist Democracy'. *Telos*: 44–67.
Patriarch Kirill of Moscow. 2011. *Freedom and Responsibility: A Search for Harmony — Human Rights and Personal Dignity*. London: Dartman, Longman and Todd.
Popper, Karl. 1945. *The Open Society and Its Enemies*. London: Routledge.

Powers, Kirsten. 2015. *The Silencing: How the Left is Killing Free Speech*. Washington, DC: Regnery Publishing.
Projections of the Ethnic Minority Populations of the United Kingdom 2006–2056. 2010. Department of Social Policy and Intervention. University of Oxford.
Qutb, Sayyid. 1964. *Ma'alim fi al-Tariq*. Chicago: Kazi Publications.
Ramalingam, Vidhya. 2012. 'The Sweden Democrats: Anti-immigration politics under the stigma of racism'. Working Paper No. 97, Centre on Migration, Policy and Society. University of Oxford.
Raspail, Jean. 1973. *Le Camp des Saints*. Paris: Éditions Robert Laffont.
Revel, Jean-Francois. 1985. *How Democracies Perish*. New York: Harpercollins.
Rosen, Stanley. 1969. *Nihilism*. New Haven: Yale University Press.
Sarrazin, Thilo. 2010. *Deutschland schafft sich ab: Wie wir unser Land aufs Spiel setzen*. München: Deutsche Verlags-Anstalt.
Schmitt, Carl. 2007. *The Concept of the Political*. Expanded edition (1932), translated by G. Schwab. Chicago: University of Chicago Press.
Scruton, Roger. 2015. *Fools, Frauds and Firebrands: Thinkers of the New Left*. London: Bloomsbury.
———. 2014. *How to Be a Conservative*. Oxford: Bloomsbury.
———. 2012. *How to Think Seriously about the Planet*. New York: OUP.
Sharma, Ruchir. 2016. *The Rise and Fall of Nations: Ten Rules of Change in the Post-crisis World*. London: Allen Lane.
Sogner, Sølvi. 2016. 'Demography and Family, c.1650–1815'. In *The Cambridge History of Scandinavia*, edited by Kouri, E. I. and Olesen, Jens E., Volume 2, 1520–1870. Cambridge: CUP: 441–453.
Soral, Alain. 2011. *Comprendre l'Empire*. Paris: Éditions Blanche.
Spengler, Oswald. 1991. *Decline of the West*. An abridged version. Oxford: OUP.
Storhaug, Hege. 2011. *But the Greatest of these is Freedom: The Consequences of Immigration in Europe*. Createspace.
Sue, Derald Wing. 2010. *Microaggressions in Everyday Life: Race, Gender, and Sexual Orientation*. Oxford: John Wiley & Sons.
Sunic, Tomislav. 2011. *Against Democracy and Equality: The European New Right*. 3rd Edition. London: Arktos.
Tacchi, Jo Ann. 1997. *Radio Sound as Material Culture in the Home*. PhD dissertation, University College London.
Tallentyre, S. G. 1906. *The Friends of Voltaire*. London: Smith, Elder & Co.
The Koran. 2014. Translated by N. J. Dawood. London: Penguin.
Traub, James. 2016 (February 2nd). 'Little Sweden has taken in far more refugees per capita than any country in Europe. But in doing so, it's tearing itself apart'. *Foreign Policy*.
Tuchman, Barbara W. 1984. *The March of Folly: From Troy to Vietnam*. New York: Ballantine Books.
Turnbull, Colin. 1972. *The Mountain People*. New York: Simon & Schuster.

Vattimo, Gianni. 2004. *Nihilism and Emancipation: Ethics, Politics and Law*, edited by Santiago Zabala. New York: Columbia University Press.

Vidali-Spitulnik. 2012. 'A House of Wires upon Wires: Sensuous and Linguistic Entanglements of Evidence and Epistemologies in the Study of Radio Culture'. In *Radio Fields: Anthropology and Wireless Sound in the 21st Century*, edited by Lucas Bessire and Daniel Fisher. New York and London: New York University Press: 250–67.

Vygotsky, Lev. (1987). 'Thinking and speech'. In R. W. Rieber & A. S. Carton (Eds.), *The Collected Works of L.S. Vygotsky, Volume 1: Problems of General Psychology* (pp. 39–285). New York: Plenum Press. (Original work published 1934.)

Widfeldt, Anders. 2015. *Extreme Right Parties in Scandinavia*. London; New York: Routledge.

Woodward, Ashley. 2009. *Lyotard, Baudrillard, Vattimo: Nihilism in Postmodernity*. London: The Davis Group Publishers.

Ye'or, Bat. 2011. *Europe, Globalisation and the Coming of the Universal Caliphate*. Madison, NJ: Fairleigh Dickinson University Press.

Zakharine, Dmitri. 2010. 'Audio Media in the Service of the Totalitarian State'. In *Totalitarian Communication: Hierarchies, Codes and Messages*, edited by Kirill Postoutenko. Bielefeld: Transcript Verlag: 157–77.

Zemmour, Eric. 2014. *Le suicide français*. Paris: Albin Michel.

Žižek, Slavoj, 1989. *The Sublime Object of Ideology*. London: Verso.

INDEX

0–9

1975 Immigrant and Minority Policy (Sweden). *See* Immigrant and Minority Policy of 1975
1984 (Orwell). *See* Nineteen Eighty-Four
2014 Swedish General Election, 100, 119–120
2015 Counter-Terrorism and Security Act (UK). *See* Counter-Terrorism and Security Act of 2015 (UK)
2016 Nice truck attack, xvii, 215–217
2016 US presidential election, xii, 36, 83
2018 Italian General Election, 229
2018 Swedish General Election, 113
9/11, 73, 164

A

Abu-Lughod, Lila, 141
academia
    academics, 34–35, 78–79, 81, 154, 206
    Bias Response Teams, 78
    developments in, x, 3, 16–17, 77, 96
    diversity and, 16–17, 77, 83
    elitism and, 14–16
    EU and, 206
    freedom of speech and, 12–14, 23, 33–34, 77–79, 81–82, 135
    gender and, 13, 33–34, 52
    groupthink and, 12, 14, 30
    Islam and, 139
    Marxism and, 32, 34–35
    political correctness and, 53–54, 60, 77
    political opinions and, 25, 34–36, 83, 96
    safe spaces and, 58, 78–79
Acerbo Law, 113
Adelsohn-Liljeroth, Lena, 149
affirmative action, 53
Afghanistan and Afghanis, 106, 113–114, 117, 129, 195, 197, 240
Africa, 25, 90–91, 94, 101, 133, 164, 192, 213. *See also* North Africa
Afrosvenskarnas Riksförbund, 227
Aftonbladet, 150
Ahlul Bayt Foundation, 139
Åkesson, Jimmie, 74
Al-Khaled Samha, Mohamed, 69
Al-Shabab, 117
Alternativ för Sverige (Swedish political party), 107
alternative media. *See under* media
Al-Qaeda, 11, 98, 129
Alternative für Deutschland (German political party), xvi
Althusser, Louis, 80
America. *See* United States
Amin, Idi, 90–91
Amis, Martin, 98
Amsterdam Treaty, 211
Andersen, Hans Christian, 64
Angolan Revolution, 90–91
anti-elitism. *See under* elitism
Antifascistisk Aktion, 107
anti-globalism. *See under* globalism
anti-racism. *See under* racism
anti-semitism, 2
Apri, Ivar, 219
Arabs, 91
Arctic, 6, 88
Arendt, Hannah, 141
Argentina, 224
Arnstberg, Karl-Olov, 130
art, contemporary, 185–186
Article 50, 202. *See also* Brexit; EU
artificial intelligence, 185
åsiktskorridor, 40
Assad, Bashar al-, 164, 193
Auschwitz, 74
Austin, John Langshaw, 31

Australia, 118, 169, 238
Austria, 36, 210

B

Bach, Johann Sebastian, 60
Baltimore, 153
Bannon, Steve, 38
Barroso, José Manuel Durão, 214
Bastille Day attack. *See* 2016 Nice truck attack
Bataclan theatre massacre, 27–28
Baudrillard, Jean, 3
Bavaria. *See under* Germany
Bay of Pigs, 10
BBC, 91, 168–169, 202, 218–219
Belfast, 72
Belgium, 113, 124, 161, 210
Bell, Daniel, 169
Berdyaev, Nikolai, 179, 188
Bergen-Belsen, 74
Bergman, Ingmar, 1
Bergson, Henri, 55
Bergwall, Sture, 11–12
Berlin, 206
Berlingske, 158
Berlin Wall, 104, 203
Berlusconi, Silvio, 96, 213
Bernstein, Richard, 165–166
Bias Response Teams. *See under* academia
Bible, 71, 173, 194
Biden, Joe, 176
Bilderberg Group, 163
Bill of Rights (US). *See* Constitution (US)
bin Laden, Osama, 69
Blackburn, 195
Blair, Tony, 192
Bloom, Allan, 37
Blue Peter, 166
Boko Haram, 116
Bolton, 195
Bolton, Lissant, 141
Bonhams, 185
Booth, 226
Borgholm, 71
Bowers, C. A., 170
Bradford, 44, 195
Brave New World (Huxley), 43, 53
Breivik, Anders Behring, 194–195
Brexit, xii–xiii, xv, 79, 93, 154, 229
  causes of, 204
  meaning of, 203, 235
  response to, xx–xxi, 83, 125, 202, 207–208, 235
Bruckner, 199, 201
Brussels, xv, 6, 65, 110–112, 179, 189, 202–203, 211. *See also* globalists and globalism; European Union
Bucharest Declaration, 176
Burisma Holdings, 176
Burke, Edmund, 96–97
Burnham, James, 91
Burundi, 90–91

C

Cabinet (UK), 59
California, 156
Cambodia, 224
Cambridge, 59
Cameron, David, 59, 208
Camp of the Saints, The (Raspail), 193–194
Camus, Renaud, 75
Canada 59, 169, 196–197, 223
Castro, Fidel, 193
categorical imperative, 54
Catholicism, 43, 46, 142, 161, 218. *See also* Christianity
Ceaușescu, Nicolae, 161
censorship, xvi, xx, 5–6, 30–31, 38, 50–51, 65–68, 75, 82, 109–110, 233. *See also* freedom of speech; hate-speech
  consequences of, 194–195
  self-censorship, 21–22, 32–33, 38, 40, 44, 53, 58, 66, 84–85, 151–152, 233
  social media and, 81–82
Challenger Space Shuttle, 9–10
Chamberlain, Neville, 190–191
'Champaign socialists', 15
Chaplin, Charlie, 229
Charlie Hebdo, 98–99, 135
Chechnya, 129
Chesterton, G. K., x
child-marriage, xxi, 20
Chile, 176
China and the Chinese, 9, 20, 56, 91, 95, 97, 177, 200, 204
Choudary, Anjem, 218
Christ, Jesus, 138, 165, 173, 180
Christianity, xvii, 4, 21, 38–40, 47, 49, 54, 62, 65, 68, 72–73, 102, 111, 144, 165, 201, 224. *see also* Catholicism; Russian Orthodoxy *under* Russia
  criticism of, 201

Crusades and, 201
homosexuality and 71, 73
Islam and, 111, 133, 165, 198, 218
liberalism and, 47, 89, 102–103, 111, 180
terrorism and, 99–100
West and, 15, 73, 102–103, 136, 138, 161, 180–181, 192
Christie's, 185
Churchill, Winston, 72, 172, 196, 203
Church of Norway, 162
CIA, 110
civil rights movement (US), 165–166
Clark, Wesley, 164, 236
Cleese, John, 33, 165
Clinton, Hillary, 36, 81, 204
Clinton Committees, 81
Clowes, Edith W., 175
Cologne, 109, 122
Colombia, 224
comedy. *See* humour
Commodus (emperor), 27
Communism, 161, 179, 188, 224. *See also* Soviet Union *under* Russia
conservatism, 89, 167, 175, 187–188, 191–192, 232–234
Constitution (Swedish). *See under* Sweden
Constitution (US), 75, 154
consumerism, 1, 18, 89, 160–162, 165, 176, 183, 186. *See also* globalism
contemporary art. *See* art, contemporary
Copenhagen, 99, 139
Corbyn, Jeremy, 15, 82, 194, 221
Council of Europe. *See* European Council *under* EU
counter-*jihad*. *See under jihad* and jihadists
Counter-Terrorism and Security Act of 2015 (UK), 135
Coventry, 195
Crimea, 177
Crusades. *See under* Christianity
Cuba, 177, 193
Cuban Missile Crisis, 177
cultural enrichment, 128
cultural grammar. *See under* political correctness
cultural Marxism, 2, 34–35, 49, 60, 102–103, 223. *See also* Marx, Karl
cultural nihilism, xviii–xix, 1–6, 15–16, 23, 25, 35, 37, 38, 47, 57, 110, 126, 218, 235. *See also* post-modernism;
relativism
as anti-Western, 2, 73, 81, 163
definition of, 2
hypermorality and, 170
Islam and, 2, 39, 45, 110, 126
media and, 91, 110, 218
Russia and, 178
Sweden and, 97, 134, 137, 147
West and, 181
white males and, 60–61
cultural relativism. *See* cultural nihilism; relativism
Czech Republic, 36, 213

D

Dagens Nyheter, 127
Dansk Folkeparti (Danish political party), 100
da'wah, 138–139
de Benoist, Alain, 46–47
de Gaulle, Charles, 202
Delors, Jacques, 211
democracy, xx, 6, 46, 49, 56, 58, 64, 76, 85, 100, 115, 153–154, 185, 193
Denmark, 68–69, 100–101, 127, 138, 208, 240
Derby, 43
Descartes, René, 30
Det Konservative Folkeparti (Danish political party), 100
dictatorship of virtue, 165–166
diversity, xxi, 12, 15–20, 41, 53, 55, 76–77, 82, 163, 196–197, 209
meaning of, 17–18, 169, 197
as racist term, 169
training, 43
undiversity and, 197
use of term, 17–20, 85, 134, 169, 232, 234
Domitian (emperor), 27
Dostoevsky, Fyodor, 170
Drummond, Nicholas, 153, 178

E

Eagle Death Metal, 27
Eastern Europe. *See under* Europe
East Germany, xiii, 102, 104. *See also* Germany; Western Germany
ECB (European Central Bank). *See under* EU
Eco, Umberto, 36–37
eco-colonialism, 95

economics, 186–187
Ecuador, 91
Edinburgh University, 58
Egalia School, 49
egalitarianism, 93–94, 152
Egypt, 176, 213
el-Faisal, Abdullah, 195
Eliot, T. S., xiv, 89, 179
elitism, 14–15, 76
anti-elitism, 90
Enemedia. *See under* media
Enlightenment, 4, 54, 63, 96, 224
environmentalism, 21, 92, 94–95, 117, 186–187
equality, xi, xix, 15, 25, 39, 52, 76–77, 85, 93, 95, 134, 209, 231. *See also* egalitarianism
Erdoğan, Recep, 55–56, 109, 192–193
Eritrea and Eritreans, 113, 137
Erlander, Tage, 121–122, 225
Ethiopia, 213
ethnopluralism, 235
EU (European Union), 6, 56, 92–93, 95–96, 152, 156, 167, 175, 180–182, 198, 202–214, 236. *See also* Europe
border control and, 36, 110, 189, 193, 230
Brexit and, 203–205, 207–208
Constitution and, 207–208
crisis and, 205, 210
democracy and, 6, 17, 95–96, 111–112, 191, 204–205, 207–210, 212–214, 237
ECB (European Central Bank), 210, 213–214
economy and, 204, 210
Euro Crisis and, 213–214
European Commission, 17, 93, 156, 163–154, 202, 207–213, 230
European Council, 100, 209–210, 213–214
European Parliament, 207, 210, 220
expansion of, 213
federalisation and, 212, 214
freedom of speech and, 38, 66, 71, 96
functioning of, 207–213
globalism and, 202–206, 209
Greek crisis and, 211
immigration and, 210–211
Islam and, 213
Monetary Union and, 210
political union and, 6, 181, 205–206, 208, 210
popularity of, 191

presidency of, 211–212
Russia and, 176–178
state sovereignty and, 163–164, 176, 205, 207–208, 213–214
strategy for building of, 205–206, 208–209
Treaties of, 207–212
Turkey and, 55–56, 192–193
tyranny and, 207
eudaimonia, 16
Eurasian Economic Union, 175
Euro Crisis. *See under* European Union
Europe. *See also* EU; West
Christianity and, 182, 189
colonialism of, 91
divisions in, xviii–xix, 42, 106–107, 138–139, 182, 190, 235
Eastern Europe, 25
election fraud and, 36
EU and, 182
honour and, 105
immigration and, xv–xix, 65, 105, 111, 125–126, 164, 182, 189, 206, 234
Islam and, 129, 182, 189, 213, 240
population of, 227
race and, 168
Russia and, 175–176
state of affairs in, 48, 111
terrorism and, 99–100, 125–126
Western Europe, xiii, 48, 66, 89–90, 92, 126, 136, 138–139, 154, 168–169, 174, 183, 190
European Central Bank. *See under* EU
European Commission. *See under* EU
European Convention on Human Rights, 71, 115, 213, 237
European Council. *See under* EU
European Court of Human Rights, 57
European Court of Justice, 38
European Parliament. *See under* EU
European Union. *See* EU
Europol, 125–126
Evola, Julius, 37, 187–188, 199
Exeter College, viii

F

Facebook, 69–70, 108, 130
Fahd (king), 139
family, 49, 116–117
Farage, Nigel, 65, 191, 202, 232, 236
fascism, 48, 52, 59, 85, 108, 134–135, 207

female genital mutilation, 55, 90, 116
feminism, 13-14, 23, 25, 38, 60, 67, 76-77, 162. *See also* genders
  female genital mutilation and, 116
  Islam and, 4, 38, 115-116, 240
  Sweden and, 49-50, 115-117
Fico, Robert, 189
Finland, 108, 118, 120, 137, 149, 222
First Amendment (US), 75, 77
Fleischer, Peter, 107
Florida, 109
Foreign Policy, 129
Foucault, Michel, 34, 62, 64-65
FRA law (Sweden), 156-157
France, xvi, 60, 69, 110, 147, 190-191, 202, 205
  censorship in, 183
  EU and, 207
  fragmentation in, 106-107
  immigration and, 205
  Islam in, 27-28, 57, 74-75, 216-218
  terrorism in, xvii-xviii, 27-28, 98-99, 109, 161, 183, 206, 215-217
  values of, 183
France2 (French television channel), 44
Francis (pope), xvii
Frankfurt, 169
Frankfurt School, 48
freedom, xi, 5, 32-33, 45, 49, 59, 85-86, 162, 232-233. *See also* freedom of opinion; freedom of speech; freedom of thought
  groupthink and, 11, 21-22
  infringements on, xvii-xviii, 32-33, 181
  political correctness and, 48-49
  use of, 236
freedom of opinion, 73-74, 194
freedom of speech, x, 5-6, 22, 25, 39, 43-43, 64-86, 140, 236. *See also* censorship; hate-speech; *see also under specific nation names*
  Islam and 72, 82
  limits on, 65, 236
  parrhesia and, 64-65
freedom of thought, 26, 30, 45, 73-74
Freedom Party of Austria, 101
Fried, Hédi, 143
French Revolution, xi
Future of Europe Group, 212-213

G

G8, 180
G20, 180
G40, 180
Gaddafi, Muammar, 164, 192-194
Georgia, 176
Guatemala, 176
Gay Games, 92
Gehlen, Arnold, 3, 47, 169, 233
Geller, Pamela, 75, 85, 218
genders. *See also* feminism
  academia and, 13, 33
  discrimination and, 13
  distinctions and, 19, 50, 93, 145
  education and, 49-51
  female genital mutilation, 55, 90
  gender theory, 33
  Islam and, 115-116, 137-138
  language and, 22-24, 32-33, 50, 84-85
  marriage and, 19
  number of, 49-51
  relations between, 23, 25, 67
  Sweden and, *see under* Sweden
gender theory. *See under* gender
Geneva Convention, 101, 131
Germany, xiii, 62, 93, 110, 127-128, 202, 210, 220. *See also* East Germany; West Germany
  Bavaria, xvi
  guilt and, 90, 168-170, 224
  hate-speech and 70, 82
  immigration and, xvi, 62-63, 93, 101-102, 109, 114, 130, 186, 205
  rape and sexual molestation in, xvi, xviii, 122
  refugee night flights and, 109-110
  rights and, 154
  terrorism in, xvi, xviii, 62-63
globalism and globalists, xv-xvi, 6, 18, 36, 57, 66, 175, 202-214, 230-231
  agenda of, xiii, 18, 57, 164, 185, 223, 234-236
  conditions of, 230
  consequences of, 89
  crisis of, 179
  democracy and, xx
  immigration and, 164
  language and, 231-232
  opposition to, xx, 36, 191, 202-204, 230-233, 235, 241
  Russia and, 175-176, 178

Goldberg, Johan, 48
Goldman Sachs, 163, 213–214
Goldsmith, Zac, 196
Goldsmiths, 58
Google, 107, 156
Gorbachev, Mikhail, 176
Gospel. *See* Bible
Gothenberg, 125
Gramsci, Antonio, 102–103, 141–142, 223
Graves, Robert, 215
Greece, 180, 204, 213–214
Green, Åke, 71, 73
Greenhill, Kelly, 193
Green Movement, 92–93
Green Party (German political party), 169–170
Grimshøj, 69
grooming gangs, 43–44
groupspeak, 20, 42
groupthink, x, xix, 5, 8–26, 42, 35, 46, 48, 50, 62–63 143, 175, 203, 230, 236
   academia and, 12
   freedom and, 11, 29–30, 66
   parrhesia and 65
   psychological corruption and, 9–10, 40, 49
   totalitarianism and, 9
Guadeloupe, 146–147
guilt. *See under* West

H

Hadlow, Martin, 141
halal meat, 44–45
Hamas, 222
Hamburg, 170
Hamlet (Shakespeare), 198
Harvard University, 77–78
hate-crimes, 5–6, 81, 150
hate-speech, 5–6, 37, 45, 66–68, 70, 72–73, 75, 77, 82, 85, 129–130, 167, 188, 237
Hedegaard, Lars, 85
Hertford College, 61
Heterodox Academy, 25
Heidegger, Martin, 2, 191
Herder, Johann Gottfried, 165
High Arctic. *See* Arctic
hijrah, 138
Hitler, Adolf, 74, 96
Hobbes, Thomas, 34
Hofer, Nobert, 101
Holocaust, 70, 74

Holland. *See* Netherlands
Hollande, François, 205, 211
Hollywood, 18
homophobia. *See under* homosexuality
homosexuality, 38, 82, 143
   Christianity and, 71
   homophobia, 201
   immigration and, 115
   Islam and, 73, 116, 136, 184, 195, 201
   marriage and, 204
   in non-Western countries, 20
honour, 54, 105, 188
honour killing, 20, 105, 136
Hotel Negresco, 215–216
Hotel Ukraine, 177–178
Houellebecq, Michel, 136
House of Commons Library (UK), 211
House of Lords (UK), xx
Hughes, Jesse, 27
human rights. *See* rights (human)
Human Rights Declaration. *See* Universal Declaration of Human Rights
humour, 23, 33, 54, 64, 74–76, 78, 138, 165, 229–230
Hungary, 36, 190, 202
Hunt, Tim, 32, 35
Hunter, James Davison, 92
Huntford, Roland, 21, 155
Hussein, Saddam, 164
Huxley, Aldous, 8, 94
Hyde Park Corner, 110
hypermorality, 47, 169–170

I

Iceland, 206
IKEA, 217
IMF (International Monetary Fund), 202
Immigrant and Minority Policy of 1975 (Sweden), 120–121
immigration, xiii–xviii, 47, 59, 113–140, 234
   causes of, 129–130, 132, 175, 192–193, 205
   censorship and, 70
   colonialism and, 198–199
   costs of, 114, 226
   crime and, 120–121, 123, 132
   demographics and, 113–114, 196–197
   demographics of, 118–119
   economy and, 47–48, 186
   ethics and, 193
   integration and, 197–198

minors and, 114, 119, 128, 153
motives behind, 21, 117, 132, 206
as Ponzi scheme, 117
rape and sexual molestation and, 123, 147–148
taxation and, 118
welfare and, 57, 117
India, 204
Indonesia, 133
inequality. *See* equality
interracial marriage, 162–163, 168
Inuit, 6, 87–89
Iran, 89, 139, 176, 221
Iraq and Iraqis, 102, 113, 124, 128–130, 137, 147, 153, 175, 184, 226
Ireland, 72, 207, 210
irony. *See* humour
ISIS, 11, 68, 83, 109, 114–115, 125–127, 129, 139, 206, 216–217
Islam, xiv–xv, 2–4, 14, 20–21, 101, 106, 182. *See also* Al Qaeda; *jihad* and jihadists; Qur'an; *shari'ah*
   blasphemy and 68–69, 96, 129–130, 133–134, 138, 240
   censorship and, 51, 66, 68–69, 71–72, 82, 85, 108–110
   Christianity and, 111, 133, 161, 165, 195, 198, 218, 240
   crime and, 43–44, 68, 116, 123–124
   da'wah and, 138–139
   dhimmi and, 200
   dress and, 240
   electoral fraud and, 36
   female genital mutilation and, 55, 90, 116
   feminism and, 4
   freedom and, 200–201
   groupthink and, 11
   hijrah and, 138
   homosexuality and, 73, 116, 184, 195, 201, 240
   honour and 54, 105
   Islamophobia, 41, 45, 80, 116, 123, 133, 201
   Jews and, 69, 195
   jihad and, 99, 116, 184, 215–217
   multiculturalism and, 4, 135–136, 184–185, 190
   political correctness and, 28, 36–38, 45, 51, 73, 133, 162
   radicalism and, 11, 51, 85, 124–126, 133, 135, 185
   rape and sexual molestation and, 43–44, 68, 116, 137
   secularism and, 4, 183, 195
   Sunni, 138
   terrorism and, xvii–xviii, 10–11, 27–28, 36, 68–69, 74–75, 85, 98–100, 124–125, 139, 161, 183, 215–217
   totalitarianism and, 96, 133
Islamic Relief Worldwide, 222
Islamophobia. *See under* Islam
Ismail, Abu Bilal, 69
Israel, 139, 222
Italy, 36, 93, 177, 204, 210, 213, 229

J

Janis, Irving L., 10
Jantelagen, 39–40
Japan, 117–118, 200
Jibali, Al, 195
jihad and jihadists, 10–11, 68, 82, 85, 99, 109, 125–127, 129–130, 136, 138, 184–185, 201, 213, 215–217, 221–222. *See also* Islam
counter-*jihad*, 130
jizya, 54
Johnson, Boris, xv
Judaism, 73
Juncker, Jean-Claude, xx, 180, 202–203, 212

K

Kaddor, Lamya, 170–171
Kafka, Franz, 25, 71
Kalb, James, 89, 144, 160–161
Kant, Immanuel, 54, 142
Kaplan, Mehmet, 221–222
Kennedy, John F., 10, 83
Kenya, 90–91
KGB, 59
Khan, Sadiq, 125, 195
Kiev, 178
Kim Jong-il, 8–9
Kirill (patriarch), 180, 189
Knudsen, Anne, 158
Korea. *See* North Korea; South Korea
Kosovo, 193
Kurds, 109

L

labelling. *See under* language
Lahouaiej-Bouhlel, Mohammed, 216
Langballe, Jesper, 69

language, 224. *See also* censorship
  labelling and, 14, 29–32, 39, 47, 54, 62,
    107, 168, 191, 198, 207, 226, 232
  manipulation of, xxi, 5, 31, 45, 52, 77,
    79, 134, 153, 166, 168–170, 201, 217,
    231
  multiculturalism and, 141–143, 146, 196
  objectifying language, 22–24
  policing of, 22, 24–25, 40, 42–43, 45,
    61, 74–77, 82–83
  private 40, 61
  semantic buckler, 201
  speech act, 31
  use of, xii, 16, 38–39, 78, 224, 231
Länstidningen, 74
Lebanon, 131
Le Bon, Gustave, 155
Left (political). *See* liberalism
Leicester, 72–73, 197
Le Pen, Marine, 232
liberal fascism, 48, 62
liberalism, xi–xii, xv, 2, 4. *See also* Left
  (political)
  agenda of, xvi–xvii, 17, 21, 49, 61,
    74–75, 85, 89, 93, 120, 164, 194,
    198, 234
  authoritarianism and, 18, 30–31, 38, 61,
    89–90, 97, 152, 190, 195, 238
  Christianity and, 89
  definition of, xiv, 89
  diversity and, 20–21, 43
  environmentalism and, 21, 169
  elitism and, 15–16, 76
  freedom of speech and, 64, 66, 70, 79,
    83–84, 194
  groupthink and, 5, 10–12, 15
  intolerance of, 21–25, 31, 47, 79, 108, 134
  Islam and, xiv–xv
  language and, 153, 168, 201, 231
  mentality of, xix, 10–12, 89, 91–92, 134
  religion and, 47, 180
  self-destruction of, 95, 132–133, 139–140,
    154, 161, 163, 182, 229
  strategies of, 16, 28–29, 31–32, 74–75,
    107, 134, 139–142
  universalism and, 16, 46, 89, 97
liberty. *See* freedom
Liberty GB, 72
Libya, xxi, 175
*Libya: The Strategic Gateway for the Islamic
  State* (ISIS), 206

Life of Brian, The, 165
Lindgren, Astrid, 50
Lisbon Treaty. *See* Treaty of Lisbon
Lithuania, 120
localism, xv, xx
Löfven, Stefan, xv, 129–130
London, 58, 68, 72, 125, 196
Löwith, Karl, 2
Lübeck, 70
Lutheranism, 224
Luton, 72–73, 197

M

Ma'alim fi al-Tariq (Qutb), 54
Maastricht Treaty, 208, 210–211
MacDougall, David, 91
Macedonia, 180
Macron, Emmanuel, 65
Malaysia, 133
Malmö, 125, 138
Malmström, Cecilia, 128
Manchester, 195
Marklund, Liza, 143
Marshall Plan, 224
Marx, Karl, xi. *See also* cultural Marxism
Marxism, 13, 16, 31–32, 34, 39. *See also*
  cultural Marxism; Marx, Karl
mass immigration. *See* immigration;
  migration crisis
Mau-Mau Uprising, 90–91
Mauritania, 91
May, Theresa, 236–237
Maydan Square, 178
McLuhan, Marshall, 142
McConnell, James, 72
McDonald's, 18
Mecca, 138
media, xxi, 38, 154. *See also under* Sweden
  agenda of, 91, 102, 119–122, 139, 149,
    185, 203
  alternative media, 145, 238
  Brexit and, 202–203
  Enemedia, 218
  Governments and, xviii, 109–111, 122,
    144, 149, 217–218, 238
  manipulations of, 178, 195, 203, 217, 225
Media Matters, 127
Medina, 138
meritocracy, 15–16
Merkel, Angela, xvi, xx, 65, 93, 102, 109,
  129–130, 160, 205–206

Me Too Movement, x
micro-aggression, 77
Middle East, 11, 101, 105, 113, 120, 123, 131–133, 137, 164, 175, 200, 241
migration crisis, xiii, xxi, 82, 101–102, 129–130, 175, 211, 234, 240–241. *See also* immigration
Migrationsverket, 128, 131
Milbank, John, xiv, 89
Miljöpartiet (Swedish political party), 73, 101–102, 144, 221
Mill, John Stuart, 81
Milošević, Slobodan, 193
missaktning, 71
Muhammed, 68, 74, 138, 165, 195
modern art. *See* art, contemporary
Monty Python, 58, 102
Morgan, Nicky, 82
Mosesson, Hans, 143
Mozart, Wolfgang Amadeus, 63
Mrázak, Rudolf, 141
MTV, 18
multiculturalism, 6, 18, 20, 31, 39, 42–43, 45–49, 61–62, 65, 85, 92, 98, 101, 106, 126, 160–171. *See also under* Sweden
aims of, 61, 164, 166
Islam and, 184–185
minorities and, 153
opposition to, 189–190, 200, 229, 241
relativism and, 167
religion and, 161–162, 164
results of, xi, xiii–xiv, 101, 129, 160–164
Russia and, 178
universality and, 46–47, 98, 200
West and, 167–168, 200
Murdoch, Iris, 103
Muslim Brotherhood, 54, 73
Muslims. *See* Islam
Mussolini, Benito, 113

N

Nationalalteatern, 143
national imaginary, 141
National Museum (Stockholm) 51
NATO (North Atlatic Treaty Organization), 176–177, 236
Nawaz, Maajid, 63
Nazism, 66, 74, 127, 146, 152, 158–159, 161, 167–168, 223–224
Netherlands, 106–107, 190–191, 207, 210
NetzDG, 82

New World Order, 204
New York Times, 240
NGOs (non-governmental organisations), 95, 119, 202, 222, 226
Nice, xvi, xviii
Nice Treaty. *See* Treaty of Nice
Nicholas II (czar), 216
Nietzsche, Friedrich, xix, 1–2, 12–13, 105, 135, 165, 230–231
nihilism. *See* cultural nihilism
Niger, 91
Nigeria, 90–91, 116
Nigerian Civil War, 90–91
Nineteen Eighty-Four (Orwell), 83–84
no-platforming, 107
Nørgård, Finn, 99
North Africa, 11, 105, 113, 123, 132–133, 137, 164, 175. *See also* Africa
North Korea, 8–9, 89, 171, 200
Norway, 50, 100–101, 127, 137, 162, 206, 226
NRK (Norwegian Broadcasting Company), 50
NSA (National Security Agency, USA), 157
Nyheter i dag, 127

O

Obama, Barack Hussein, xviii, xx, 79
objectifying language. *See under* language
OECD (Organisation for Economic Co-operation and Development), 120
Offenbach, Jacques, 27
Official Secrets Act, 64
OFII (French Immigration Service), 183
Ohlsson, Birgitta, 126–127
Oldham, 195
open society, 29–30, 70, 209
Orbán, Viktor, 190, 194, 202
Organisation for Economic Co-operation and Development. *See* OECD
Orlando massacre, 108–109
Orthodox Church. *See under* Russia
Orwell, George 45, 52, 77, 81, 85, 156, 227, 237
Osborne, George, 59
Östersund, 74, 219
Ottoman Empire, 106
overpopulation. *See* population growth
Overton Window, 111
Oxford, viii, 12, 43–44, 60, 139
Oxford University, viii, 12, 83, 198

P

P1 (Swedish radio station), 143, 147, 220
P2 (Swedish radio station), 98, 129–130, 146
Pabst, Adrian, xiv, 89
Pakistan and Pakistanis, 101, 133, 195–196, 200, 240
Palaiseau, 162
Palestine, 222
Palme, Olaf, 121
George, Papandreou, 213
Pabst, Adrian, 233
Paris attacks of 2015, 206
Paris, 27, 44, 98–99
Parliament (UK), 38
parrhesia, 64–65, 79, 93
penitent State, 199
Pickles, Eric, 36
Pippi Longstocking (Lindgren), 50
PISA (Programme for International Student Assessment), 120
Plato, 23
political correctness, 3, 5, 14, 27–63, 106, 162
  academia and, 53, 57–58
  censorship and, 50–51
  cultural grammar and, 36–37, 45
  effects of, 29–30, 37, 41–44, 52
  freedom and, 48–49, 51, 66, 194
  homogeneity and 54
  language and, 28–32, 35–36, 40, 66
  objectives of, 29–30, 42
  multiculturalism, 165
  tolerance and, 29, 42, 47, 51
  totalitarianism and, 48–49
  use of, 28–29, 37
  victimhood and, 34–35, 78
politics of folly, 51, 75, 167
polygamy, 20
Popper, Karl, 30, 70
population growth, 87–88, 94–95, 117
populism, 191
Portugal, 204
post-modernism, 33–35, 55, 59, 79–80, 92, 96, 154, 167, 196. *See also* cultural nihilism; relativism
Powers, Kirsten, 85
prejudice, 34, 37, 55, 61
press. *See* media
Prevent legislation (UK), 81
Programme for International Student Assessment. *See* PISA
progress and progressivism, 94–96, 160–162, 167, 170, 179, 209, 233–234
Protestantism, 224
Protocol on Privileges and Immunites of the European Communities, 210
Protocol Relating to the Status of Refugees, 193
Public Order Act of 1986, 67–69
Purdue University, 77
Pushkin, Alexander, 60
Putin, Vladimir, xviii, 127, 175–177, 179–180, 185, 188, 190–192, 202–203, 214
Pyongyang, 8–9

Q

Qur'an, 10–11, 164–165. *See also* Islam
Qutb, Sayyid, 54

R

race, 145–146, 167, 197–198, 227
Racial and Religious Hatred Act, 68
racism, 14, 31–32, 39–40, 43–44, 54, 58, 66, 119–120, 122–123, 128, 133, 139, 145–146, 168–169, 227
  anti-racism, 66, 128
  immigration and, 197–198
  reverse racism, 75
Radio 3 (UK radio station), 98, 146
Radio 4 (UK radio station), 143
rape and sexual molestation. *See under* Germany; immigration; Islam; Sweden
rap music, 66–67
Rasbiologiinstitutt, 146
Raspail, Jean, 193–194
Reagan, Ronald, 176
Reding, Viviane, 211
Rees-Mogg, Jacob, 59–60
Refugee Air, 102
refugee crisis. *See* migration crisis
Reinfeldt, Fredrik, 119, 207, 223
relativism, 7, 45–46, 50, 54–55, 47, 90, 162, 166, 223–224. *See also* cultural nihilism; post-modernism
religion, 11, 47, 52–53, 96–97, 142, 161, 172–175, 223. *See also* Christianity; Islam; secularism; *see also under* Sweden
Revel, Jean-Francois, 152
reverse racism. *See under* racism

Revolutionära Fronten, 107
Rhodes, Cecil, 58–59
rights (human), 15, 24, 39, 46–48, 71, 96–97, 115, 147, 231
　democracy and, 193
　history and, 46–47, 96–97
　prioritisation of, 47
　victimhood and 47, 147
River War, The (Churchill), 72
Robinson, Tommy, 110
Rochdale, 43
Roma, 127, 131
Roman Catholic Church. *See* Catholicism
Romania, 161, 176–177
Rosen, Stanley, 2
Rotherham, 43
Rousseau, Jean-Jacques, xviii, 96, 99
Rubens, Pieter Paul, 51
Rushdie, Salman, 85
Russia, xviii, 25, 56, 97, 127, 154, 157, 172–180, 185, 188–192, 200, 204, 220, 224
　EU and, 175–176
　foreign policy of, 175–180
　freedom of speech and, 189–190
　globalism and, 175–176, 178, 180, 185, 192, 200, 204
　Islam and, 175
　liberalism and, 174, 176, 178
　NATO and, 176–178
　New World Order and, 203–204
　patriotism and, 188, 191
　political correctness and, 189, 191
　Putin and, *see* Putin, Vladimir
　Russian Orthodoxy, 172–174, 179–180, 220
　Soviet Union, xiv, 37, 39–40, 48, 59, 76, 132, 151–152, 162, 172, 179, 189–190, 214
　Syria and, 204
　tradition and, 172–176, 188, 220
　Ukraine and, 176–178
　US and, 176–177, 204
　West and, 188
Russian Orthodoxy. *See under* Russia
Rwanda, 90–91

S

Sabuni, Kitimbwa, 227
Sahlin, Mona, 220–221
same-sex marriage legislation, 67
Sandberg, Kristian, 143
Sandelin, Gunnar, 130
Sarkozy, Nicolas, 17, 75, 162–163, 168
Sarrazin, Thilo, 234
Sartre, Jean-Paul, 2
satire. *See* humour
Saudi Arabia, 36, 91, 138–139, 220
Scandinavia, 97
Scargill, Arthur, xv
Schäuble, Wolfgang, 207
Schengen (Agreement and Area), 110, 189, 206. *See also* EU (European Union)
Schmitt, Carl, 182, 222
Schopenhauer, Arthur, xx
Schulz, Martin, xx, 96, 207–208
science, 181
Scruton, Roger, 24, 57, 95, 179, 234
SD. See *Sverigedemokraterna*
Second World War. *See* World War II
secularism, 2, 4, 19, 30, 39, 45–47, 49, 51, 54, 65, 89, 106, 161, 164, 179, 184, 196, 229. *See also* religion
security, 194
self-censorship. *See under* censorship
September 11. *See* 9/11
Serbia, 180
Serrano, Andres, 138
sexism, 26, 32–33. *See also* genders
Shakespeare, William, 60, 198
shari'ah law, 11, 44–45, 54, 117, 133–139, 164–165, 185, 190, 199–200, 239–240
Sharma, Ruchir, 39
slave morality, 135
slave vanity, 231
Slough, 72–73, 197
Slovakia, 184, 189, 213
Snowden, Edward, 156–157
Sobi Bor, 74
sobornost, 192
social justice, 80–82
social media, xvi, 30, 32, 43, 67, 81–82, 84, 108, 194, 217
Socrates, xv, 62, 64
Södermalm, 136–137
Sogner, Sølvi, 158
Solzhenitsyn, Aleksandr Isayevich, xiv
Somalia and Somalis, 105, 113, 117, 129–130, 137
Soros, George, 109, 127, 164, 192, 230
Sotheby's, 185

Soumission (Houellebecq), 136
South Africa, 91, 213
South America, 25, 91
Southern, Lauren, 68
South Korea, 9, 32
Soviet Union. See under Russia
Spain, 69, 82, 210
Spectator, 219
Spengler, Oswald, 1, 37
Springare, Peter, 123
Stalinism, 39, 66
Stasi, x, xiii
St Chad's College, viii
stereotypes, 51–53, 61, 63
Stockholm, xvi, 49–51, 60, 103, 125, 127, 136–137, 170, 219, 240
Stockholm University, 60
Sudan, 72
Sunni Islam. See under Islam
surveillance, 152. See also under Sweden
Sutherland, Peter, 163–164
Sverigedemokraterna (SD, Swedish political party), 41, 74, 100, 103–104, 107–108, 112–113, 118, 120, 158, 219, 226
Sweden, viii, xiii, xx, 2, 5, 21, 97
    arms sales and, 147
    begging in, 131
    Brexit and, xv
    censorship in, xvi, 18–19, 21–22, 51, 63, 100, 111
    child marriage in, xxi
    Constitution of, 50
    crime in, 51, 120–122, 125, 219
    cultural nihilism and, 97, 134, 137, 147
    culture of, 58–59, 104, 117, 133, 221–222
    democracy in, 104–105, 111–113, 127–128, 150, 154, 157–158, 200, 239
    demographics in, 102, 111, 113–114, 119, 123, 158, 227
    as dictatorship 107–108
    education in, 120, 155
    election fraud in, 100–101
    equality and, 39–40
    espionage and, 157
    EU and, 207
    eugenics in, 158–159, 225, 227
    feminism and, 49, 73, 107–108, 115–117, 145–146, 148

    fragmentation of, 101, 105–107, 136–137, 142–143
    freedom in, 154–155
    freedom of speech in, 39–42, 71, 76, 111, 145, 150
    future of, x–xi
    gender in, 49–51
    Government of, xv, 73
    groupthink in, 11–12, 21, 40, 49, 145, 158, 239
    guilt and, 224–225
    immigration and, xiii, xv–xvi, xviii, xxi, 3, 21, 31, 40–42, 47, 65, 100–105, 108–140, 186, 219–220, 240–241
    integration and, 112, 221, 239
    Islam in, 4, 65, 73, 101, 111, 135–138, 144, 220–221, 225–226, 239–240
    language in, 21–22, 31–32, 98, 107, 142–143, 146
    media in, xiii–xiv, xvi, 18–19, 42, 51, 73, 76, 99, 102–104, 108, 111, 119, 130, 144, 148–150, 155, 158, 217, 219–220, 226, 238
    as microcosm of Europe, xiv
    multiculturalism in, xiii–xiv, xvi, xxi, 21, 97, 100–102, 105–106, 113, 121, 135–136, 145, 155, 168, 221–222, 225, 227
    Nazism and, 224–225, 227
    no-go areas in, 125
    Parliament of, 51
    political correctness in, 40, 42
    past of, xiv
    racism and, 31–32, 39, 139, 145–147
    radio in, 98, 119, 141–151, 220, 239
    rape and sexual molestation in, xviii, 44, 51, 120–122, 125, 127, 137, 147–148, 219–220
    religion in, 40, 49, 54–55, 111–112, 142, 144, 154–155
    riots in, 128
    standard of living and, 112, 114
    surveillance in, 107, 111, 156–158
    taxation in, 129–130
    terrorism and, xvi, xviii, 125, 217
    totalitarianism and, 107–108, 151, 155
    unemployment in, 186
    welfare in, 103, 130, 237–238
Swedish Integration Board, 111
Swedish Media Council, 150

Swedish National Council for Crime Prevention, 123
Swedish Trade Union Confederation, 150
Switzerland, 154, 206
Syria and Syrians, xvi, 68, 102, 113, 124, 128–130, 132, 138, 153, 175, 184, 192–193, 197, 204, 206, 221–222, 226

T

Taliban, 58–59
Tallentryre, S. G., 64
Taylor, Harry, 68
tech companies, 26
television, 18, 109, 130, 152, 155, 176, 185, 241
terrorism, xvi–xvii, 7, 98–99, 124
Thatcher, Margaret, 205, 211
Thucydides 57
Timmermans, Frans, 163
tolerance, xix, xxi, 17, 29–31, 42, 52, 55, 60, 82, 115, 134–136, 153, 209, 232, 234
To Live With Herds, 91
Toronto, 196
totalitarianism, 8–9, 151–152
　freedom of speech and, 65–66, 76
　language and, 18, 65–66, 82–83, 134
　liberalism and, 18, 48, 53, 58–59, 61, 70, 89, 134, 190, 195, 238
　mindset of, 16, 49, 58, 151
　political correctness and, 42, 48–49
　surveillance and, 152, 155–158
　technology and, 155–156
　tolerant dictatorship, 155
totalitarian mindset. *See under* totalitarianism
tradition, 231–233
Treaty establishing a Constitution for Europe, 207–208
Treaty of Amsterdam. *See* Amsterdam Treaty
Treaty of Lisbon, 207–209
Treaty of Nice, 207
Treaty of Rome, 208, 210
Treaty on the Functioning of the European Union. *See* Treaty of Rome
Trudeau, Justin, 196–197
Trump, Donald, xiii, xv, 29, 35–36, 38, 65, 83, 125, 133, 180, 191, 202–204, 229, 232, 236
trygghet, 103, 112, 139–140

Tuchman, Barbara W., 51
Turkey, 55–56, 109, 131, 177, 192–193
TV. *See* television
Twitter, 82, 108

U

Uganda, 20, 91, 197
UK (United Kingdom), 21, 38, 59–60, 98, 114, 131, 180–181, 190–191
　academia in, 53, 58–59, 81
　Brexit and, xx, 79, 83, 202–203, 208–209, 211
　crime in, 124–125
　demographics in, 195–198, 235
　electoral fraud and, 36
　female genital mutilation in, 54
　freedom of speech in, 71–72, 110
　grooming gangs in, 43–44, 110
　immigration and, 197–198
　Islam in, 43–44, 68–69, 71–72, 110, 124, 195, 197, 199, 201
　media and, 149, 218–219
　population of, 227–229
　racism and, 43
　shari'ah and, 199
　terrorism in, 124
　travel bans and 68, 85, 125
UKIP (UK political party), 168–169
Ukraine, 176–178
Ullenberg, Erik, 58
ummah, 11, 57
UN (United Nations), xiv, 112, 114–115, 183, 240
UN Convention on Refugees and Asylum, 115, 193
Undercover Mosque, 195, 200
UN Human Development Index, 112, 114
United Nations Office on Drugs and Crime (UNODC), 122
United Kingdom. *See* UK
United Nations. *See* UN
United States of America. *See* US
Universal Declaration of Human Rights, 46
universities. *See* academia
University of California (UCLA), 77–78
University of Durham, viii
University of Minnesota, 77
University of Passau, 211
US, 39, 169

US (cont'd.):
  academia and, 23, 53, 58, 77–78, 81
  border control and, 36
  Christian Right of, 184
  democracy and, 154, 176
  foreign policy of, 175–176, 220
  freedom of speech and 75, 241
  future of, xiii
  mass shootings in, xviii, 42
  politics in, 36, 81
  Russia and, 176, 190–191
  surveillance and, 153, 156
Usama, Abu, 195

V
Valdai Club, 191–192
Van der Belen, Alexander, 101
van Gogh, Theo, 69
Van Rompuy, Herman, 212
Vattimo, Gianni, 2
Velvet Revolution, 213
Venstre (Danish political party), 100
Vergangenheitsbewältigung, 224
victimhood and victims, 20, 24, 28, 30, 34–35, 43, 45, 47, 72–73, 104, 132–133, 141, 154
  ethnicity and, 72, 104–105
  freedom of speech and, 84
  identity and, 134
  Islam and, 99, 104, 132–133
  reversal of, 137
  Swedes and, 104–105
Vidali-Spitulnik, 146
Vikings, 39
Vlaams Blok (Belgian political party), 113
Volkswagon, 10
Voltaire, 64
Volvo, 168
von Berg, Stefanie, 169, 233
Vygotsky, Lev, 39–40

W
Wales, 197
Wallenberg family, 218
Weinstein, Bret, 35
West. *See also* Europe
  Christianity in, xiii, 15, 136, 180–181, 192, 198
  freedom in, 66, 182, 189–190
  future and, 7, 94–95, 183, 229–241
  globalism and, 180
  guilt and, 34, 58–60, 90–91, 105, 135, 146–147, 168–170, 188, 199, 224
  hatred of, 163
  liberalism and, 89
  religion and, xiii, 15, 136, 164–165, 174, 181, 198, 200, 233
  suicide of, 190–191
  state of, xvii, 33–34, 38–39, 81, 89, 133, 166, 179
  tradition and, 179, 233–234
  value of, 15
Western Europe. *See under* Europe
West Germany, 169. *See also* East Germany; Germany
Weston, Paul, 72
white genocide, 169
white priviledge, 61–52
Widfeldt, Anders, 224
Wikan, Unni, 137
Wikileaks, 124, 157, 175, 179–180
Wilders, Geert, 65, 85
Williams, Rowan, 199
Wilson, Edward O., 87
Winchester Crown Court, 72
Winter War, 222
Wittgenstein, Ludwig, 61
Wolodarski, Peter, 127
Woodward, Ashley, 3
World War II, 147, 224
Wunstorf, 109

X
XKeyscore, 157

Y
Yale University, 77
Yanukovich, Viktor, 176
Yazidis, 118
Yiannopoulos, Milo, 27
Yugoslavia, 236

Z
Zakharine, Dmitri, 155
Zand, Emad, 102
Zimbabwe, 91
Žižek, Slajov, 29, 48, 59, 122–123
Zusammengehörigkeit, 182

OTHER BOOKS PUBLISHED BY ARKTOS

SRI DHARMA PRAVARTAKA ACHARYA	*The Dharma Manifesto*
JOAKIM ANDERSEN	*Rising from the Ruins: The Right of the 21st Century*
ALAIN DE BENOIST	*Beyond Human Rights*
	Carl Schmitt Today
	The Indo-Europeans
	Manifesto for a European Renaissance
	On the Brink of the Abyss
	The Problem of Democracy
	Runes and the Origins of Writing
	View from the Right (vol. 1–3)
ARTHUR MOELLER VAN DEN BRUCK	*Germany's Third Empire*
MATT BATTAGLIOLI	*The Consequences of Equality*
KERRY BOLTON	*Revolution from Above*
	Yockey: A Fascist Odyssey
ISAC BOMAN	*Money Power*
RICARDO DUCHESNE	*Faustian Man in a Multicultural Age*
ALEXANDER DUGIN	*Ethnos and Society*
	Eurasian Mission: An Introduction to Neo-Eurasianism
	The Fourth Political Theory
	Last War of the World-Island
	Putin vs Putin
	The Rise of the Fourth Political Theory
MARK DYAL	*Hated and Proud*
KOENRAAD ELST	*Return of the Swastika*
JULIUS EVOLA	*The Bow and the Club*
	Fascism Viewed from the Right
	A Handbook for Right-Wing Youth
	Metaphysics of War
	The Myth of the Blood
	Notes on the Third Reich
	The Path of Cinnabar
	Recognitions
	A Traditionalist Confronts Fascism
GUILLAUME FAYE	*Archeofuturism*
	Archeofuturism 2.0
	The Colonisation of Europe
	Convergence of Catastrophes

OTHER BOOKS PUBLISHED BY ARKTOS

	A Global Coup
	Sex and Deviance
	Understanding Islam
	Why We Fight
Daniel S. Forrest	*Suprahumanism*
Andrew Fraser	*Dissident Dispatches*
	The WASP Question
Génération Identitaire	*We are Generation Identity*
Paul Gottfried	*War and Democracy*
Porus Homi Havewala	*The Saga of the Aryan Race*
Lars Holger Holm	*Hiding in Broad Daylight*
	Homo Maximus
	Incidents of Travel in Latin America
	The Owls of Afrasiab
Alexander Jacob	*De Naturae Natura*
Jason Reza Jorjani	*Prometheus and Atlas*
	World State of Emergency
Roderick Kaine	*Smart and SeXy*
Peter King	*Here and Now*
	Keeping Things Close
Ludwig Klages	*The Biocentric Worldview*
	Cosmogonic Reflections
Pierre Krebs	*Fighting for the Essence*
Stephen Pax Leonard	*Travels in Cultural Nihilism*
Pentti Linkola	*Can Life Prevail?*
H. P. Lovecraft	*The Conservative*
Charles Maurras	*The Future of the Intelligentsia & For a French Awakening*
Michael O'Meara	*Guillaume Faye and the Battle of Europe*
	New Culture, New Right
Brian Anse Patrick	*The NRA and the Media*
	Rise of the Anti-Media
	The Ten Commandments of Propaganda
	Zombology

OTHER BOOKS PUBLISHED BY ARKTOS

TITO PERDUE	*The Bent Pyramid*
	Morning Crafts
	Philip
	William's House (vol. 1–4)
RAIDO	*A Handbook of Traditional Living*
STEVEN J. ROSEN	*The Agni and the Ecstasy*
	The Jedi in the Lotus
RICHARD RUDGLEY	*Barbarians*
	Essential Substances
	Wildest Dreams
ERNST VON SALOMON	*It Cannot Be Stormed*
	The Outlaws
SRI SRI RAVI SHANKAR	*Celebrating Silence*
	Know Your Child
	Management Mantras
	Patanjali Yoga Sutras
	Secrets of Relationships
GEORGE T. SHAW (ED.)	*A Fair Hearing: The Alt-Right in the Words of Its Members and Leaders*
OSWALD SPENGLER	*Man and Technics*
TOMISLAV SUNIC	*Against Democracy and Equality*
	Homo Americanus
	Postmortem Report
	Titans are in Town
HANS-JÜRGEN SYBERBERG	*On the Fortunes and Misfortunes of Art in Post-War Germany*
ABIR TAHA	*Defining Terrorism: The End of Double Standards*
	The Epic of Arya (2nd ed.)
	Nietzsche's Coming God, or the Redemption of the Divine
	Verses of Light
BAL GANGADHAR TILAK	*The Arctic Home in the Vedas*
DOMINIQUE VENNER	*For a Positive Critique*
	The Shock of History
MARKUS WILLINGER	*A Europe of Nations*
	Generation Identity

Made in the USA
Monee, IL
03 May 2026

49438597R00173